THE (BOOK) Of FIRST CORINTHIANS

CHRISTIANITY
IN A HOSTILE CULTURE

Advancing the Ministries of the Gospel
AMG *Publishers*

God's Word to you is our highest calling.

TWENTY-FIRST CENTURY
BIBLICAL COMMENTARY SERIES®

THE BOOK OF FIRST CORINTHIANS

CHRISTIANITY
IN A HOSTILE CULTURE

DAN
MITCHELL

GENERAL EDITORS

MAL COUCH & ED HINDSON

TWENTY-FIRST CENTURY BIBLICAL COMMENTARY SERIES is a registered
trademark of AMG Publishers.

ISBN-13: 978-0-89957-819-4
ISBN-10: 0-89957-819-5

Cover Design by ImageWright, Inc.
Editing and Text Design by Warren Baker
Editorial assistance provided by Weller Editorial Services, Chippewa Lake, MI

Printed in Canada
15 14 13 12 11 10 –T– 7 6 5 4 3 2

To my wife, Nancy,
who has given me
"the greatest thing in the world"

And to Douglas B. MacCorkle,
now with the Lord,
pastor, professor, mentor, friend
who taught me the joy of discovery

Twenty-First Century Biblical Commentary Series®

Mal Couch, Th.D., and Ed Hindson, D.Phil.

The New Testament has guided the Christian Church for over two thousand years. This one testament is made up of twenty-seven books, penned by godly men through the inspiration of the Holy Spirit. It tells us of the life of Jesus Christ, His atoning death for our sins, His miraculous resurrection, His ascension back to heaven, and the promise of His second coming. It also tells the story of the birth and growth of the Church and the people and principles that shaped it in its earliest days. The New Testament concludes with the book of Revelation pointing ahead to the glorious return of Jesus Christ.

Without the New Testament, the message of the Bible would be incomplete. The Old Testament emphasizes the promise of a coming Messiah. It constantly points us ahead to the One who is coming to be the King of Israel and the Savior of the world. But the Old Testament ends with this event still unfulfilled. All of its ceremonies, pictures, types, and prophecies are left awaiting the arrival of the "Lamb of God who takes away the sin of the world!" (John 1:29).

The message of the New Testament represents the timeless truth of God. As each generation seeks to apply that truth to its specific context, an up-to-date commentary needs to be created just for them. The editors and authors of the Twenty-First Century Biblical Commentary Series have endeavored to do just that. This team of scholars represents conservative, evangelical, and dispensational scholarship at its best. The individual authors may differ on minor points of interpretation, but all are convinced that the Old and New Testaments teach a dispensational framework for biblical history. They also hold to a pretribulational and premillennial understanding of biblical prophecy.

The French scholar René Pache reminded each succeeding generation, "If the power of the Holy Spirit is to be made manifest anew among us, it is of primary importance that His message should regain its due place. Then we shall be able to put the enemy to flight by the sword of the Spirit which is the Word of God."

The church at Corinth was far from the ideal model of a first-century apostolic church. It had been planted in one of the most difficult and challenging cities in the Roman world. It was to this burgeoning young church, with all of its potential and all of its problems, that Paul wrote his first letter to the Corinthians. Leon Morris observes: "Here we have a typical Pauline letter. The apostle praises his correspondents for their Christian virtue, and rebukes them soundly for their many failings."

The challenges facing the new community of believers in Corinth are not unlike the challenges facing the twenty-first century church. As the great apostle speaks to them regarding matters of Christian faith, life, and ministry, so he speaks clearly and loudly to us with them. Thus he would remind us of the gospel "by which...[we] are saved" (15:2). Then he would challenge our generation to be "steadfast, immovable, always abounding in the work of the Lord" (15:58).

Contents

CHAPTER 1

Background of First Corinthians

The fundamental challenge Paul confronted wherever he carried the gospel was this: "How can those who have been called to belong to Christ be faithful to their new Lord while they must still belong, in so many ways, to this present age?"[1] What church of any age has not struggled with this question? Over the centuries, Christians have responded to this challenge from one extreme to another. On the one hand, there is the temptation to just *drop out*. In the ancient world, the Egyptian hermit-monk Anthony followed that attractive option. And some in Corinth thought this was what Paul was teaching (cf. 1 Cor. 5:9ff.). Not only did the apostle reject this teaching, but common sense tells us that it could never be a consistently effective means of fulfilling the Great Commission. This form of extreme separatism still exists today in many forms, from pharisaical and cultic groups to entire societies insulated from the world around them.

The opposite extreme is to try to create the kingdom of God on earth and, with it, replace all human systems of government. Following Augustine, many have sought to obliterate the "kingdom of the world" by universally establishing the "kingdom of God" on the earth. Many modern-day theonomists, postmillennialists, and amillennialists continue to follow this misguided teaching. It is misguided for two dominant reasons: First, it is not possible to establish God's kingdom without the *King*. A simple straightforward reading of New Testament prophetic passages such as the Olivet Discourse (Matt. 24—25), 1 Corinthians 15, or Revelation 20 makes this clear. In such texts it is hardly possibly to conclude anything other than that it would be only after the return of Christ to the earth that the universal messianic kingdom would or could be established. But beyond this, such teaching contradicts the clear example and teaching of Christ, who did not ask fallen humanity to come to Him. Rather, He came to *us*. And as His Father sent Him, so He sent His followers into the world. "*In the world, but not of it,*" is the principle Jesus taught. It is this latter point that Paul emphasizes in his letter to the Corinthians. We are not called to "go out of the world" (5:10), nor has the kingdom come that we might now "reign as kings" (see 4:8). Rather, we are "saints," drawn into fellowship with a crucified Christ and called to be agents of His love in a lost and sinful world.

This was precisely the question confronting the fledgling congregation in Corinth. That it was a major concern to them and to their spiritual father, Paul, is evident in that fully one-third of 1 Corinthians is devoted to dealing with it, and nearly half of 2 Corinthians is given over to further related instruction.

Inasmuch as these practical questions have remained with the church from its inception into the twenty-first century, can there be any question of its importance and relevance to believers today? While the church faces new challenges, the issues of church unity, sexual immorality, marriage, divorce, litigiousness, modesty, authority, spiritual gifts, and hope are issues every pastor deals with while confronting the day-to-day problems of modern-day Christians who still struggle to live clean in Corinth.

Falling second in the body of the Pauline epistles, 1 Corinthians both complements and contrasts the great doctrinal epistle that precedes it. Whereas Romans emphasizes matters of biblical theology, the Corinthian letters are concerned with practical theology and its application to a particular local assembly. Yet this is not to say that Romans is not a practical epistle (as chapters 12—15 demonstrate). Nor is this to suggest that Paul does not give attention to doctrine in 1 Corinthians. In fact, it is a *theological* frame of reference from which he launches this letter and in terms of which the entire issue is placed before its recipients. What does it mean and how is it possible to be God's church in Corinth?[2] Furthermore, the instructional and doctrinal sections of this epistle are larger than many entire books of the New Testament (note especially chapters 7—15).

With this in mind, the predominant thrust of 1 Corinthians is that of a pastor concerned with the spiritual welfare of a wayward assembly. And that concern does not appear to be misplaced, as a closer look at the city and culture of Corinth shows.

Corinth, Old and New

Corinth was a wealthy commercial center located on a narrow neck of land (four miles wide) that connected the Peloponnesus and Northern Greece. Situated as it was, it became a crossroads for travel and commerce both north and south, east and west. It had two harbors; one (Lechaeum) faced toward

Italy in the west, and the other (Cenchreae) faced toward Asia in the east. The wealth of Corinth was acquired by hauling freight and smaller vessels across the isthmus and by politicians who levied tolls on the commerce.

The history of the city of Paul's day may be divided into two periods—the *old* and the *new*. The old city (which gave to the world the classic Corinthian pillar) was founded ca. 1500 B.C. and was destroyed by the Roman general Lucius Mummius in 146 B.C. A century later, the new city was rebuilt on the same location. The old city of Corinth rose to wealth and fame during the period of the Greek city-states. It was known for its cosmopolitan culture and luxurious temples. On the gray, rocky hill to the south of the city (called Acrocorinth), the shining sanctuary to Aphrodite was located. Visible far out to sea, this temple was once serviced by a thousand slave girls who doubled both as temple prostitutes and as entertainers for the city's night life.[3] The destruction of the old city (together with the sacking of Carthage) largely became the means by which Rome rose to wealth and power.

The new city was built by Julius Caesar in 46 B.C. and was elevated to the status of a Roman colony with the title *Colonia Laus Julia Corinthiensis*. When Paul came to Corinth in A.D. 50–51, it was again a thriving metropolis, the capital city of Achaia, under the principate of the emperor Claudius (41–54) and ruled by the Roman proconsul Lucius Junius Gallio.[4] Its population, vastly different from the old city (a mixture of Roman, Greek, and Oriental), was nearly half slaves. This rich cosmopolitan city boasted that it was heir to the glories of ancient Greece. "Its walls enclosed an area two and a half times as large as Athens . . . . It was the most important administrative and commercial and was full of people on the go at all times."[5]

> As Paul approached the city, he would first have seen the imposing mountain of Acrocorinth towering above the city to its south crowned with fortification walls and a temple of Aphrodite (Strabo, *Geography* 8.6.21). He would have passed through widely scattered suburbs to arrive in the forum, full of reminders of the Roman administration. Latin inscriptions were everywhere. A temple on the western slope of the forum was dedicated to the family of the Julii and another was dedicated to Livia, the wife of Augustus. At the eastern end, a Roman basilica accommodated the law courts, and at the southern edge, in front of a colonnaded row of shops almost 500 feet long (the largest in the empire!) was the *bema* ("tribunal"), where the Roman governor conducted official public business (Acts 18:12–17).
>
> If Paul was in Corinth in the spring of 49 or 51 C.E., he might have seen the Isthmian games. These were among the four major panhellenic festivals

and were celebrated at the shrine of Poseidon on the isthmus every two years. The reward for winning in these games was a crown of celery, and Paul was moved to comment that these athletes worked "to receive a perishable wreath, but we an imperishable" (1 Cor. 9:25).[6]

The city knew every type of religion its pluralistic society could bring to it. Excavations of the city have discovered sanctuaries of the followers of Dionysus, Asclepius, Demeter, and Core. Each year in her honor the Cult of Isis held a festive spring procession from Corinth to the harbor in Cenchreae. "Isis was also known to her devotees as the goddess who granted to women powers equal to those of men."[7] There was also a synagogue and sizable contingency of Jews. Gallio's treatment of the leader of the synagogue (see below) in consequence of his hostility toward Paul's work and this "new religion," suggests that a significant premium was attached to the acceptance given to all religious views. The proconsul was clearly making the point that any further efforts such as this would not be tolerated in his court.

It is precisely for such reasons that Christianity was able to thrive in the cities of those days. And it is for the same reason that it did not thrive in rural districts (Latin, *pagan*, means "rural," "country"). These so-called "pagan" (literally, "backwoods") superstitions that prevailed in the outlying areas were nearly impenetrable by new ideas and religious teachings for many centuries. By contrast, the people in the cities had been uprooted from their homelands and their ancient cultures and were open to new ideas and new values. In such an environment, the church would take root. Ironically, in our day, the outlying areas of America have been so well seeded with Christianity that it is from this rural heartland that biblical values are maintained. Nonetheless, what Paul knew about the receptivity of the city folk to his preaching is still true, and we would do well to consider the importance of maintaining a strong witness in the inner-cities as a strategy for advancing the gospel in our own day.

The Isthmian games were held in the stadium in alternate years. These were second in popularity only to the Olympics. This sport culture evidently rubbed off on Paul during his lengthy stay, for he uses metaphors of the athlete and of athletic competition here and in his other letters (cf. 9:24–26; Gal. 2:2; 5:7; Phil. 2:16). The *bema* seat, used by Gallio and at athletic events, has even found its way into the language of theology to articulate the final judgment of believers, known uniquely in Scripture through Paul's letter to the Corinthians (cf. 1 Cor. 3; 2 Cor. 5).

An outdoor theater accommodating 20,000 people was the arena for the gladiatorial games and contests with wild beasts. A smaller indoor theater (capacity of 3,000) housed plays and concerts. From such a cultural hub, a

strong gospel witness might well be heard all over the world. It was no wonder Paul felt constrained to bear testimony to such a city.

But the moral depravity evident throughout the city most vividly reflects
the spiritual need of Corinth. The vile character of the old city carried over into
the city of New Testament times. The Greek word *korinthiazomai* (literally, "to
act the Corinthian") came to mean "to commit fornication."[8] Corinth was a
seaman's paradise and a moral cesspool. In this Las Vegas of ancient Achaia,
divorce was commonplace and its results in broken lives evident even in the
homes of believers.[9] "Easy" women roamed the streets, and the moral air was
polluted with the luring aroma of sin. It was famous for all that is debauched.
It was, no doubt, an inspiration for the catalog of sins in Romans 1:18–32
(written by Paul while a guest of Gaius in this wicked city). It was from this
filthy slough of sin that Paul's converts were extracted (cf. 1 Cor. 6:9 11).

I Was With You in Weakness and in Fear

Paul was often given to self-deprecation, with suggestions that he was not
much of a physical specimen (1 Cor. 15:8; 2 Cor. 10:10; Gal. 4:13–16). In one
ancient description of him, possibly dating from the living memory of those
who knew him, Paul is described as "a man small of stature, with a bald head
and crooked legs, in a good state of body, with eyebrows meeting and nose
somewhat hooked, full of friendliness; for now he appeared like a man, and
now he had the face of an angel."[10] Most Christian artists and writers have tend-
ed to characterize Paul in less than complimentary terms. While we may never
know exactly what he looked like, it is evident that the strength of Paul's message was not in his physical presence, but in the finished work of Jesus Christ.

Luke records the origin of the Corinthian church in Acts 18:1–17. Paul
came to Corinth in A.D. 50 after a very unfruitful evangelistic effort at Athens
(Acts 17:16–34). Many think Paul's experience at Athens influenced his
methodology as he moved on to Corinth. According to Luke's account, Paul
had only modest success there. One wonders if Paul considered his efforts to
be a failure altogether. His use of familiar Greek philosophy and poetry, as
well as cultural icons at Athens, gave way in Corinth to one simple truth—
Christ crucified.

When Paul came to Corinth, he *determined* (The Greek term *krino*, "to
judge" or "decide," suggests that the distressed apostle deliberated carefully on
the matter and made a strategic decision) to preach nothing but "Jesus Christ,
and Him crucified" (1 Cor. 2:2). Here he would rely only on the gospel. And
on this foundation alone God would build a thriving assembly in this heathen city. It may not be too far-reaching to suggest that 1 Corinthians 2:2

offers a window into this great missionary's heart and developing methodology as they are informed by his theology and experiences. In this epistle he engages in sustained theological reflection on the gospel in relation to knowing Christ and making him known[11] in a hostile and alien setting.

Probably running short on cash on his arrival, Paul accepted the hospitality of the godly Aquila and Priscilla, exiled Jews from Rome. During the week, he worked with them making tents (Acts 18:1–4). To this day, the term *tent-maker* is used to describe those who, following Paul's example, serve the Lord bivocationally. On the Sabbath, Paul went to the synagogue, where he "reasoned with" the Jews and Greeks concerning Christ (see Acts 18:4).

After the arrival of Silas and Timothy, Paul no longer required secular employment, and therefore devoted himself entirely to aggressive evangelistic effort. One of his earliest converts was Crispus, the synagogue leader. Subsequently, the man's entire household believed, along with many others in the city (Acts 18:8). Incurring opposition from the Jews, he was forced to find another meeting place. Providentially, this turned out to be the home of Titus Justus (probably the "Gaius" of 1 Cor. 1:14), right next door to the synagogue!

Later the Jews had Paul arraigned before Gallio (probably at the bema seat in the main square), where the proconsul dismissed the charges and demonstrated his contempt for the Jews by looking the other way as their new leader, Sosthenes, was flogged in the street. (See my comments on Sosthenes at 1:1.) In all, Paul ministered in Corinth for eighteen months (Acts 18:11), during which time he also wrote 1 and 2 Thessalonians. It is noteworthy that another church was subsequently started in the eastern port of Corinth in Cenchrea (cf. Rom. 16:1). Whether Paul had a hand in this during his first visit or at a later time is not known for certain. At the conclusion of Paul's first visit, the leadership of the assembly was assumed by Apollos, an eloquent preacher from Alexandria (Acts 18:24—19:1). Assured that the church was in good hands, Paul then moved on to Ephesus, where he enjoyed the longest ministry he was ever to have in any one place.

Many Tutors . . . Not Many Fathers

In his own words, Paul's relationship with the Corinthian church was akin to that of a parent with a rebellious child. To understand the occasion for the writing of 1 Corinthians, it is necessary to outline Paul's ongoing involvement with this congregation after his departure for what became a sustained and fruitful ministry in Ephesus. While it is true that much of this is open to debate, the best that can be done here is to outline the most conspicuous details.

1. It was reported by those of Chloe's household that there were quarrels between some of the brethren (1 Cor. 1:11).

2. Although Paul promised a second visit (1 Cor. 4:19), he did not have occasion to see them again before writing 1 Corinthians.

3. After his initial visit described above, Paul wrote the church a letter, in which he apparently warned the Corinthians not to associate with immoral people (1 Cor. 5:9). This letter was misconstrued by the people and required further explanation in 1 Corinthians 5:10–11. There is no incontrovertible evidence that this previous letter has survived or is incorporated in any way into the text of the canonical book of 1 Corinthians as suggested by some.[12]

4. A letter was sent to Paul containing several questions (note the recurring phrase "now concerning," 1 Cor. 7:1, 25; 8:1; 12:1; 16:1). The first reference adds, "the things about which you wrote," which makes it clear that Paul is referencing their letter in his detailed responses throughout the remainder of his epistle.[13] This letter may well have been delivered to Paul by the three men mentioned in 1 Cor. 16:17 (see my comments on this text).

5. After writing 1 Corinthians, Paul sent Timothy to check into conditions in the church with the threat that, if necessary, he would come in person to deal with their carnality (1 Cor. 4:17–19; 16:10–11; Acts 19:22). It is not known whether Timothy ever made it. He may have also requested Apollos (who had since moved on) to take time out to help with the situation (1 Cor. 1:12).

6. With the problems apparently unresolved, Paul was forced to make good on his threat and pay a brief but painful visit (2 Cor. 2:1–4; 12:14; 13:1–2).

7. Upon his return, Paul sent a third letter to Corinth that was of such a severe nature that he later seemed to have regretted writing it (2 Cor. 2:4). This letter was carried by Titus, who was to meet Paul at Troas to give him a status report. This (along with the earlier letter mentioned in 1 Cor. 5:9) had been lost and may well have been destroyed after Paul's final visit with them.[14]

8. When Paul failed to meet Titus at Troas, his anxiety was so great that he was unable to preach, though he had the opportunity (2 Cor. 2:12–13). He hurried on to Macedonia, where he met Titus en route. Titus's report was very encouraging. Paul immediately sat down and penned 2 Corinthians to express his great relief at improved conditions (2 Cor. 2:13–14; 7:5–16) and to deal with some of the remaining problems in anticipation of another visit.[15]

9. Paul followed this letter with his last recorded visit when he spent the winter in Corinth on his way to Jerusalem with the collection for the poor (Acts 20:1–4).

Many Questions, Deeper Concerns

From the foregoing, we see that 1 Corinthians was occasioned by at least two factors. First, from two sources, Paul had received word of divisions in the church (1 Cor. 1:11; 16:17). This sectarianism probably arose more out of the sophist spirit in Corinth than from Judaistic tendencies (as at Galatia). Factions had long characterized the Greek culture.[16] The Greeks split over politics, sports, and philosophy.[17] Thus, it is not surprising to see them carrying this habit over into the church. Paul showed them that this was incompatible with the gospel of Christ (1 Cor. 1:18–25). It was counterproductive to their impact as the new community upon their sinful city. And it was folly when compared with the eschatological destiny of the saints when "the trumpet will sound" (1 Cor. 15:52). An important subtext of this discussion also relates to Paul's authority as their spiritual father and an "apostle" of Christ.[18]

Second, Paul had received a letter from the assembly requesting answers to a series of questions. He felt obliged to respond. In addition to these factors, there were apparently other reports not recorded that were of concern to him. Thus, with pen in hand, Paul purposed to rebuke the party spirit in the assembly and to encourage them to moral purity and spiritual unity.

Paul, Called an Apostle

The authorship of 1 Corinthians is so well attested that only a brief sketch is necessary here. External evidence derives from references to the epistle from the first century onward. Clement of Rome, *Epistle of Barnabas* (3:1, 16), the *Didache* (chap. 10), Polycarp, Hermas, Justin Martyr, Athanagoras, Irenaeus, Clement of Alexandria, Tertullian, the Muratorian Canon, Marcion and the Old Syriac and Old Latin texts all attest to the authority and Pauline authorship of 1 Corinthians.

Internal evidence is equally strong. The writer calls himself Paul (1:1; 3:4, 6, 22; 16:21). The epistle harmonizes well with Luke's accounts in Acts and with the other Pauline letters. Frequent mention is made of contemporaries of the mid first century (thus eliminating a second-century forgery). This, without doubt, is a genuine product of Paul, the apostle to the Gentiles.

I Will Remain in Ephesus until Pentecost

The date and the place of the writing of this letter are also easily discerned. Paul himself tells us that 1 Corinthians was written from Ephesus (1 Cor. 16:8–9, 19). The subscription in the TR and the King James Version is probably due to a misunderstanding of 1 Corinthians 16:5. If it were written toward the end of Paul's stay at Ephesus, the time would be spring of A.D. 55. This is suggested since he says he planned to stay in Ephesus till Pentecost (1 Cor. 16:8) and he was in Jerusalem on or about Pentecost in A.D. 56 (Acts 20:16). In the interim, he visited Corinth briefly (2 Cor. 2:1–4), spent some time in Macedonia (Acts 20:1–6), wrote 2 Corinthians (fall A.D. 55), and came to Corinth a few weeks later and stayed about three months. He spent the Passover season of A.D. 56 in Philippi on his way to Jerusalem (Acts 20:6).

Called into Fellowship

The theme of 1 Corinthians, Paul's longest epistle, is that believers are "called into fellowship with His Son, Jesus Christ" (1:9). This *koinonia* into which they have been called is not about church dinners and cell group get-togethers. It is about participation with their Savior in a community and a task that sets them apart from all others. And it is precisely this fellowship that links them with abiding love to the cross and the resurrection. Because of the cross they are no longer of this world. And a proper understanding of the resurrection will help them to know that they cannot hope to realize the glories of the kingdom until the King is come and they shall receive "of God" that which they can never hope to realize by human innate capacity or achievement.[19] It is precisely on this point that their spiritual father takes them to task. He is deeply disturbed that these believers do not seem to understand the nature of the gospel, which focuses on the cross and the empty tomb, not on pneumatics and self-exaltation.

Certain terms are used repeatedly, such as *knowledge, wisdom, discern, love, holy,* and *sanctify.* These terms betray the priority issues on the writer's mind. From this spiritual reservoir Christian leaders from Paul's day to this have drawn refreshing words of counsel, admonition, and comfort for troubled saints.

Throughout this epistle and the one that follows it, Paul reflects the intense concern of a spiritual father struggling to bring his problem children back into fellowship and submission. In this respect, the images he employs are striking: "brother," "father," "children," "nursing mother," "servant."[20] Thus the great thrust throughout is practical, taking the form of instruction, correction, reproof, or edification. But throughout, one sees the heart of this great pastor-apostle reaching out to his wayward flock with firm resolve but always with loving affection

What Does It Mean to Be "the Church of God at Corinth"?

Whether it is doctrine, reproof, correction, or instruction in righteousness, throughout this epistle Paul is answering the question of what it means—individually and corporately—to be a saint in a sinful world. He deals with these issues in turn as they serve his purpose to call the Corinthians "into fellowship." He gives both unsolicited advice (chaps. 1—6, 15) and solicited advice (chaps. 7—14). The Corinthians had requested his counsel on a series of problems with which they were dealing, and Paul responded to these, but not until he directed their attention to a few problems of which they weren't aware or at least didn't care to bring up. This letter follows a pattern familiar to Paul (cf. 2 Tim. 3:16) of reproof (chaps. 1—4), correction (chaps. 5—6), instruction (chaps. 7—15), and teaching (chap. 15). His chapter on the resurrection is directed to a doctrinal problem a certain individual in the assembly seemed to have with the concept of the bodily resurrection (chap. 15). This is the only doctrinal "error," as such, that Paul had to deal with in the epistle, and it does not appear to have been one of the questions asked of him.

However, as others have observed, it is a mistake to suggest that the theological, or for that matter, the practical issues raised and developed in this epistle are considered by the writer in an ad hoc manner. Throughout the epistle there is a "theological pulse."[21] This is a common pattern in all of Paul's letters, yoking his doctrinal teaching with practical advice. Most of his shorter letters can be easily broken into two sections: the doctrinal and the practical. In this—much longer—epistle it would seem that the writer has woven the doctrinal and practical into a tapestry of theology and exhortation. After a brief introduction, the book opens with a discourse on the wisdom of the cross (1:18—2:16), which forms the foundation for the rebuke of factionalism, the challenge to unity, and the admonition to purity. Then there is the practical teaching on spiritual gifts (chaps. 12—14), which pivots on the theology of love (chap. 13). And finally there is the chapter on the resurrection (chap. 15), which serves as the eschatological bookend to match the opening discussion of the gospel. Together they effectively embrace the entire epistle.

There is a mistaken notion in modern Western thinking that "theory" and "practice" have little or nothing to do with each other. Some—even in evangelical churches—take pride in their disdain for theology in favor of giving people "practical" instruction on how to deal with issues in their lives, families, and churches. A visit to the average Christian bookstore will easily demonstrate the popularity of such fare. Paul shows us that he would reject such compartmentalized methodology. Right thinking and right action are two sides of the same coin. Without doctrine we are left to drift with the tides of modernity—victims of every "wind of doctrine." Without the faithful appropriation of truth in action, we are locked in an ivory tower far removed from the realities of the world into which we are called to serve Christ. Paul's writings give us the perfect balance of doctrine/theology and practical instruction. Never does he place a wall of separation between these.

The theme of the epistle, as noted above, is captured in 1:9, "God is faithful, through whom you were called into fellowship with His Son, Jesus Christ our Lord." In a nutshell, this is the essence of Paul's message to the Corinthians. And it is this truth by which he calls them to "discern what is involved in belonging to Christ within the context of an unbelieving society. In one way or another, all the problems addressed in these chapters reflect the difficulties that arise because believers are called to be agents of God's love in a world to which they do not ultimately belong, and which in Paul's view, is swiftly passing away."[22]

SECTION 1: REPROOF

I Exhort You, Brethren

1 Corinthians 1—4

CHAPTER 2

To the Church of God at Corinth
1 Corinthians 1:1-9

Preview:

By opening his letter with an assertion of his love for the Corinthian church, Paul makes it clear that they hold a special place in his heart. God has enriched them. And not only so, but He continues to confirm the gospel in them and to call them into fellowship with His Son, Jesus Christ our Lord.

Greetings (1:1-3)

Bad news! About all Paul hears from his recent church-plant in Corinth is discouraging. They struggle with disruptive members. They don't know how to respond to flagrant violations of community—let alone *godly*—standards. And they disagree with one another over basic issues that should have been resolved long ago. How could this be happening?

They couldn't have asked for a more promising start. Their founding pastor was none other than the great missionary evangelist and church planter, the apostle Paul himself. Their subsequent pastor was the eloquent preacher Apollos. They had enjoyed the evident support of the magistrates to worship freely and share their faith without fear. They had strong leadership and were wonderfully gifted by the Holy Spirit to do the work of the ministry.

Yet none of these strengths and opportunities seem to matter. It is rumored that they have run off their pastor. There are threats of a church split. Some have raised questions about their leadership and even about Paul's

15

integrity. In some cases, his words are being taken out of context and miscon-strued. This "apostle to the Gentiles" has a job to do, and being the leader that he is, he heads toward the problem, not away from it. Whatever it takes, whether with pen or in person, he is not going to let these issues ferment any longer without taking action.

What would come of Paul's efforts was one of the most practical and perennially useful epistles in all of the New Testament. To be sure, all of Scripture is profitable, but most pastors and church leaders find themselves drawn to certain key texts when addressing various issues and problems in their churches. It is difficult to imagine anyone in church leadership in any age who has not found the letters of Paul to the Corinthian Christians to be a wealth of instruction and help on issues and concerns that sadly remain prob-lematic in our assemblies to this day.

Paul, Called . . . an Apostle

The salutation of this letter, on the one hand, is standard for Paul's letters. He identifies himself and his recipients and offers greetings on behalf of himself and his companions. But, on the other hand, he adds to his salutation things that are significant to his readers. He makes a not-so-subtle declaration that his audience could not have missed. He writes not simply as a friend and for-mer associate in the ministry, but with a clear assumption of authority by virtue of his calling—by none other than the Lord Himself—as an "apostle." He is not merely asserting this of himself, nor is he speaking of "what will be, but what is."[1] When he adds, "by the will of God," his appeal is to the high-est authority granting him the right to speak. This of course anticipates and answers those who had questioned his authority (cf. 9:1–2; 2 Cor. 10:10). Paul develops this theme further in chapter 9. Here the important matter is that he has differentiated himself from others by grounding his claims in the speech and activity of both God and Christ. As such, he does not merely stack up as first among equals. He stands out as singular in his calling from God and his role in bringing the church to Corinth.[2]

Paul has similar intent in the mention of "Sosthenes our brother." Paul joins the well-known brother, Sosthenes with him in writing. This man was not a fellow apostle, nor is there any evidence that he could be a coauthor of this letter. Acts 18:8 mentions Crispus, the synagogue ruler when Paul first arrived, as one of the first converts. Sosthenes is the name of the man who had been elected to take his place and subsequently had been flogged in a public display in the town square. Now a "Sosthenes" appears as a fellow Christian and minister of the gospel. In light of the opposition facing Paul at the Corinthian church, it is no doubt possible that he uses Sosthenes, probably a native Corinthian, to help ingratiate himself with his readers. On this point, Grosheide notes:

> Some think [Sosthenes] is one of Chloe's household (v. 12). We prefer the opinion that Sosthenes is the man referred to in Acts 18:17. *Brother* makes clear that Sosthenes has become a Christian since the facts related in Acts 18. However the word *brother* alone cannot express the fact that Paul intends to inform the Corinthians of the conversion of Sosthenes. He was probably the ruler of the Jewish synagogue mentioned in Acts 18:17, although this cannot be established beyond question.[3]

We should not be dogmatic, but if Grosheide's hunch is correct—and I believe it is—Sosthenes was more than a mutual acquaintance. He was a well-respected authority—known to the readers in his role as the former leader of the synagogue. Now he appears as a companion and supporter of Paul's ministry in Ephesus. This suggests why he is mentioned at all and why he is mentioned specifically in this context. We know that Paul is not above "dividing the Sanhedrin" when it becomes necessary (cf. Acts 23:6–10). In this case, we can be sure that he secured the favor and approval of those who followed their former leader in his indirect approbation of the writer.

What is at stake here is more than Paul's reputation in the early Christian community. What stands or falls with his authority is his *word*, which under the inspiration of the Holy Spirit is providentially destined to serve as normative Scripture to guide both this wayward congregation and the Church at large (see 2:12–13). If it could be demonstrated that his authority was a self-serving usurpation, then it could be shown that his teaching was also in question. The writer considers this fact to be of critical importance and therefore finds it necessary to establish the fact beyond question at the very outset (see also 1 Cor. 9:16; 2 Cor. 3:4–6). And this is why he wastes no time getting to the point.

To the Church of God Which Is at Corinth

Believers in "the church," at Corinth are called out and called together. On the theological significance of this expression see my introduction above. "Both 1 and 2 Corinthians are addressed 'to the church of God which is at Corinth' (1 Cor. 1:2; 2 Cor. 1:1), a turn of phrase that is both unique to these letters and evocative of the most basic challenge that Paul faced in dealing with this congregation: What does it mean and how is it possible to be *God's* church *in Corinth*?"[4] What Paul asserts, namely, that his calling is from God Himself, he also conveys indirectly to the Corinthians. They are not merely *the church*, they are *God's* church. This is so because they are His work, having been "sanctified in Christ Jesus" (1:2) and gifted abundantly by His Spirit (1:7). Here Paul has special reference to the Corinthian's correct *standing* before God. That is, they were set apart for God's special use. His aim in the epistle is to bring their *state* into closer alignment with this standing.

Yet the believers remain "in Corinth." When God saves them, he doesn't take them immediately on to heaven. Nor does he bring them into a "kingdom of heaven" on earth—a point to which Paul will come later (cf. 4:8). Instead, they are to remain in Corinth—a wicked city—as "saints." Here they are to build a new community, proclaiming the crucified Christ, building on His foundation with "gold, silver, and precious stones" (see 3:10–15), anticipating Christ's return (1:7), "always abounding in the work of the Lord" (15:58).

Paul knew from his prior experience in Athens how frustrating it was to try to be a *philosopher* when God had called him to be a *prophet*. He already knew what Tertullian more than a century later would declare—that there could be no concord between "Athens and Jerusalem." The church established in Corinth was not a Greek thing, it was a God thing. But it was a God thing in Greece. And if it was to flourish as God intended, it would have to do so God's way. And God's way would be characterized by the "wisdom of the cross," not the "wisdom of the world" (cf. 1:18–31).

Paul then adds that these believers in Corinth are "saints by calling, with all who in every place call on the name of our Lord Jesus Christ." Leon Morris responds correctly to the suggestion of some that this language is meant to widen the salutation to include all Christians. "[T]he Epistle gives no sign of being intended as a circular or a general manifesto. It sticks stubbornly to local issues."[5] Indeed, the local issue to which the writer points is "saints by calling" in solidarity with "all" others who "call upon the name of our Lord Jesus Christ." This looks ahead to the latter section of chapter 1, where the writer finds it necessary to attack the spirit of factionalism that characterized their group. He will make it clear before he is finished that there is only one Spirit by whom we are all baptized into one body (12:12, 13). The Church is one organism into which every saint is placed and in which each exercises the gifting that is sovereignly given for the edification and support of the whole.

More important, the language in this epistle is significant to Paul's agenda. As early as Genesis 4:26 we read, "Then *men* began to call upon the name of the LORD." Jesus used the "serpent in the wilderness," (cf. John 3:14; Num. 21:8–9) to recall an Old Testament motif by which to describe what He would do for the salvation of the world. In similar fashion, Peter recalls the words of the prophet Joel to declare that "everyone who calls on the name of the Lord shall be saved" (cf. Acts 2:21; Joel 2:28–32). Again, Paul uses similar language in Romans 10:13: "Whoever will call upon the name of the Lord will be saved."

The gospel is not a complicated thing. Nor is it something that is found at the end of a long journey. It is especially not something the "wisdom of this world" will be able to ferret out. It is available to those who "call upon the name of the Lord." It is for those who simply *ask.* As Moses lifted up the serpent in the wilderness, they were only to "look and live." It is so simple that it would be construed by the wise of this age as "foolish" (see 1:18).

There is still one more needle imbedded in this sentence. Since the Corinthians are claiming the family *name,* Paul expects that they will live in conformity to the family *way.* The emphasis, of course, is on the unity of all who call upon the name of the Lord. The instruction establishes first of all that there is no legitimate place for this type of division in the body. Second, it establishes that if one is in the body, there will be a natural affinity with all others who share that common faith. And third, it establishes boundaries. Those who are bound together in one *koinonia* may not be joined to harlots or idols (cf. chaps. 5, 6).

Grace and Peace

With "grace" Paul contemplates all that is understood in God's love as it is exercised toward sinners. "Peace" has in mind those benefits that come from the exercise of God's love. Note that grace and peace come from "God our Father and the Lord Jesus Christ." Here the Father and the Son are shown to be of equal status yet clearly distinguished (cf. Phil. 2:6). Together the words of the greeting form a wonderful précis of the essential truths of the gospel as emphasized by Paul throughout this epistle and in all his writings. It is a natural fit for this one who considered himself the "chief of sinners," and who knew the power of the cross for everyone who believes—to the Jew first and also to the Greek. The gospel is all of grace, grounded in the purpose of God and the finished work of Jesus Christ. And in its appropriation through the Holy Spirit there is first of all, "peace *with* God" (in reconciliation and justification, cf. Rom. 5) and then the "peace *of* God" that passes understanding (cf. Phil. 4:7). The great apostle blesses his readers with this greeting and at the same time offers it as a doxology of praise and as a prayer for its reality to those upon whom it is bestowed.

Thanksgiving (1:4–9)

One of the benefits of reading 1 Corinthians is that it offers a paradigm for problem solving. We already know that Paul is deeply concerned about this church. In fact, he is at odds with many of the people, and it is probably not a stretch to say that he is hurt and angry. Yet he begins with a prayer of thanksgiving for all the good things God has done and continues to do in and for them ("I thank my God always concerning you"). And as one reads on, it is evident that this is not merely a ploy to throw them off balance. He has a genuine love and concern for them to which he returns time and time again throughout this letter and in his subsequent dealings with them. Indeed, the greatest example of the enduring quality of love as taught in chapter 13 is Paul's undying love and affection for these people as he express-es repeatedly in these letters to them (cf. 16:24; 2 Cor. 2:4; 11:11; 12:15). Thus, what follows takes the form of genuine thanksgiving to God for spe-cific benefits enjoyed by the Corinthian assembly. At the same time Paul is looking for evidences that confirm to him (and his readers) that God is gen-uinely at work in the life of their church (cf. 1:6). As these evidences are doc-umented, he has genuine cause for rejoicing and a positive outlook on their prospects as individuals and as a church.

First, there is confirmation of Christ's work (1:4–6). "I thank my God always . . . for the grace of God which was given you in Christ Jesus" (v. 4). The direction of Paul's thanks is to God. The very fact that a church should have been brought into existence at all in so wicked a place as Corinth was evidence of God's grace and power (cf. Rom. 1:16). The regularity of Paul's prayer is expressed in the term "always." No doubt this is somewhat hyperbolic, but it is probably not an overstatement that, at least for the moment, Paul is sufficient-ly concerned about this church that they are on his mind constantly and in his prayers "always." Pastors will do well to follow his example. Sometimes it is dif-ficult to leave problems behind. In fact, anyone in whom God has placed a "pas-tor's heart," knows how impossible it is sometimes to *let go.* Paul had learned the power of prayer for himself as well as for those for whom he prayed. In the face of so many obstacles to the work in Corinth, he could be positive and upbeat, because he knew that "God is faithful" (1:9). As he had already written to the believers at Thessalonica, "Faithful is He who calls you, and He also will bring it to pass" (1 Thess. 5:24). This is a good illustration of what the theolo-gians like to call the "communion of the saints." That is, he gives thanks to God for the mutual benefits that he extends to all believers. In this case, it is for "the grace of God which was given." This looks to the next verse, which in turn hints at the important topic developed later in chapters 12—14.

The reason for Paul's thanks was that the Corinthians had been "enriched" in Christ "in all speech and all knowledge." The extent of this enrichment is expressed in verse 7: They "are not lacking in any gift." While the term *gift* has a wide variety of meanings, here it probably has reference to spiritual gifts. The reference to "all speech and all knowledge" (v. 5) clearly anticipates Paul's lengthy discourse on tongues, in which "knowledge" is conspicuously absent from, rather than conjoined to, the gift. That they are mentioned together here sets the stage for what Paul will say later.

"The testimony concerning Christ" (v. 6) is not the Corinthian's witness *to* Christ, but their witness *of* Christ through the convicting work of the Holy Spirit (cf. John 16:8–14).[6] They have witnessed the saving work and power of Christ in their lives because of Paul's faithful preaching of the gospel. This work is confirmed in the fact that God's grace was given (1:4), God's supply is evident (1:5), and God's gifts are manifested (1:5–6).

Second, there is confirmation in the coming of Christ (1:7–8). Since the gospel had been faithfully preached and received by the Corinthian believers, they are now privileged to wait upon the second coming of Jesus Christ, who in turn "shall also confirm" (v. 8) them. Historically, the gospel had been confirmed in them. Now they anticipate the prospect of that blessed event when Jesus Christ shall also declare them blameless before the throne of God. In the meantime, they are "awaiting eagerly" (v. 7) (without arrogance, cf. 4:5). They are to watch for "the revelation of our Lord" (it hasn't happened yet, cf. 4:8, 9). And they would be found "blameless" (because Christ has been made unto us "righteousness and sanctification, and redemption," cf. 1:30). Life is not a sprint but a marathon.

The expression "the day of the Lord Jesus" or "the day of Christ" occurs in 1 Corinthians 5:5; 2 Corinthians 1:14; Philippians 1:6, 10; 2:16; and 2 Thessalonians 2:2. These expressions, in contrast to the "Day of the Lord," refer to God's future program for His Church (cf. Is. 2, 13; Ezek. 13, 30; Joel 1—2; Zech. 14; et al.). The Day of the Lord is a more general term for God's future judgment upon Israel and the nations—including the Tribulation period (Zech. 14:1–4). But as Spiros Zodhiates has noted, "Two different programs are in these two expressions . . . but they fall within the same time period."[7] They both officially begin when Christ returns for His church.

Finally, Paul confirms that the Corinthian believers have been "called into fellowship with His Son, Jesus Christ our Lord (1:9). Just as Paul directed his thanksgiving toward God, so the ground of his thanksgiving is that same God. For, it is He who "is faithful." And it is also that same One by whom they "were called." The term *fellowship* includes both union and communion. The Corinthian believers had been brought into *union* with the Lord Jesus Christ. Accordingly, this great truth implies that they had been brought into *communion* with one another. It is on this basis that Paul attacks their sectarianism as incompatible with their calling and character as part of the new community, which functions under the headship of Christ. As noted above, this is the theme of this epistle and the central truth around which all that follows is centered.

Study Questions

1. In what specific ways does the culture of Corinth contribute to the issues and concerns developed in Paul's writings to this church?

2. Suggest some ways that the Corinthian culture has modern-day parallels.

3. It is speculated that the apostle Paul wrote several letters to this church. How many were there? How do you account for some of them possibly being lost?

4. What two factors prompted Paul to sit down and write 1 Corinthians?

5. State and explain the key verse of this epistle. How does this relate to Paul's theme throughout?

6. In what specific way(s) did the Corinthian believers misunderstand the gospel?

7. What leadership principles can be gleaned from Paul's approach to the issues in this church?

8. Who was Sosthenes? Is it possible that Paul has a "hidden agenda" for mentioning him? What might that be?

9. Explain Paul's greeting. What is the significance of "grace" and "peace?"

10. Suggest at least four topics that Paul introduces in the first nine verses of his letter.

CHAPTER 3

Dealing with Division
1 Corinthians 1:10–31

Preview:
Against the spirit of factionalism, Paul carefully presents the wisdom of the cross. As humble saints, our only boast is in the Lord Jesus, who is made unto us wisdom, righteousness, sanctification, and redemption.

In Paul's instruction to Timothy (2 Tim. 3:16), he encourages his young protégé with assurances that, although he is young and inexperienced, he nevertheless has in his possession the Scriptures that were "inspired by God" and are "profitable for teaching, for reproof, for correction, for training in righteousness." In this hard-hitting letter to the Corinthians, the apostle Paul demonstrates the practical value and functional power of the inspired Word for teaching in the local church. Not surprisingly, since both letters are from the same pen, each of these qualities of "profitability" is demonstrated here in turn as God's Spirit directs its composition.

In this opening section that I have titled "Reproof," the first major concern to which Paul turns his attention is the divisive spirit in Corinth.

Paul's Exhortation (1:10–17)

"Now" (v. 10) is adversative. Paul is not simply "moving right along" with a benign agenda. Rather, it is with such language that he plants his feet and stiffens his back for what is certain to be a confrontation. The language here calls to mind Galatians 2:11, when little Paul stood up to the big man—Peter—to call him to accountability because "he stood condemned." Whatever else may be said of Paul, the one quality he can never be denied is courage. And in situations such as in Corinth there is no question why God selected him for the job. Even before he opens his mouth, he is a lesson in leadership and conflict management.

Although these believers have been called to *koinonia* with Christ, there is a problem. Paul introduces his appeal for unity with "I exhort you, brethren, by the name of our Lord Jesus Christ" (v. 10). The writer does two things here. First, he "exhorts" (Greek, *parakalein*, "beseeches") them as "brethren." The image is that of a coach who calls a player to come "alongside." The player knows the coach isn't there to pay him a compliment. His purpose is probably to let him know what he needs to do to improve his game. It is easy to picture Paul putting his arms around these people and saying something like, "Now, dear brothers, don't you think it is time to put an end to this conflict?"[1] He is about to exhort them to unity, which is characteristic of brethren in Christ. And although he does not want to be heavy-handed about it, he has to let them know that their behavior is unacceptable and that they need to work together to succeed.

Paul then, asserts his authority with an appeal to the "name of our Lord" (cf. 2 Thess. 3:12). The believers' reverence and love for Christ should induce them to yield obedience to the apostle. Since Paul's own integrity has been called into question, it is appropriate that he defer authority to Christ. Grosheide accurately captures the tone and the force of this text.

> The name of Jesus Christ is uttered and in that way, not merely through Christ, but through the utterance of His name the apostle exhorts. The use of "through" can thus be explained (Rom. 12:1). By uttering the name of the Lord Jesus Christ Paul recalls to the mind of the Corinthians the sufferings and the glory of the Mediator and the fruits thereof for the children of God. . . . The apostle's exhortation is a very earnest one. He admonishes the Corinthians to place themselves before the face of the Lord. This does not surprise us when we consider the seriousness of their sin.[2]

The readers must not miss Paul's point. When a prophet speaks the *word* of God, the authority is not in the messenger, it is in the *God* of the word. As an apostle, Paul's word is authoritative, not because of his own authority, but because of the One who commissioned him (cf. 9:16; 2 Cor. 3:4–6).[3] Those who speak prophetically today, who faithfully preach the Word of God, share this authority—not in quite the same way as Paul (since he was given to *write* Scripture and we are not), but certainly in terms of the authority of the text preached. It is no less the Word of God today than it was in the first century. And it speaks with no less authority today. But a further caution is in order: "Clearly, his sense of apostolic authority is matched with an equally strong sense of his accountability to the One by whom he has been commissioned (e.g. 1 Cor. 4:1–5)."[4] To whom much has been given, much shall be required.

Paul exhorted further, "That you all agree [Greek, *legete*: "call," "assert," "maintain"], and there be no divisions among you" (v. 10). Quarrels had split the congregation into factions, so Paul's appeal is to unity in the fellowship. But the language here suggests more than mere speech; it cuts deeper, to "intent." The believers are to be in "agreement" together, which requires a more in-depth examination of themselves. And so he adds, "that . . . you be made complete [note the use of this term, *katartizo*, in Mark 1:19, translated "mending"] in the same mind and in the same judgment" (v. 10) (literally, "thought" or "opinion").

It is doubtful that Paul wants to eliminate diversity from the congregation. His instruction regarding the diversity of gifts (chapter 12) speaks eloquently to that point. In fact, it is with the celebration of diversity that he attacks the divisive spirit circulating around the diverse ministries of Peter, Christ, Apollos, and himself. What he challenges the Corinthians to do is to "mend" their relationships and attitudes toward one another and work toward developing a spirit of unity and cooperation. It is only arrogance and a misunderstanding of the nature of the gospel that permits them to put asunder what God has joined together.

A pastor once remarked, "I would have a great church if it wasn't for people!" Although spoken in jest, his comment points to the great challenge of leading a diverse group of people that never really "arrives" but is always in a state of "becoming." The spiritual mix of the Church is more like Brazilian *feijoada* than a gourmet dinner. Restaurants all over Brazil save their leftovers each week and throw them in a pot with black beans to be served on Wednesdays. They call it *feijoada*. It's their version of "Irish stew." In the church, God brings people of all socioeconomic and ethnic backgrounds together and gifts them to work on each other to "stimulate one another to love and good deeds" (Heb. 10:24).

In a wider circle, the Church functions like family. No one has the opportunity to select who his or her family members will be. Neither do we have the right to decide who will sit on the other end of our pew or participate in our small groups. Nonetheless, our contemporary churches have fallen prey to this sin. We have divided over generational lines, worship styles, color, ethnic background, socioeconomic status, and other diversity issues. The apostle would give the same counsel he gave the Corinthians: "Let there be no division." What God has joined together, let no man put asunder. Paul will come back to this before the chapter is over and will be less diplomatic than he is here (cf. 1:26–31).

"Chloe's *people*" (v. 11), possibly slaves of Chloe's household who were in Ephesus on business, had brought word to the apostle concerning the condition of the assembly at Corinth. The report was that "there are quarrels among you." The term *eris* is translated in our text only here as "quarrels." Elsewhere it is translated "strife" (cf. 3:3; 2 Cor. 12:20; Gal. 5:20). It does not suggest "schism" yet, but it is clearly not something that should be going on in the church.[5] His intent is "that . . . there be no divisions" (Greek, *schismata*). Schism conveys the idea of "rending apart." The situation is not that bad yet, but the writer is directing them to mend their ways lest it reach that point.[6]

Word does not appear to have come directly from Chloe, but from those who worked in her household. "I have been informed" (v. 11), suggests that there was significant conversation between Paul and his guests from Corinth. They filled him in on conditions there in such a way that he could not doubt the accuracy of their report. Nor could he ignore it any longer. Paul is careful not to betray confidences, but he is just explicit enough to show them that he has gathered firsthand information and is able to speak directly to the issues before the church.

A word should be said here about the levels of Gentile society represented in the church. Here it is evident that in securing the truth about the Corinthian church, Paul gives as much credence to the servants "of Chloe" as he would the person of highest stature. In fact, he reminds them that most of them are "baseborn" anyway (cf. 1:26–29). Early Christians seem to have come from all levels of Gentile society except the very highest. Upper-class women seem to have outnumbered the upper-class men. It is likely that the women enjoyed a higher status in the Christian community than they had in the culture generally. Some of the more prosperous members acted as patrons—supporting churches in their homes and bringing entire households into the assembly (Acts 11:14; 16:15; 18:8). Also, freedmen, slaves, and others whose positions were somewhat ambiguous in society were attracted to the Christian community because of the elevated status they enjoyed there and of course the promise of their role in the coming kingdom of Christ.[7] On this front both Paul and James (cf. Gal. 3:26–29; James 2:1–3) agree that in Christ all stand as equals—whether in terms of our common need (Rom. 3:23) or in terms of our status as members of the body. Contemporary objections by critics to the contrary misunderstand the nature of the Christian gospel and the facts of Christian history.

As to the factionalism in the Corinthian church, there appear to have been four rival parties. "Each one of you" (v. 12) suggests that everyone had chosen sides. Some professed to follow Paul, perhaps as the most sublime teacher, and some followed Apollos, the gifted orator from Alexandria. Others claimed Peter, or "Cephas."[8] These may have been Judaists, or, more likely, they were those who preferred Peter, believing he represented greater authority, for he was with Christ in His earthly ministry. Then there were those who renounced all the others and claimed only Christ. What special advantage this last party claimed is not certain. But they were as much sectarian as the others, for they degraded the Lord to the level of a party leader (also notice 2 Cor. 5:15; 10:7; and 11:23).[9]

Apollos—Paul's Fellow Servant in the Ministry

- *An Alexandrian Jew, eloquent in speech and "mighty" in scriptural teaching (Acts 18:24)*
- *Accurately taught the things concerning Jesus (Acts 18:25)*
- *Acquainted with the ministry of John the Baptist (Acts 18:25b)*
- *Spoke boldly in the synagogue at Ephesus (Acts 18:26)*
- *Taught the way of God more clearly by Priscilla and Aquila (Acts 18:26b)*
- *Introduced to Paul at Corinth (Acts 19:1)*
- *Followed by some who wanted to create division among the apostles (1 Cor. 1:12–13)*
- *Called a servant of God who "watered" after Paul had "planted" (1 Cor. 3:4–6)*
- *A mere man who was not to receive inflated honor (1 Cor. 3:22)*
- *To be sent by Paul at a later time to minister to the Corinthians (1 Cor. 16:12)*
- *Part of a traveling team of ministers who were sent by Paul to serve others (Titus 3:13)*

"Has Christ been divided?" (v. 13). The implied answer in the Greek text is "No." There is but one Christ. "Paul was not crucified for you, was he?" He goes on, "Or were you baptized in the name of Paul?" (v. 13).

In view of the divisions in the assembly, Paul is thankful that very few in Corinth were even baptized by him (1:14–16). No one could ever accuse him of trying to gather a following for himself in this way. The implication of this is significant: Baptism is not necessary to salvation; otherwise the apostle would have been giving thanks to God that he participated in the salvation of so few.

Baptism was not part of the apostle's commission; rather, he asserts, "Christ did not send me to baptize, but to preach the gospel" (v. 17). Paul concludes his exhortation regarding the divisions in the assembly with a call to evangelize "not in cleverness of speech, that the cross of Christ would not be made void" (Greek *Kenoo* means "to empty or deprive of substance") (v. 17). This looks ahead to the next segment of his argument where he deals with the problems of human wisdom as opposed to divine. The success of the gospel lies in the plain doctrine of a crucified Christ. Paul was not about to ascribe its power to the flourish of oratory or the intricacies of Greek philosophy. In spite of his learning at the feet of Gamaliel, Paul puts his learning aside when he preaches the simple gospel of Christ. This truth needs no artificial dress. It alone carries with it the "power of God for salvation" (Rom. 1:16). Having exhorted the people to unity, the apostle now goes on to correct a misconception they have regarding the nature of the gospel by demonstrating his own example in proclaiming this powerful but simple truth (vv. 18–25).

Paul mentions the cross of Christ ten times in his letters. The cross cannot be ignored. It is the great emblem of the salvation Christ accomplished for us.

Paul's Doctrine of the Cross

The cross of Christ cannot be made void by clever speech (1 Cor. 1:17).

The cross represents the power of God to save, but it is foolishness to those who are perishing (1 Cor. 1:18).

The cross is a stumbling block to Jewish legalism (Gal. 5:11).

The teaching of the cross brings persecution (Gal. 6:12).

Paul's only boast is in the cross (Gal. 6:14).

The cross brings reconciliation for both Jew and Gentile (Eph. 2:16).

Christ was obedient to the point of death on the cross (Phil. 2:8).

Those who walk contrary to the pattern of Paul are enemies of the cross (Phil. 3:18).

Christ made peace through the shedding of His blood on the cross (Col. 1:20).

On the cross Christ canceled out the certificate of death (the Law) that was against us (Col. 2:14).

Paul's Proclamation (1:18–25)

Paul directs his attention first to the "word of the cross" (vv. 18–20). "For" (v. 18) introduces the reason he did not come merely with wise words. The content of Paul's message was the cross, not wisdom as defined by "this age" (1:20). It is "to those who are perishing foolishness" (v. 18). In the cross's effect on people, Paul singles out two groups: "those who are perishing" and "us who are being saved" (v. 18). Those who perish deem the word of the cross foolishness. The word of the cross was met with scorn and contempt by people of great wit and learning. They are like those who cried out on Golgotha's hill, "He saved others; let Him save Himself if this is the Christ of God" (Luke 23:35).

Paul identifies the other group with the words "to us who are being saved" (v. 18). The language here is strongly reminiscent of our Lord's instructions regarding the broad way that leads to destruction and the many who enter by it, and the narrow way that leads to life, while few find it (Matt. 7:13–14). To the saved, the pure and simple message of the cross is the "power of God" (v. 18).

In verses 19 and 20 Paul further buttresses his argument by the appeal from Scripture (Is. 29:14; 19:12; 33:18). The "wise" of Corinth are no more effectual to the saving of souls than the "wise" of Judah in staving the threat against Sennacherib. The activity of God is greatly stressed in these verses God will "destroy" (v. 19) human wisdom and make the wisdom of this world "foolish." But where is the wisdom of God, and how is it demonstrated? Paul's answer to this question is given in verses 21–25. It is the wisdom of the cross.

It is evident that "the world through its wisdom did not *come to* know God" (v. 21). By leaving humans to their own wisdom, God demonstrates human folly. Sinful humans are not only incapable of knowing God; they have degraded Him to the level of the creature (cf. Rom. 1:21–23). "Where is the debater (Greek, *suzetetes*, "disputer," "sophist") of this age?" (v. 20). Why are these Corinthian believers taken up with sophistry when history affirms that through such "wisdom," the knowledge of God is impossible? By way of contrast, Paul says that the knowledge of God is possible only to "those who believe" (v. 21). Here is the wisdom of God. Salvation comes through "the foolishness of the message preached" (v. 21). The emphasis of the apostle here is not on the "act" of preaching, but on the "content" of preaching (that is, the message of the cross, cf. v. 18 above). It is not "preaching" as such that is foolish (as some have discerned from the KJV reading); it is that which is preached—the cross—that is foolishness.

Sophia in the New Testament and *hokmah* in the Old Testament both signify the idea of "skillfulness." This root idea is seen in Exodus 36:1–2, where the term is associated with the skill of the craftsman. Duane Litfin observes:

> A wise person, according to the Bible, is one who lives skillfully by obeying God's Word (1 Corinthians 1:21). There is a wisdom of the world that will lead us astray, the Apostle Paul says, but Jesus Christ is the "wisdom of God." In Him may be found "all the treasures of wisdom" (Colossians 2:3). Those who obey His Word will live skillfully; their lives will show the marks of fine craftsmanship. These are the ones who are wise indeed.[10]

Here too, the wisdom of God displayed on the cross is linked with something God is doing, rather than just information or ideas (as we typically think of wisdom). The truth of human depravity, the truth of God's love, the truth of God's plan, and the truth of God's holiness are all part of the mix. But the wisdom of God in the cross is seen in what He does about all this. What seemed impossible—to satisfy the holiness of God and justify sinners—is a work so wonderful, says Peter, that it is a matter into which "angels long to look" (1 Pet. 1:12).

Adding to the significance of this "wisdom" in the context of the epistle as a whole, Victor Paul Furnish correctly notes:

> The decisive point in Paul's discourse on the wisdom of the cross, which stands within the chapters where he is appealing for unity, is expressed in his statement that because "the world did not know God through wisdom, God decided, through the foolishness of our proclamation, to save those who believe" (1:21). In this context, being saved (note the present tense participle in 1:18) means, first, being delivered from the self-deception that merely human wisdom can attain the knowledge of God. And it means, second, being drawn into a relationship to God where a trustful believing is possible. The "foolishness" of the apostle's proclamation is that this saving power of God is at work in the most unlikely of places, the cross (1:18), and in the most unlikely of figures, a crucified Messiah (1:24; 2:2). He does not mean, however, that either the knowledge disclosed in the cross or the trustful believing that it makes possible actually constitutes salvation. In fact, he never employs the noun "salvation" in this letter, but only the verb, and always in such a way as to make it clear that believers are *"being* saved" (1:18; 15:2).[11]

The question is asked, "What precisely is the power of the cross through which believers are being saved, and through which they may hope to come into the fullness of the knowledge of God?"[12] The answer is already anticipated when Paul makes reference to God's grace that is given to them (1:4) and their relationship to God as "saints" (1:2). This is further developed in 1:26–30, where it is seen that Christ Jesus is made unto us wisdom, righteousness, sanctification, and redemption. Furnish concludes: "It is thus through the power of God's grace operative in the cross that one is delivered from the wisdom of this age, and granted, in Christ (who is 'the power of God and the wisdom of God,' (1:24) a new identity and a new life."[13]

This insight is critically important in distinguishing Paul's gospel from competing Gnosticism, but also from all other forms of religiosity that would render the obligations of the gospel in human terms and achievement. What the wisdom of the world cannot understand is that the human problem is not simply a "personal" problem (or a social problem, for that matter). It is a situation before God that must be resolved. And for that reason, the solution must come from above, not from below. That God *must* do so is foolishness for the Greek mind since both their gods and their associated *leges sacrae* (obligations) were of their own making.[14]

That God *would* do so in this manner is also incomprehensible and a stumbling block to the Jews who were looking for more dramatic demonstrations of God's mighty power. "Jews ask for signs, and Greeks search for wisdom" (1:22). For Jews, it was necessary that the message be accredited by physical wonders. The Greeks, on the other hand, required intellectual elegance. Both found it equally difficult to accept a dead man on a cross as an eternal Savior. "But to those who are the called, both Jews and Greeks, Christ [is] the power of God and the wisdom of God." The superiority of the cross is seen in that it is both a sign and wisdom—but only to the "called" (these are to be identified with those above who "believed," v. 21).

Interestingly, in our modern world, each of these issues stands out as an obstacle to the gospel, but each in a quite different way. Moderns continue to perpetuate the mistaken notion of the Greeks that salvation is a personal matter and (if acquired) a personal achievement. Or, with the Jews, they stumble at the absence of miraculous signs. But what is most problematic for the modern secular mind is the scandal of the cross itself. The spirit of the age cannot accept the idea that God would identify with humankind in weakness, suffering, and death. If God would show Himself, it must be with such strength as to abolish all enemies. The irony of such thinking is that if God were to do that, we would *all* perish. The world remains blind to the truth, not because God has not shown Himself, but because what He has shown is simply not acceptable. He should not have come in a manger, but on a throne. He should not have identified with the weak, but with the strong. He should not have been poor, but powerful. The further irony of this kind of thinking is that the world need only wait for His *second* coming to see the mighty display of His power and majesty. But sadly, when they do see Him, it will be entirely too late for those who could not accept the Savior unless He could come to them on their own terms (2 Thess. 2:7–12).

The factional spirit at Corinth was wrong because it represented an attitude that was incompatible with the gospel of Christ and because it represented a misunderstanding of the nature of the gospel. Paul goes on, now, to show that it is wrong because the experience of the believers themselves shows the folly of such a haughty spirit.

Paul's Exultation (1:26–31)

If boasting is ever to be legitimated, it must not have anything to do with who we are! "For" introduces the negative side of Paul's argument. "Consider your calling, brethren, that there were not many wise according to the flesh, not many mighty, not many noble." Look around you, declares their spiritual father, and tell me the kind of people God is calling. Are you considered the wise, mighty, or noble of Corinth? He answers his own question—"Obviously not." The nature of Paul's argument here tells us that most of the Corinthian congregation were poor and of the lower element of society. They certainly had very little to offer in themselves.

"But God has chosen the foolish things of the world . . . and God has chosen the weak things . . . and the base things" (literally, "nobodies," v. 27). There are no "nobles" here—just baseborn. The selection of God is designed to bring to silence the wisdom of man. He selects the foolish to shame the wise; the weak[15] to shame the strong; and the "nobodies" to shame the "things which are strong" (the "somebodies"). Paul is not saying this to insult them. Rather, he is reminding them that their salvation was not a socioeconomic matter. Probably only a few members of their congregation were well-to-do while many more were not. Paul's suggestion that most of their numbers are "weak" hints at his discussion of the "weak" and the "wise" in 8:7–13 and suggests the approach he will use against those who are arrogantly offending the "weak." On God's relation to the poor in Scripture, Blomberg observes correctly: "Scripture nowhere guarantees salvation for all people under a certain socioeconomic level. But it does consistently reflect God's special concern for the poor, oppressed, and the marginalized people of the world."[16] Paul's readers were not the recipients of the grace of God because of their status in society—and their relationship with Christ was not likely to change that! The wisdom of God does not respond to such frivolous concerns. It responds to needs much deeper than these, and it offers riches much more precious.

The adversative, "But," introduces the positive side of Paul's argument. He concludes that all the riches of salvation are lodged in Jesus Christ. All that the Corinthian believers are, they owe to Him. Thus, it is not in oneself, party alignment, or in supposed human ability that any believer ought to glory. "But by His doing you are in Christ Jesus" (v. 30). To answer the implied question, "What am I in Christ?" Paul tabulates those qualities of His that now belong to the believer. First, there is "wisdom" (v. 30). True wisdom is not found in gnostic speculation or sophistry, but is demonstrated in God's work on the cross for the redemption of sinful humanity. "Righteousness" (v. 30) is a legal concept and has in mind that righteousness that is registered to the believer's account the moment he or she believes (Rom. 5). "Sanctification" (v. 30) has in mind that which Paul has already introduced in 1:2 in the words "sanctified in Christ Jesus." This contemplates the work of Christ *in* the believer. It has in mind both a positional and a progressive truth. In justification, there is the idea of righteousness *applied* to one's account. In sanctification, the idea is that of righteousness *activated* in the believer's life, equipping him or her for service in the body. Then, as if to save the best for last, Paul adds "redemption."

If the order of these terms is logical, Paul probably would have had in mind the eschatological prospect of the resurrected body. However, in this case, it is more likely that he has injected this as a factor that underlies all the above—it is offered as a climax. The twenty-four elders put it this way, "Worthy art Thou to take the book, and to break its seals; for Thou wast slain, and didst purchase for God with Thy blood *men* from every tribe and tongue and people and nation" (Rev. 5:9). It was the atonement that opened the way for God to extend His grace to sinful humans, and pour out upon them such benefits as wisdom, righteousness, sanctification, and redemption. But in light of the situation in Corinth, it is evident that Paul intends to emphasize the eschatological element as well. These believers needed to be reminded that redemption is not complete until Christ comes and we are "changed"—a point to which he will come later in this letter (cf. 15:51–57). They had the mistaken notion that they had already arrived. Paul needed to remind them again and again that this was not the case.

"That" (v. 31) indicates purpose. If there is to be boasting, it is to be properly directed—that is, to "the Lord." If the gospel were shackled with human contingencies, this would not be possible. But because salvation is of Jehovah, to Him alone must be the praise.

Study Questions

1. Suggest several ways Paul establishes his authority in dealing with the problems in this church.

2. Paul mentioned four distinct factions in this church. State and explain each.

3. If you were to identify the "positions" taken by those who divide your church, what would they be?

4. Explain Paul's position on baptism. Why is it that he makes such a point about baptizing so few in their group?

5. Specifically, why is it that Jews and Greeks each in their own ways reject the simple truth of the gospel?

6. What is it that is suggested by Paul as "foolishness" against the wisdom of the world?

7. Why is it that the world fails to know God through its wisdom?

8. How then, in Paul's view, does anyone come to know God?

9. In Paul's discussion, what is it, specifically, that God has used to "shame the wise"?

10. Christ is said to have been made to us wisdom, righteousness, sanctification, and redemption. Explain the significance of each of these for Paul.

CHAPTER 4

Developing True Spirituality
1 Corinthians 2:1-16

Preview:

Paul proclaimed the gospel of Christ crucified constantly in his ministry to the Corinthians so that their faith would stand in God's power, not men. In so doing, he brought them into a relationship with the Holy Spirit, the source of all true spirituality.

Having denounced the divisive spirit that characterized the Corinthian assembly, the apostle Paul, in chapter 1, has shown that the uniqueness of the Christian assembly is its unity. Chapter 2 is related to the preceding in that while the former deals with a worldly *attitude*, the latter deals with worldly *wisdom*. Paul's message demonstrates *divine* wisdom, which is unlike any wisdom the Corinthians had ever known. This wisdom is (1) demonstrated by divine power (2:1–5), (2) hidden in divine mystery (2:6–9), and (3) secured only in a relationship with the Holy Spirit (2:10–16).

In the Corinthian church, as in our own day, there were many who had confused true spirituality with internal power structures or intellectual prowess. They attached membership in the "Cephas party," the "Apollos party," or some other party to special spiritual status. To be spiritual, then, meant that they supported the "correct" spiritual leaders. In so doing, they failed to appreciate those in the body who were not as discriminating as they were. A subtle pride of association crept into their thinking. And those who did not "belong" to their superior group languished from neglect and, in some cases, abuse. Still others were overly impressed with eloquence and philosophical reasoning.

Such were given to a different kind of spiritual pride in their learning and in the superiority of their ideas.

It is now known that the literary styles and conventions of the upper class-es were available to the lower classes in the Roman Empire of Paul's day. The public performances of rhetoricians were in great demand. And all levels of the population were regularly entertained with the recitation of all sorts of literary works.[1] No doubt, even among the common people, this contributed to an appreciation for the more artful turn of phrase—something perhaps for which Apollos was known. Or, what is more of concern to the apostle here is that they were taking special pride in these spiritual sophistries. It was not the elegance of their arguments that troubled their spiritual father; it was the arrogance of their hearts. And he takes special pains to show that this is entirely out of step with both his example and his teaching. The power and wisdom of the cross operate at a different level than the power and wisdom of the world. True spir-ituality is not a product of overscrupulous separation from questionable brethren. Nor does it come with wisdom as the world defines it. Rather, true spirituality comes about through a relationship with the Holy Spirit.

Pentecostal Power (2:1-5)

"And when I came to you, brethren, I did not come with superiority of speech" (v. 1). Paul reflects upon his initial ministry with the Corinthians. His message was not characterized by eloquence (although he certainly was capa-ble of it). Instead, it was a declaration of the "testimony of God" (to be pre-ferred over "mystery"). This was not Paul's testimony of God, but God's testi-mony of Himself (namely, "the cross"). First Thessalonians 1:9-10, written at Corinth shortly after Paul's arrival to the city, offers us a window into his mind during his early ministry there. Shortly after hearing the good report of Timothy regarding the situation at Thessalonica, Paul is moved to celebrate the robustness of their faith—"how you turned to God from idols to serve a living and true God, and to wait for His Son from heaven, whom He raised from the dead, *that is* Jesus, who delivers us from the wrath to come." What is especially curious about this is not so much what is said, but what is not said.

Paul confronted paganism everywhere he went. On Cyprus he confront-ed the Jewish magician (Acts 13:6-12). At Lystra he and Barnabas were con-fused with Hermes and Zeus (Acts 14:8-13). At Philippi he was opposed by a spirit of divination (Acts 16:16-40). And in nearly every major city (Athens, Corinth, Ephesus, etc.), he presented the gospel as God's salvation from their false gods. But the order is always as Paul has it here: "to God from idols." His method of evangelism was fairly uncomplicated. He came "proclaiming" the positive "testimony of God." There is always the temptation in such circumstances to become overly preoccupied with what we *reject* as believers in Christ. But Paul resisted the temptation and simply laid out the truth of *what God did.* John expresses the principle well with the words: "For God did not send the Son into the world to judge the world, but that the world should be saved through Him" (John 3:17). The Gospel writers all note well that the reason Jesus was received by publicans and sinners was because He offered to save them, not condemn them. And so it is with Paul. He does not try to meet them on their ground nor on his own terms. He brings them to a "hill called Mount Calvary" (chap. 1) and to the empty tomb (chap. 15), and lets the evidence of God's work speak for itself.

The implication "I determined" (literally, "I concluded," v. 2) is that Paul gave careful thought to his approach and resolved to lay aside the ornaments of speech and philosophical skill to announce "Jesus Christ, and Him crucified" (v. 2). In the words of Fred Zaspel:

> The practical value of this is immense. Do we want the people who hear us to be saved? Then we preach Christ. Do we want them to grow in grace? Then we preach Christ. Do we want them to gain increased victory over sins, to be more faithful to Christ, to His church, to their families, more loyal on the job, more joyful, loving, temperate, peaceful and virtuous? Then we acquaint them more with Christ. Unpacking, working out the implications of "Christ crucified" we provide them with all the "stuff" which the Holy Spirit uses to bring them "from glory to glory" (2 Cor. 3:18).
>
> Preachers today speak often of "balance" in ministry, and by that so many mean to say they are careful to balance subjects out equally. Paul tells us that if Christ is not the whole of our message, then we are not balanced at all. We do not relegate Him to certain aspects of the Bible or to certain aspects of life only. No, He is our only theme. This, Paul is convinced, is the only message that works. That man who does not preach Christ to his people is little better than a secular moralist. "Christ crucified" is the distinctive of the Christian message. He is our only theme, yes, and He is the whole of it.[2]

Not only was Paul's message of divine wisdom, but his method also reflected the same. There is such an awesome sense of obligation to the calling and content of God's initiative in the preaching of the gospel that it induces weakness, fear, and much trembling (v. 3). This was entirely counterintuitive to those who thought that the power of a presentation was in the forcefulness of the speaker or the cogency of the argument. On that account this attitude of the apostle was a stumbling block and an offense (cf. 2 Cor.

10:10). But there were some important reasons why, in his preaching, Paul felt that he had to get out of the way.

Paul resolved to come "not in persuasive words of wisdom, but in demonstration of the Spirit and of power" (v. 4). With a deep sense of his own inadequacies, Paul carried on a ministry characterized by modesty and humility. Paul was determined, as John the Baptist was, that "He must increase, but I must decrease" (John 3:30). The "power" he would demonstrate would not be his own; it would be the power of divine wisdom. Paul's mention of the Holy Spirit here is also significant. Then, as now, the significance of "Pentecostal power" is not understood. The Corinthians thought they knew a lot about the Spirit, for as no other church in apostolic times, they had experienced the gifts of the Spirit (cf. Paul's reminder of this fact in 1:7). But they still had a lot to learn, and Paul will have many things to say about this important subject. It is difficult not to sense the irony in his speech here. This church, as many even in our own time, had developed a kind of perverse pride in their experience of grace (Greek, *Charismata*, "grace gifts"). Those special spiritual endowments that are given by the Holy Spirit to *unite* the church were being used to *divide* the church. Before he is finished, Paul will see to this matter as well (cf. chap. 12—14).

Paul's motive is "that your faith should not rest on the wisdom of men, but on the power of God" (v. 5). Paul knows that his clever speech and polished oratory can save no one. Furthermore, he knows that if they are merely drawn by the logic of his arguments, their faith will be at the mercy of the next preacher who comes along with a cleverer presentation. Paul's motive is that their faith should "rest" and that it should rest in the "power of God." Grosheide correctly notes, "Faith refers here to the act of believing, since the content of faith is not mentioned in this context."[3] He adds, "If Paul had preached human wisdom and if the Corinthians had become Christians on that basis, then human wisdom would have been the ground of their faith. But instead God had given wonders from heaven and that had worked faith in their hearts."[4] Even though it would cost him in terms of "respect," the writer saw to it that a proper foundation would be laid on which they could place their faith (cf. 3:10-12).

I have a lawyer friend who loves to divide the world into two easily recognizable categories. He says, "There are two kinds of people in the world—those who breath, and those who don't!" Or he may say something like, "There are two kinds of people in the world—those who work and those who don't." Humor aside, in the text before us, a similar distinction can be seen. There are two kinds of Christians—those who try to save themselves and those who let God do it for them. Paul knows that the faith of those who take it into their own hands will always be subject to anxiety, doubt, and "every wind of doctrine" (Eph. 4:14). But for those who put their faith in God's power to save them, their faith, in the words of Lidie H. Edmunds, "has found a resting place."

> My faith has found a resting place, Not in device or creed;
>   I trust the ever-living One, His wounds for me shall plead.
> Enough for me that Jesus saves, This ends my fear and doubt;
>   A sinful soul I come to Him, He'll never cast me out.
> My heart is leaning on the Word, The written Word of God,
>   Salvation by my Savior's name, Salvation thru His blood
> My great Physician heals the sick, The lost He came to save;
>   For me His precious blood He shed, For me His life He gave.
> I need no other argument, I need no other plea
>   It is enough that Jesus died, and that He died for me.[5]

If They Only Knew (2:6–9)

"Yet we do speak wisdom" (v. 6). David K. Lowery observes: "In Paul's disclaimer about his own brilliance he did not mean that God puts a premium on ignorance and rejects wisdom of any sort. There was a wisdom taught by the Spirit which Paul wanted his readers to grasp firmly."[6] But this is a wisdom that is "not of this age" (v. 6). It is only open to the "mature" (v. 6), for it is "in a mystery" (v. 7), hidden from "the rulers of this age" (v. 8), and not attainable through "natural" (v. 14) means, but "spiritual" (v. 15).

What Paul proclaims is the only true wisdom. "We speak" (literally, "Go on speaking." Contrast the historical aorists in verses 1–3; Paul wants them to know that his message has not changed). "We" (v. 6) is not an editorial we, but is plural. The writer's message is not a novelty; it is what all faithful preachers of the gospel are speaking.

This wisdom could only be fully appreciated by "those who are mature" (v. 6; cf. 1 Cor. 14:20; Phil. 3:15; and Heb. 6:1). Paul cannot resist the use of irony here. This term is used in extrabiblical literature to speak of those who had been initiated in the mystery religions. It "could here refer to those who believed Paul's message, the mystery of God (v. 1), and so be translated as "those who believe God's message."[7] As has been rightly observed, "[t]he reason why Paul uses this word here is not that he would recognize many kinds of Christians, some more and others less initiated. . . . This distinction is rather between those in the Corinthian church who valued highly the wisdom of the world and despised the preaching of the apostle and those who had freed themselves of the world and recognized Paul's preaching as true wisdom."[8]

"The Only True Wisdom" of Scripture

Believers are not to be wise in their own conceits (Rom. 11:25)

Wisdom comes from God (Rom. 33)

Believers are to speak as wise men (1 Cor. 10:15)

There is a fleshly wisdom opposite to godly wisdom (2 Cor. 1:12)

Wisdom unto salvation "is lavished" upon us (Eph. 1:9)

Believers should walk not as fools but as wise (Eph. 5:15)

Paul prays that believers be filled with spiritual wisdom (Col. 1:9)

Coming to Christ the lost are taught salvation wisdom (Col. 1:28)

The Word of Christ should "richly" dwell within by wisdom (Col. 3:16)

Believers should walk with wisdom (Col. 4:5)

Believers are to be wise (careful) to maintain good works (Titus 3:8)

Believers may ask for wisdom (James 1:5)

Believers should walk in the gentleness of wisdom (James 3:13)

Godly wisdom, unlike "earthly" wisdom, comes from above (James 3:15)

Wisdom from above is ...
> *Pure*
> *Peaceable*
> *Gentle*
> *Reasonable*
> *Full of mercy and good fruit*
> *Unwavering*
> *Without hypocrisy (James 3:17)*

God is the only wise God (1 Tim. 1:17; Jude 1:25)

But this wisdom was "not of this age, nor of the rulers of this age, who are passing away" (v. 6). One of the mistakes commonly made in both Paul's day and ours is to link the gospel ministry to cultural fads and charismatic personalities that are always "passing away." Used bookstores are filled with bestsellers that were written only two or three decades ago stating the now stale agenda of the revolutionary boomers of the sixties and seventies. No one even wants these books anymore except as relics of an era long past and well for-gotten. During those decades, Christian churches and organizations were spawned that celebrated many of these same values and cultural icons, lead-ing to new styles of music and worship; and congregations sadly split along these lines. Today this has resulted, ironically, in ministries that are complete-ly out of touch with "gen-Xers" and "millennials." Paul would remind us here that the message is unchanging. And if we would rely on the truth and wis-dom of the gospel as did he, we would not need to worry about "keeping up." Fads are constantly in process of decay.

"But we speak God's wisdom in a mystery" (v. 7), writes Paul. In contrast to the groping speculation of fallen man, Paul's message is the unchanging truth of God. But it is a mystery accessible only to those who are in right rela-tion with Him. "In" has an instrumental force. That is, "mystery" refers to the work or purpose of God hitherto unrevealed (Rom. 16:25–26), by which His truth is now made known. In this case, the reference is to "the hidden wis-dom, which God predestined before the ages to our glory" (v. 7). The coun-sels of God concerning our salvation are from eternity and are directed toward the same everlasting glory (cf. Rom. 8:28–32; Eph. 1:4; Phil. 1:10). Two pro-found realities stand out here. The first is that there is an *inner life* in God that stands in a direct relation to His creatures. The writer contemplates a reality in God, prior to the "sixth day," when God considered the *telos,* or "goal" (see *teleios,* "mature," above) toward which the man and woman who were to be "in his image" would be directed. The second is that this delicious *divine plot* was "to our glory." Recently, my twelve-year-old granddaughter, Julie, hatched a plot to give her mom a baby shower. For weeks the family was caught up in comedic plotting and scheming to bring all of Mom's friends together with-out Mom finding out. Julie wanted the moment of the "revelation" to be a total surprise. Her reward was the joy (and as it turned out, tears) that her mom expressed when she walked into the room, especially when she realized that it was Julie's doing to honor her in this way. There is something of this kind of plotting in this text. It conveys the idea that God's love for His crea-tures hatched such a plan to create us; but more than that, He will one day honor us in glory when we are finally united as a bride to His Son.

That this wisdom was hidden from humans had the horrible consequence (though certainly known to God) that the "Lord of Glory" was crucified. (On the expression "Lord of glory" [literally, "the Lord whose attribute was glory"], see Ps. 29:1; Acts 7:2; Eph. 1:17; James 2:1.) Over this happy scene evoked in the truth of the divine plan, the black cloud of human sin loomed to throw its fiercesome shadow upon it. God's creatures, out of ignorance, committed the ultimate "parental abuse." They defied Him, denied Him, and crucified

His Son. "All that God has prepared for those who love Him" (v. 9) was cast aside. It was something the human mind and imagination could not conceive. Paul employs the language of Isaiah 64:4 to demonstrate that the wisdom of God is not of human origin and also to contrast the thought of verse 10.

Your Spirit Is Showing (2:10–16)

In a wonderfully succinct way, Lowery summarizes the force of what follows. "The blessings of salvation were prepared by the Father, carried out by the Son, and applied by the Spirit (Eph. 1:3–14) to all believers who as a result love God (1 John 4:19). The only way the Corinthians could know this was by the Spirit, who knows and reveals these deep things of God about salvation."[9]

There is a war against truth today. This is not so much against certain *truths*, but against the idea that there is any such thing as *truth* at all. In the last century, truth was reduced to *power* with disastrous consequences. In more recent decades, the notion that anyone has a corner on truth has been under severe attack. People speak of *my* truth or *your* truth but nothing of *the* truth. Truth has been reduced to mere personal opinion. As a consequence, we have lost the moral consensus that was once a part of our culture, and efforts to restore it have been viewed at best with suspicion and at worst as bigotry.

Paul lived in a similar world where the ideas of Christianity were situated against a plethora of spiritual visions—all of which competed for attention, credibility, and the control of people's minds. The error of many in the Corinthian church was to view the truth of the gospel as just another (if superior) religion. Paul develops the thought here that what God has revealed is in an entirely different league. He does not speak of Christian spirituality as if it were our own version of a common experience shared by all other religions. True spirituality involves a relationship with the Spirit and with truth. "The Spirit searches all things, even the depths of God" (v. 10). And what is beyond human comprehension (v. 9) is made known to those who "have received, not the spirit of the world, but the Spirit who is from God, that we might know the things freely given to us by God" (v. 12).

Revelation

We can know the truth, first of all, because "to us God revealed *them* through the Spirit" (v. 10). The Spirit shows God's truth. The world does not know this truth (v. 9), but we do! (The phrase "to us" is emphatic.) This is what the theologians speak of as the doctrine of *revelation*. The Spirit "searches all things" and knows "even the depths of God" (v. 10). The truth revealed comes from the secret chambers of the very mind of God. No wonder the things of God are unknown to the natural mind. Paul uses a simple illustration. He asks, "Who among men knows the *thoughts* of a man . . . ?" (v. 11).

When a pitcher hurls a baseball at ninety miles per hour, hitting the batter, how can we know for sure if it was done intentionally? The umpire whose job it is to watch every move can't always tell. The batter who may be writhing in pain as he hobbles to first base probably has an opinion, but he can't be sure either. The spectators in the stands can't say for sure even though they all saw it happen. But one person does know—the pitcher himself. He knows exactly what his intent was whether he reveals it or not. In the same way, these inner thoughts of a man are known only to "the spirit of the man, which is in him" (v. 11). God's thoughts are only known by the "Spirit of God" (v. 11). And it is this Spirit that "we have received" (v. 12).

Inspiration

Second, we can know the truth because God has given this revelation in *words*. Paul declares that these "things we also speak" (v. 13). That is, the things revealed by the Spirit are now spoken by the apostle. And such are "not in words taught by human wisdom, but in those taught by the Spirit" (v. 13). There is an inherent objectivity to this truth. It is given in words. Later Paul would write to Timothy, "All Scripture is inspired by God" (2 Tim. 3:16). And Peter would add, "No prophecy [revelation] was ever made by an act of human will, but men moved by the Holy Spirit spoke from God" (2 Pet. 1:21). This is the doctrine of *inspiration*. Revelation speaks of the *source* of God's truth. Inspiration has to do with the *nature* of God's truth.

But Paul sees these two working together. If the "thoughts" are from God, the "words" become vehicles by which those thoughts are made known. Under inspiration, when Paul speaks, he is not working with the raw material of "human wisdom" (v. 13). Rather, he is speaking words "taught by the Spirit, combining spiritual *thoughts* with spiritual *words*" (v. 13). The term *sugkrino*, "combining," occurs only here and in 2 Corinthians 10:12. In classical Greek, it was always used in the sense of "to compound" or "to interpret" (cf. Gen. 40:8 LXX). In other words, spiritual truth is conveyed in language that is given by God's Spirit. This would not be the case if he uttered the revelations of the Spirit in the speech of human wisdom.[10] True spirituality is not to be identified with a spiritually elite group or the skill of philosophical reasoning.

Later in 1 Corinthians, Paul will also show that it is not to be associated with unusual spiritual gifts either. This latter distinction will be especially important in drawing the distinction between the Spirit Himself and those evidences that bespeak His special work in the believer's life. True spirituality is an endowment granted to every believer as an outcome of cultivating a relationship with the indwelling Holy Spirit. It is He who teaches us with the very words—Scripture—that God has given to guide us. In other words, there is an instrumental character to the artistry of the Holy Spirit in bringing the Word to bear on each believer's life. The psalmist understood this well when he said, "Thy word is a lamp to my feet, and a light to my path" (Ps. 119:105).

The Natural

True spirituality is now contrasted with "a natural man" (v. 14). The term here is interesting. *Psuchikos* ("soulish," "of the mind") contrasts with the person (*anthropos*, "man" is generic) who might be labeled *Spirit-minded*. In this context, the word links with "the spirit of the world" (v. 12) and "human wisdom" (v. 13). The natural man is the one whose thinking is of this world. This one may be said to be *worldlyminded* (cf. Jude 19). He or she is incapable of receiving "the things of the Spirit of God; for they are foolishness to him, and he cannot understand them, because they are spiritually appraised" (v. 14). When something is "appraised," it is examined or called to account. It is questioned and evaluated. The natural man, who does not have the Spirit of God in him, is incapable of even asking the right questions. His only response is ridicule. Such ideas are perceived as "foolishness" (cf. Luke 8:13; James 1:21). The natural man is incompetent. Again, the fundamental idea of "appraised" is that of "examination" or "scrutiny."[11] It is used only by Paul and Luke and is used mostly of "judicial examination" (cf. Luke 23:14; Acts 4:9; 1 Cor. 9:3; 10:25, 27). It speaks of the impatient human spirit that prejudges the truth and wants to anticipate the full judgment. The natural man does not even have the ability to sift the facts.

Paul's message was not of human contrivance. He was a channel, simply communicating God's truth. Faithful communicators of the gospel today do the same thing. We take of that truth, God's Word, and communicate it to others. This truth is contained in the record God has given to us—the Bible, the eternal and unchanging truth of God. And it is the foundation of all true spirituality.

The Spiritual

"But he who is spiritual appraises all things" (v. 15). The *pneumatikos* (the "spiritual one") in context refers to those persons who have the indwelling Holy Spirit (v. 12), who know the "thoughts of God" (v. 11) because they have been taught through "words" of the Holy Spirit (v. 13), granting them an understanding of those "things freely given" by God (v. 12). Such persons appraise or "judge" all things. The difference between the natural and the spiritual is primarily that spiritual persons have been exposed to God's revelation, have received it, and have founded their faith upon it. These persons can now judge both earthly and heavenly things. They have discernment with respect to what is and what is not of the gospel and salvation, and whether the truth of God is being taught. These persons do not lose the power of reasoning. Nor does Paul renounce reason and logic. As noted above, he does not place a premium on ignorance. Rather, he simply wants it known that revelation stands *above* reason. Human imaginations are judged by the objective truth of God. The natural person, by contrast, turns this equation around and subjects all matters of the spirit to what is considered the superior human intellect. Discerning all things, the spiritual person is "appraised by no man," (v. 15)—that is, anyone who is unspiritual is incapable of judging his or her thinking.

A Truly Spiritual Person . . .

- *Produces spiritual fruit by the Spirit (Gal. 5:22–23)*
  - *Love*
  - *Joy*
  - *Peace*
  - *Longsuffering (patience)*
  - *Gentleness*
  - *Goodness*
  - *Faith*
  - *Meekness*
  - *Temperance (self-control)*
- *Exhibits a spiritual gift (or gifts) by the Spirit (1 Cor. 12:4–11)*
- *Is led by the Spirit (Rom. 8:14)*
- *Receives the witness of the Spirit that he belongs to God (Rom. 8:16)*
- *Does not grieve the Spirit (Eph. 4:30)*
- *Is filled (or controlled) by the Spirit (Eph. 5:18)*
- *Takes up the sword of the Spirit-the Word of God (Eph. 6:17)*
- *Prays in (or by) the Spirit (Eph. 6:18)*
- *Does not quench the Spirit (1 Thess. 5:19)*
- *Is "matured" (perfected) by the Spirit (Gal. 3:3)*

Paul will come back to the *pneumatikos* again and again in this epistle to speak of that which was "sown" in them by his gospel (see 9:11); their spiritual "food"—Christ (10:3-4); their spiritual "gifts" (12:1; 14:1, 12); and the spiritual "body" given in the resurrection (15:44-46). Introducing the subject here anticipates repeated correctives he offers throughout his letter on this matter.

Paul concludes his description of the truly spiritual person by saying, "We have the mind of Christ" (v. 16). This answers the question he draws from

Isaiah 40:13, "Who has known the mind of the Lord?" The answer is, "We do!" In using the plural "we," the writer no doubt includes himself and all true believers. We should not miss the relationship, imbedded in this claim, with what goes before it. Believers have the Holy Spirit, and it is He who knows the "thoughts" of God and has communicated those thoughts through words. Through Paul and the other apostles and New Testament prophets (cf. Eph. 2:20), these truths were communicated, and many were inscripturated to form the New Testament. We have the mind of Christ because we have His words and thoughts stirred up in our minds through the indwelling Holy Spirit (see Col. 3:16–17; cf. also Eph. 3:17; James 4:5). True spirituality is being in tune with Christ through the indwelling Holy Spirit and in possession of His Word, by which we are instructed in all matters of godliness and Christian discipline.

Study Questions

1. How does true spirituality relate to the "wisdom of the cross"?

2. How would you describe Paul's attitude and approach when he preached to the Corinthians? Why do you suppose he felt this way?

3. On what did Paul wish for his reader's faith to "rest"?

4. In the writer's view, who are the "mature" ones? How do they relate to the "wisdom of the cross"?

5. Tabulate several principles for evangelism that you discern in this text. How do you plan to put these principles into action in your own life and ministry?

6. According to this text, what is it that the human mind and heart are incapable of knowing? Who does know it?

7. Characterize the "natural man." Who is this person? Is such a person saved or unsaved? Explain.

8. Characterize the "spiritual man." Specifically, what is it about this person that makes him or her "spiritual"?

9. Based on this chapter, suggest several specific ways that you might begin to acquire the characteristics of the spiritual person.

10. What does it mean to have the mind of Christ? How does this relate to having the Holy Spirit?

CHAPTER 5

Developing Maturity
1 Corinthians 3:1–23

Preview:

The greatest problem with the believers in Corinth was their lack of spiritual maturity. Instead of being spiritual, they were fleshly minded and incapable of receiving the "solid food" that Paul and Apollos attempted to offer them. Paul uses analogies of a farmer and a building to show that the Christian life is a process that requires dedication and character.

The topic of maturity was introduced in chapter 2 when Paul spoke of the "mature" as those who are capable of receiving the wisdom of God—wisdom that had been hidden in a mystery that could be understood only after God's manifestation of Himself on the cross. There Paul spoke of two mentalities that represent polar opposites in terms of their relationship to God and their relative ability to know and act upon God's truth.

At one extreme is the person who is controlled by the thinking of the world. This person may have great "natural" abilities but is profoundly limited when it comes to knowing the things of God. The "teacher" of the wisdom of God (the Holy Spirit) is absent. And this person is utterly mystified (to expand on Paul's metaphor, cf. 2:7) when it comes to spiritual matters. Since this person cannot understand such things, they are passed off as "foolishness." We need not reflect very far on our own experience to realize that we have all known people like this. Very often they are highly esteemed and gifted individuals in great citadels of learning. And occasionally the honest ones will actually admit that they wish they could have such simple faith, but even in their admission there is derision. For to them, such "simple" faith equates with "simple-mindedness." They just cannot go there. The opposite extreme is the "spiritual" person, the person who has the Spirit of God and is attentive to His Word. This person, who has the "mind of Christ," is supremely equipped to discern "all things."

But now Paul introduces a third kind of person. This is the person who, unfortunately, best reflects the majority of his readers. And, sadly, it is altogether likely that it reflects the vast majority of practicing Christians down through the ages. They are not utterly abandoned to the thinking of the world. But on the other hand, they seem to have a long way to go before they can be considered abandoned to God. Their lack of spiritual maturity even hinders the ministry that Paul had hoped to have with them. If the "natural" person is known for a *lack of understanding* in spiritual matters, and the "spiritual" is know for *discernment*, the "carnal" person is evidenced by *divisiveness*.

Since L. S. Chafer's classic *He That Is Spiritual*,[1] much attention has been given to these categories for defining various types of individuals. At one extreme are those who suggest that these represent different species of humanity.[2] At the other end of the spectrum are those who see only a quantitative difference in terms of each individual's knowledge of the things of God. In the former case, regeneration is the answer. In the latter, pedagogy is the answer. Zodhiates has rightly noted that one of the realities of ministry is that a pastor must evaluate the relative capacity of individuals to receive the message he wishes to deliver. But he also notes, "A preacher finds it a painful experience to give baby food to an adult. But if an adult is sickly and weak, then he must be given food that his condition can take. This was the condition of the Corinthians."[3] In my view, this is what Paul means by these classifications. In the words of Anthony Thiselton, they represent different *"dispositions* or *stances"*[4] that individuals may adopt. "A *sarkikos* person is characterized by self-concern and self-centeredness; a *psychikos* human is one who does not seem to show concern for the things of the Holy Spirit, but simply lives life *(psyche)* as it comes; a *pneumatikos* person is motivated and characterized by the presence and shaping of the Holy Spirit of God (2:14—3:4)."[5]

The Problem of Carnality (3:1-4)

In chapter 1, Paul had already denounced the Corinthians' divisive spirit. The reader could well have anticipated that Paul would come back to this before he was finished. That he places it so high on his agenda lets us know how concerned he is about it. "And I, brethren, could not speak to you as to spiritual men, but as to men of flesh, as to babes in Christ" (v. 1, *napioi*, "non-speakers" or "infants"). This strongly contrasts with the "mature" of 2:6. The pronoun "I" is emphatic (*kago*, "But, I")—the contrast is with the spiritual persons above. Paul, nonetheless, calls them brethren, not simply to ingratiate himself with them, (though they were a carnal lot), but to reemphasize that their behavior is not becoming *who* they are in Christ. It is important to observe that they cannot be robbed of their relationship with their Savior in spite of their immaturity and sin. Using the historical aorist, the apostle observes that even on his first encounter with them, despite his lengthy stay, he was never able to speak to them as a spiritually mature assembly. Paul calls this to mind briefly in order to compare the present state of the Corinthians with their beginnings in the faith—a comparison that must have filled them with shame.

As newborn babes this condition would be natural and to be expected (1 Pet. 2:2). But, at this stage in their development, it is embarrassing. They still are acting like spiritual babies.[6] He adds, "I gave you milk to drink, not solid food; . . . for you are still fleshly. For since there is jealousy and strife among you, are you not fleshly, and are you not walking like mere men?" (vv. 2–3). In his diagnosis of their spiritual condition Paul brings together a litany of pejorative terms: "fleshly," "babes," "milk to drink," "jealousy," "strife," and "*mere* men." The carnal (*sarkikos*) person is one who has been born of the Spirit, but who conducts life as if he or she were in the "natural" state. The term as Paul uses it is akin to the Old Testament usage of speaking of life in its transitory condition—"flesh and blood" that cannot inherit God's kingdom (cf. 15:50).[7] The warfare between the flesh and the Spirit receives significant emphasis in Paul's writings (cf. Rom. 7:14—8:13; Gal. 5:17).

In 1 Corinthians the subject appears here and in 15:44–46. In the latter text, Paul contrasts the present body (natural) with the glorified body (spiritual). The conflict is not so much between two natural inner forces within the believer. It is between the Spirit of God and our own natural and "fleshly" tendencies. The factions, who have destroyed the unity in Corinth, indicate that these believers were not walking by the "generative power" of the Spirit, but were walking by the "generative power"[8] of the flesh. They were acting just like fleshly men, with no uplifting power of the Holy Spirit. Paul does not say that they "are" men, but they are "like" men (the inference here is "natural" men; cf. 2:14). Since they are the "church of God which is at Corinth . . . saints by calling" (1:2), the writer is loathe to say of them that they are no longer to be considered God's children. On the contrary, it is precisely for the reason that they are saints of God that their spiritual immaturity is so unacceptable. They have the Holy Spirit of God dwelling within them. They should be letting that Spirit guide their attitudes and actions. Indeed, when they are glorified, this spiritual goal will be realized (15:48–49). But their behavior is far from this ideal. "For when one says, 'I am of Paul,' and another, 'I am of Apollos,' are you not *mere* men?" (v. 4). In what follows the writer will show that the party alliances and carnal attitudes are entirely out of step with the very people they purport to follow—namely, Paul himself, Apollos, and the other apostles.

Sowing and Reaping (3:5–9)

"What then is Apollos? And what is Paul?" (v. 5). Paul comes now to the crucial question: What are these men around whom the Corinthians had built their little coteries? The stress is on function, not status; otherwise, he might have asked, "*Who* are these men?" The answer follows. They are "Servants through whom you believed." They are simply ministers serving the Lord. The apostle was not there to extend his own influence and popularity; rather, he was in Corinth in obedience to God (see especially Acts 18:9–10).

"I planted, Apollos watered, but God was causing the growth" (v. 6). Each believer is used to accomplish specific tasks in the economy of God, but in the process, God simultaneously gives the increase. While human instruments can be used to plant and cultivate things, only God can make things grow. "So then neither the one who plants nor the one who waters is anything, but God who causes the growth." The biblical principle of sowing and reaping is not a metaphysical law. It is about investment, service, and ownership.

Three principles stand out in this text. The first is the importance of *faithfulness*. Paul and Apollos were not advancing their own kingdom; they were simply doing the work God had called them to do. Undeterred by the obstacles, one planted the seed and the other came behind to provide life-giving water.

The second principle is the principle of *diversity*. Neither Paul nor Apollos was called to the same work. Each was unique. Each had an important role to play in the life of this church. In the analogy given, if there had been only sowing at Corinth and no watering, there could have been no harvest. If there had been only watering and no sowing, there would have been nothing to grow. Growing churches God's way entails each member exercising his or her individual gift(s) as the Spirit has so assigned them. This is the subject of an extended analysis in chapters 12—14.

Finally, there is the principle of *ownership*. The work is God's and so is the harvest. This is the third principle, often missed by modern pundits of church growth. While it is important to establish a vision, write our mission statement, and take the time to develop a strategic plan, in the final analysis, church growth is a God thing. When people forget this, the results often parallel those at Corinth. The leadership of the church will also do well to remember this principle as Lowery has summarized.

God alone was the source of blessing (3:5–9) and ministers were only servants accountable to Him (3:10–17). Since that was so, a minister needed to beware of cultivating the praise of men—as certain leaders in the
Corinthian church apparently were doing (3:18–23), and needed instead
to seek by faithful service to gain the praise of God (4:1–5).[9]

"Now he who plants and he who waters are one" (v. 8). *Heis*, "one," could
be understood as "individual," or as "a unity." Either idea could be reasonably
seen in the context, but it is more probable that the sense here underscores the
individuality of each worker. This is seen especially in the clause that follows it:
"but each will receive his own reward according to his own labor" (v. 8). Just
as there are differences in the quality and workmanship of craftsmen, even so
there are differences among God's ministers. And each is uniquely accountable to God.

The function of this argument is interesting. The Corinthians were typical
of many immature Christians we observe in our churches today. Often when
young believers begin to study the Word of God and to learn the essentials of
the faith, they will readily attach themselves to the elementary teachings of
their mentors (as with Cephas, Apollos, etc.). Later, when another person
explains a doctrine or a text of Scripture in ways that seem to contradict their
only other understanding of it, they will become alarmed and offended and
will often take action against these "novel" ideas. Part of developing maturity
is in teaching people to appreciate that the true church is much wider than
their narrow (not to say narrow-minded) ideas. And since it is God's church,
and it is He who assigns the workers, we must be content to allow Him to
reward each according to His own standards.

And so Paul concludes, "For we are God's fellow workers; you are God's
field, God's building" (v. 9). To be a fellow worker with God is an amazing
concept. In Christian theology, nothing quite matches the knotty problem of
the synergy between the sovereignty of God and the actions of free moral
agents. Yet nothing is more evident in the text of Scripture as here observed.
The field, the building, indeed the work is all of God. Yet He assigns that
work to human agents, just as he places those same agents into the super-
structure of the building. This is the imagery that dominates the remainder
of the chapter. The use of the architectural metaphor is best understood if
one remembers the magnificent temples and buildings common in Corinth.
The important thrust of this metaphor applies to the believer's works (as will
be shown).

One final observation needs to be made here. There is a subtle shift in the
use of pronouns. Paul says "we" are God's fellow workers. Then he adds, "you"
are God's field, God's building. In our translation, we miss what the original

recipients of this letter most likely had to understand as an assertion of the writer's apostolic authority. *You* are the field, and *we* are the field hands. *We* (Paul, Apollos, Cephas, et al.) are working together with God in the work of the ministry. But *you* (that is, the church) are, in effect, the result of that work (cf. Eph. 2:20). Most expositors are inclined to draw the broader inference from the text to suggest that *all believers* are so designated. When it is limited to those who labor, as did Paul, the analogy is appropriate.

The Church Is a Temple (3:10–17)

The present chapter pivots on verse 9. It is here that Paul shifts from the field metaphor, to the building or temple metaphor. And having already hinted that they are a "result," and he, along with their other mentors, is the "cause," he opens with a terse reminder: "According to the grace of God which was given to me, as a wise master builder I laid a foundation, and another is building upon it" (v. 10). Paul has already given assurances that the grace of God has been abundantly experienced in this assembly (cf. 1:4–5). Not the least of those blessings of God's grace was Paul's initial effort in establishing them in the faith. He was, by God's grace, the "master builder."

The Bema Judgment of Believers' Works

All believers will appear before the "bema," or judgment seat, of Christ for the receiving of rewards (2 Cor. 5:10).

All believers will be openly presented to the Lord (2 Cor. 5:11).

The Christian life is built on the foundation of Jesus Christ (1 Cor. 3:10–11).

The believer must build carefully on Christ (1 Cor. 3:10b).

The believer is to build a solid Christian life, not one with "wood, hay, straw" (1 Cor. 3:12).

The believer's works will be tested as to their [spiritual] quality (1 Cor. 3:13).

Solid works will be rewarded (1 Cor. 3:14).

Worthless works will be consumed (1 Cor. 3:15).

To preach the gospel brings a reward (1 Cor. 9:18).

Christ will judge believers as to how they have treated one another (James 5:7–9).

Holding on to the truth brings a reward (2 John 1:8).

The foundation is always the least noticed yet the most important part of any building. Just as "seeds" determine what grows to maturity, a foundation establishes the dimensions and shape of the building placed upon it. Paul had laid the foundation of this church. In so doing, he "became [their] father through the gospel" (4:15). By adding, "another is building upon it" (3:10), he is asserting that there is continuity between his work and those who followed him. This is vital. Although the building may include many stories, only those that are built on the foundation are going to stand. But more important to the writer, only that which is established on the foundation is given legitimacy. Later Paul will deal with his detractors more directly, but for now he wants his readers to begin to develop the skill of "discrimination." In their immaturity, they are still unable to discern true shepherds from hirelings (John 10:11–13). When churches attach more importance to results or to personalities, they are driven by "the wisdom of the world" (1:20), not the wisdom that is manifested in the truth of the gospel. Far more important to the life of the church is that those in leadership are building on the foundation and according to the master plan, so Paul adds, "Let each man be careful how he builds upon it" (3:10). The adverb "how" has in mind the *manner* in which this task is to be undertaken. Again, the point is that the church is God's, and the most that can be said of us is that we are charged by Him to do His work.

The warning is necessitated by the nature of the foundation, "which is Jesus Christ" (v. 11; cf. Acts 4:12; Luke 6:46–49). The accomplishments of Jesus Christ for us and for our salvation are "once-for-all" (cf. Heb. 9:27—10:13). There is a qualitative difference between His work and ours. It is for this reason that Paul emphatically adds, "No man can lay a foundation other than the one which is laid" (v. 11). In this respect, no one can add to or subtract from His work. Curiously, it is only in the matter of suffering that Paul is willing to suggest that we share in the work of Christ—or as he puts it, "Now I rejoice in my sufferings for your sake, and in my flesh I do my share on behalf of His body (which is the church) in filling up that which is lacking in Christ's afflictions" (Col. 1:24; compare a similar usage of this expression in 1 Cor. 16:17). Paul is not saying that his suffering adds to the atonement of Christ. Rather, he is saying that his suffering is an extension of the sufferings of his Lord. Luke captures something of this truth in his introduction to the book of Acts: "The first account I composed, Theophilus, about all that Jesus began to do and teach" (1:1). By implication, what follows of the exploits, persecution, and even martyrdom of the early church leaders, recorded in Acts, is a continuation of the work of Christ. Ironically, it is precisely in this respect that the Corinthians had missed it (cf. chap. 4).

Since the foundation is laid and the building is under way; since the master plan is God's, it is important that we understand the believer's relationship to the ongoing task. In this instance, it is necessary to look at Paul's conclusion and then come back to his instruction relative to it. His conclusion is given in 3:16–17. "Do you not know that you are a temple of God . . . ?" "You" in this sentence is plural. The meaning is this: You (collectively as the church) are a temple (singular). And as a temple you have the Spirit of God dwelling in you. Woe to you if your work is such that it "destroys" that temple. God will hold you accountable. In other words, the temple here is not a reflection on the individual Christian as a tabernacle of the Holy Spirit (Paul will use this same metaphor in chapter 6 to say just that), for now, the imagery is given to say something important about them as "the church of God which is at Corinth"—that is, the local church (1:2). They have an individual responsibility, but they are also accountable to one another and to God in how they proceed.

With that in mind, then, Paul begins, "Now if any man builds upon the foundation with gold, silver, precious stones, wood, hay, straw" (3:12). In building the church each will supply building materials—some may be of *superior* quality (gold, silver, precious stones), and others may be of *inferior* quality (wood, hay, stubble). Of the six types of material mentioned, three are combustible and three are incombustible (see also Deut. 4:24; Mal. 3:2; 2 Thess. 1:7; Heb. 12:29). Of these two categories, the first is abiding. The gold and silver would be for ornamentation. The precious stones such as marble, granite, and alabaster would guarantee that the structure would last for centuries. Such shining temples were visible all about the ancient city of Corinth, and some are standing to this day. The second list has materials that perish. In Corinth these were materials that likely went into the poorest huts in which perhaps many of these believers actually lived (cf. 1:26–28). By contrast, these will not withstand a trial by fire. All of these building materials represent "each man's work" (3:13). Someone might well argue that straw keeps the rain off my head as well as granite. Perhaps so, but it will not withstand fire as well as stone. There is coming a time when the permanence of our work will be openly displayed for what it is, "for the day will show it" (v. 13). This is the *day* of the Judgment Seat of Christ (cf. 1:8; 4:5; 2 Cor. 5:10). "Fire" is figurative for judgment—more specifically, the absolutely righteous judgment of God. Fire is used here, not for its enlightening power, but for its consuming power. It will "test the quality of each man's work" (v. 13).

"Remains . . . reward . . . burned . . . loss" (vv. 14–15)—the judgments are broken into two categories. If a person's work remains undamaged by the fire, he or she receives rewards (*misthos*, "wages"; cf. v. 8). Of course, it goes without saying that even the wages mentioned here are entirely a gift of grace (cf. Dan. 12:3; 1 Cor. 9:17; 2 John 1:8; Rev. 4:4; 11:18). If a person's work does not endure and it is consumed in the fire, that person will experience "loss." Everything the person has been devoted to in this life shall be suddenly swept away. "But he himself shall be saved, yet so as through fire" (v. 15). It is important to notice that such a one does not suffer the loss of salvation, but the loss of reward. The stress in this entire passage is not on an individual's relationship to Christ, but on service. It does not suggest that one might be in danger of losing his or her salvation,[10] but it does give a stern warning with respect to their ultimate accountability (see also Amos 4:11; Jude 1:23).

Now Paul concludes, "Do you [people] not know that you [collectively] are a temple of God, and *that* the Spirit of God dwells in you?" (v. 16). His question demands an affirmative answer. Indeed, they should know this. The temple in this context is the local church, not the individual believer as noted above (cf. 2 Cor. 6:16; Eph. 2:21). The idea that the Holy Spirit dwells in the church does not vitiate the doctrine of the omnipresence of the Holy Spirit. Nor does it suggest, as some have, that God dwells only in temples. Indeed, the Holy Spirit is everywhere, but He does not "dwell" in this special sense everywhere. His presence is made manifest in the local church inasmuch as He has taken up residence in every believer (cf. John 14:16) and has gifted each for service to the other (cf. 1 Cor. 12). In Paul's ecclesiology (doctrine of the church), he recognizes that the church is more than a collection of *individuals* who happen to belong to some "invisible" entity consisting of believers of all ages and places. The church is also a visible and tangible *community*. In this chapter Paul uses the metaphor of a building to emphasize the Church's concrete connectedness and mutual responsibility. Later, in chapter 12, he will use the metaphor of the body to show that this individual-corporate duality is also a living entity. It is an *organism* with many individual *organs* coordinated and directed by one head—Jesus Christ.

"If any man destroys the temple of God, God will destroy him" (v. 17). (Greek, *phtheiro*, conveys the idea of "dishonoring"). This is a much stronger expression than "suffer loss" above. There are two possibilities. Paul may have in mind unsaved people who may or may not be in the assembly, but who, in fact, are false believers. The prospect for such people is a fearful one. They will fall under the condemnation of God. Another possibility is that Paul is simply emphasizing that if persons are guilty of serving God in the building of His temple with materials of "dishonor," they will be destroyed in the judgment. And it follows that however much these persons are honored in this life, when they stand before God, they will be utterly empty-handed and dishonored. This seems to be the thought since he then follows with the words, "for the temple of God is holy, and that is what you are" (v. 17). Again he uses the plural "you" to designate that he is speaking of them in a corporate sense—not as mere individuals. So he has in mind the entire assembly. The force of his admonition then is that they are a holy temple, and it follows that they should be conducting themselves according to their true identity, not by the world's standards.

To summarize then, the church is composed of *people*—it is not merely bricks and mortar. It is a *habitation* of God, a place where God Himself takes up special residence. And it is *holy*. That is to say, it is deserving of reverence and respect—not as a *sanctuary*, a term often identified with the building—but as a *called-out assembly* of men and women who comprise His work. Paul's counsel stands in stark contrast to the way these people are treating each other. We would do well to heed his admonition today when party spirit and factionalism enter to terrorize our congregations.

He's Got the Whole World in His Hands (3:18–23)

Learning to trust in God and not ourselves or other people is one of life's greatest challenges. In concluding this chapter, Paul shows that human wisdom comes up empty-handed on the truly vital issues of life. Those things that are often used to divide us (such as material possessions, physical blessings, or human leaders) are already ours in Christ—freely available to all who will simply trust in Him.

"Let no man deceive himself" (v. 18). Paul urges his readers not to be led away from the truth and simplicity of the gospel by having too high an opinion of human wisdom. "If any man among you thinks that he is wise in this age, let him become foolish that he may become wise" (v. 18). Paul returns to the topic of chapter 1 and wraps the first three chapters into a bundle. The Corinthians' problem was, in John's language, "the boastful pride of life" (1 John 2:16). Do not have too high an opinion of yourself. Learn to resign your own understanding to follow the instruction of God. The way to wisdom is to submit our own understanding to God's. This entails considering our own *wisdom*, by comparison, to be mere foolishness. This does not mean that we leave our brains at the door. What it means is that, in the presence of the cross and the manifold demonstration of God's wisdom, we do not speak—we *listen*. As my friend from Texas would say, "There are two kinds of fools in the world. There are those we only think to be fools and there are those who open their mouths and remove all doubt." In the presence of the One who already knows our "reasonings" (cf. v. 20), it is best to "be still" and know that He is God (Ps. 46:10 KJV).

First, the writer establishes that "the fear of the LORD is the beginning of wisdom" (cf. Ps. 111:10). This is true because all knowledge ultimately comes from God. It is not unlikely that the writer is reflecting here on Psalm 94:8–11.

> Pay heed, you senseless among the people;
> And when will you understand, stupid ones?
> He who planted the ear, does He not hear?
> He who formed the eye, does He not see?
> He who chastens the nations, will He not rebuke,
> Even He who teaches man knowledge?
> The Lord knows the thoughts of man,
> That they are a mere breath.

There can be no comparison between God's wisdom and man's. God "catches the wise in their craftiness." (v. 19; cf. Job 5:13). But Paul continues in even stronger language. In his indictment of human wisdom, he adds, "The reasonings of the wise . . . are useless" (v. 20; *mataios*, "pointless," "meaningless"). Under the influence of logical positivism, philosophers in our time[11] have charged that the only meaningful language is given in analytic or synthetic statements capable of scientific investigation and verification. In such a climate, language about God that purported to be giving factual information was discarded as *meaningless.*[12] Our text responds to such warped thinking to show that it is not the wisdom of God that is meaningless, but it is the so-called wisdom of the world. At the beginning of the twentieth century, there was great optimism regarding the possibilities of human intelligence to solve the world's problems. A century later, in the wake of the Bolshevik revolution, ethnic cleansing, two world wars, the holocaust, the detonation of the atomic bomb, Korea, Vietnam, and now 9/11, skepticism abounds. There is serious doubt today whether the intellectual elite of our time even know the right questions—let alone the right answers! Is it any wonder that "He who sits in the heavens laughs" (Ps. 2:4) and that we should "Do homage to the Son, that He not become angry, and you perish in the way" (Ps. 2:12)?

Because all knowledge ultimately comes from God and because all human knowledge is vain, it is both *wrong* and *foolish* to trust in human wisdom. The illusion of modern science is the claim that we know more about the mysteries of the heavens than ever before. The reality is that all we know about the mysteries of the heavens is that they are more mysterious than we ever imagined. Jesus spoke eloquently to this point in His conversation with Nicodemus in John 3:11–12: "Truly, truly, I say to you, we speak of what we know and testify of what we have seen, and you do not accept our testimony. If I told you earthly things and you do not believe, how will you believe if I tell you heavenly things?"

Modern science and technology have given us things that are often described as "miraculous." We now enjoy sophisticated devices capable of repairing broken bodies and expanding the human understanding of the material universe beyond our wildest imaginations. Yet as wonderful as these inventions are, they fail to answer the deepest questions of the human heart. If life is extended, it still comes to an end. If understanding is enlarged, it is still insufficient to bring peace, hope, or joy, or to satisfy the longings of the human heart. Nearly a hundred years ago, James Hastings wrote in words that are more applicable today than they were when he spoke:

> Science cannot take the place of the Cross. Some are constantly asserting the claim of science to supersede Christianity. Many well-meaning Christians are spending the time which might be devoted to evangelistic work in [endeavoring] to reconcile the book of Genesis with the latest scientific theory . . . . The most serious question in the world is not, What think ye of Darwin? Or even, What think ye of Moses? It is, What think ye of Christ?[13]

Ironically, scientific reasoning can tell us that there is a statistical probability that God created the universe, that there is a heaven, and that there is a place like hell. But it cannot tell us how God did it. Nor can it say where heaven is or how to get there. It cannot instruct us on the location of hell or how to avoid it. Jesus is the only man in history who was personally present at creation, who has seen heaven, and who knows the reality of hell. He taught us more about these matters than any other individual recorded in Scripture. It is wrong to imagine that those who have never experienced creation *ex nihilo* would know more about it than the One who has. And it is foolish to seek directions on how to get to heaven or how to shun hell from those who know the least about it. Rather, we had better seek wisdom from Him who said: "We speak what we know," and added with authority, "I am the way, and the truth, and the life; no one comes to the Father, but through Me" (John 14:6). In the end, obedience is more important than understanding. And trust is more powerful than reason. One need not be able to understand avionics to fly in an airplane. Nor do sinners need to understand the mysteries of God in order to enjoy the blessings of being a saint. And only a fool will reject the offer until he or she can understand it.

The conclusion to chapter 3 is very much like the conclusion to chapter 1 (cf. 1:29–30). If you must boast, then by all means, boast in Christ, "for all things belong to you" (v. 21; *pas*, "all"). The individual who belongs to Christ is a child of God, and the Father will do anything for His child. None of the Father's resources will be begrudged to the believer (cf. Rom. 8:32). "All things" has in mind all these resources, even human resources, such as "Paul or Apollos or Cephas." Or they may be of "the world," or they may be related to the blessings of "life or death"; indeed they may even include "things present or things to come" (v. 22). But as for ownership, "all things belong to you, and you belong to Christ; and Christ belongs to God" (vv. 22–23). The absurdity of their dividing over allegiances to any of these men is that God gave them "all" to the Corinthians. The absurdity of wrangling over who has the greatest gifts (cf. chap. 14) is that these are all granted by the good hand of God. The child of God will lack no good thing (see Ps. 84:11). But it must be remembered that it is only because of one's relationship to Christ who is Lord of all that any of these benefits accrue.

All things are ours with one exception—ourselves. Paul says, "You belong to Christ." (v. 23). We are Christ's and "Christ belongs to God." Hastings suggests: "Christ belongs to God by right of generation. 'Thou art my Son, this day have I begotten thee.' We belong to Christ by right of purchase. 'Ye are not your own; for ye were bought with a price.'[14]

The expression "Christ belongs to God" (literally, "Christ of God") is important. It has implications for the home and the church as well as eschatological ramifications that will be discussed later in this epistle. In terms of His essential deity, Christ is not subordinate to God in the way the believer is subordinate to Christ; rather, He is the anointed one of God. He is God in flesh, "reconciling the world to Himself" (2 Cor. 5:19). It is in the performance of this *task* that He assumes a "subordinate role." In this respect, He provides an example of the structure of authority in the home and in the church (cf. 1 Cor. 11:3). Even in the establishment of His millennial kingdom, He will do so in obedience to the plan established by the Father (cf. 15:27–28). Eventually God the Father will be seen as "all in all."

Study Questions

1. Describe the individuals in this chapter who are said to be "carnal." Would you consider them to be saved? How does Paul account for their behavior? Do you know people like this?

2. How does the issue of maturity relate to the issue of carnality? Be specific.

3. How would you characterize Paul's method of church growth? Are there any principles here that could be transferred to a contemporary setting?

4. Compare and contrast the "field" metaphor with the "building" metaphor. Why might the writer mix these metaphors?

5. Compare and contrast the significance of the foundation versus the building of the temple.

6. The writer uses two types of material to describe the quality of workmanship that is invested by each person. What are these and what is the significance of each?

7. In what sense can we say that the Holy Spirit inhabits the church as temple?

8. In what sense are those who violate God's temple going to be "destroyed"? Are these believers or unbelievers?

9. Defend Paul's assertion that the "reasonings of the wise . . . are useless" against modern scientific advances in medicine and technology.

10. Since Christ is God, how is it that He is said to "belong" to God?

CHAPTER 6

Defending Servant Leadership
1 Corinthians 4:1–21

Preview:

In contrast to the Corinthians' factional spirit, Paul shows them that their "heroes" do not support them in their attempts to exalt one over the other. Rather, they were all working together as fellow workers of God. They had given their lives to carry the gospel to reach people like those at Corinth. In so doing, Paul lays out his strategies for discipleship and chides the Corinthians as only their spiritual father could do. Believers should imitate the example of the apostles as "servant leaders" instead of trying to exalt themselves over others.

Since all who ministered at Corinth were servants of God (cf. 3:5), and since the church belongs to God and is His temple (cf. 3:16–17), the Corinthians were entirely out of line in qualifying these ministers by their own arbitrary standards. It is God whom these men serve, and He must be their Judge. Paul, Apollos, and Peter were faithful ministers of Christ and, along with the other apostles, were simply obeying God in extending the gospel around the world. In this chapter, Paul shows that the wrangling in Corinth was inappropriate, unfair, and intolerable.

Servant Leadership (4:1–4)

Having established in the previous chapter that "all things belong" to those who are in right relation to Jesus Christ, Paul now goes on to show how this truth relates to himself and to all who followed him in planting and nurturing the Corinthian church. Nowadays it is typical to distinguish between *leadership* and *management.* Leadership is all about setting the vision and establishing global directions. In a military setting, this would correspond to the generals. Management functions under the leader to see to the execution of the vision. In a military setting this would correspond to the field officers. Using this analogy, Paul is suggesting that his role was not as the leader, or general—that was Jesus Christ. Paul's role was that of a manager, or field officer. He was not in charge. He was under orders. He was not setting the agenda. He was getting a job done.

First, he says, "Let a man regard us in this manner, as *servants* of Christ" (v. 1, emphasis mine). Paul had quite an arsenal of terms available for his use in making this point. *Doulos* (Rom. 1:1) spoke of a permanent servitude. *Therapon* (Heb. 3:5) stressed service in relation to persons. *Diakonos* (1 Cor. 3:5) stressed service in relation to the work. *Oiketes* (Luke 16:13) spoke of a household slave. *Uperetas* (John 7:32), or "under-rower," spoke of a person under authority. In most cases in these letters, as elsewhere, Paul uses the term *diakonos*, or "minister," "servant," sometimes simply transliterated "deacon" (1 Cor. 3:5; 2 Cor. 3:6; 6:4; 11:15, 23). Only here does Paul employ this term ordinarily rendered "officers" elsewhere in the New Testament (cf. John 18:3). More importantly, according to Paul's testimony, it is the term used by the Lord when He commissioned him. "But arise, and stand on your feet; for this purpose I have appeared to you, to appoint you a *minister*" (Acts 26:16, emphasis mine). The root meaning of the term is "under-rower," and it conveys the sense of a subordinate who is charged with a task. It speaks of one who acts under the orders of another as an "assistant" (e.g., see Luke 4:20) and officer (see Matt. 5:25).[1]

Then Paul goes on to say that he and the other apostles are to be regarded as "stewards of the mysteries of God" (v. 1). A "steward" is generally a slave in the master's household who is entrusted with property. Both terms—*servant* and *steward*—emphasize subordination to the master. However, the latter, places particular stress on accountability. He must give an account for the manner in which he carries out his master's orders. So, finally, Paul adds, "It is required of stewards that one be found trustworthy" (v. 2). In verse 2, Paul moves from the plural to the singular ("stewards"—"a man"). This is characteristic of Paul. He typically moves from principle to particular—that is, what is sought for in all stewards is that each one be found reliable and trustworthy. And what is especially important here is that the steward is viewed as accountable to no one but his master. So it is a "small thing" (v. 3) to Paul that he is now being subjected to the judicial scrutiny of individuals to whom he is, in the final analysis, not accountable.

In fact, Paul is not intimidated by "*any* human court" (v. 3; Greek, *anthropines hemeras*, "man's day"). This is an implied contrast with the Day of the Lord (cf. *kairos*, "time," v. 5). Paul is saying, "My time has not yet come."

Indeed, "I do not even examine myself" (v. 3). This is not a contradiction with 11:28. It is rather that the *final* judgment on our work is to be given by the Lord Himself. And it is He who shall render to each according to his work (cf. 3:12–15).

On this score, Paul adds, "I am conscious of nothing against myself" (v. 4). It was this sort of total commitment that gave Paul the authority to make such a statement as "Be imitators of me" (1 Cor. 4:16; 11:1). But, he continues, "I am not by this acquitted." Paul was not competent to objectively examine himself. "Man is totally irrational in his attitude and assessment of his own nature. He is a fallen creature with a heart that is desperately wicked above all else (Jer. 17:9), and a mind that has to be renewed (Rom. 12:2)."[2]

To summarize then, Paul has established that he has three roles to fulfill in his work in Corinth. He is a *minister* a field officer working under orders. He is a *steward* given the oversight of God's property ("field," "building"). And as such he is expected to be *trustworthy*. He is answerable, not to them, but to the Lord who assigned him to the task.

Thank God for Ducks (4:5)

The Lord alone is the Judge. Therefore, the examination must await His time, that is, when He "comes" (v. 5; cf. 1:7). Then He will shed light on the "things hidden" (v. 5) that Paul relates to "motives of the heart." At that time, "each man's praise will come to him from God" (v. 5). God who knows the minds and the hearts will apportion to each his due praise.

My family lives on a lake. Living here has acquainted us with many creatures native to aquatic habitats. Among these creatures are two swans, many ducks, and even more geese. Since we live in "the south," it is rare for the lake to freeze over. It is also rare for our ducks and geese to leave for the winter. But some years ago we had an especially bitter winter. What started as a cold snap continued for several weeks, stretching into months—causing the lake to develop a layer of ice. Spreading from the shoreline toward the center, over time the ice closed in to cover nearly the entire lake. As this process continued, we watched the ducks and geese, who ordinarily keep to themselves, inexorably being pushed together into the center of the lake. The cold north wind just kept blowing, and the opening in the ice grew smaller and smaller. What mystified us was that it didn't close up altogether leaving the birds stranded on the ice. Someone explained to me that the birds actually keep that from happening by beating the edges of the ice with their wings.

Since the geese are much larger than the ducks, I judged that it was they who were chiefly responsible for seeing to this task. Each day I would watch in amazement as the little opening in the center of the lake remained. And each day the shivering fowl could be seen huddling together in their still segregated groups. But one day a most unusual thing happened. As if on cue, the geese—to a feather—stretched their long necks toward the southern sky, spread their wings, and lifted themselves out of the icy water. Making one full circle, and in an ever-diminishing cacophony of sound, they tracked south and disappeared from sight.

I thought, *How sad. Now the poor ducks are going to lose their home in the lake too. And they too will have to leave.* But to my surprise, that was not what happened. The ducks stayed and continued the task of keeping the edges of the ice broken. Never once did their little pond freeze over. And they were still there in the spring when the geese returned. Later someone told me the geese never were responsible for this phenomenon. The ducks were. I had judged them by their appearance, but it was the ducks, not the geese, that had the right stuff all along.

"Man looks at the outward appearance, but the LORD looks at the heart" (1 Sam. 16:7). It is impossible for those of us who are not privy to the Lord's eternal plan to pass judgment on His agents. Yet, like the Corinthians, we still try. To us as to them, the apostle gives two pieces of advice. The *first* is that judgment is not ours to make. Leave it alone until God's time, and then God Himself will give the praise. This in itself is an amazing truth, and it bespeaks the very core of grace. God calls, commissions, enables, and empowers his agents. When the work is done, it is all of Him and all of grace. Yet, it is the agent who will receive praise from God: "Well done, good and faithful slave" (Matt. 25:21, 23).

The second piece of advice is that judgment is certain. And when it comes, even the hidden motives of the heart shall be exposed before Him with whom we have to do. It will not be our outward appearance that will make the difference. It will be our faithfulness to the work assigned by the Master. Are we with the ducks, "always abounding in the work" (1 Cor. 15:58), or the geese, just taking up space in the pond?

One final word is in order on "the things hidden in the darkness" (v. 5; Greek, *krupta tou skotous*, "the hidden things of darkness"). Nigel Turner argues that this should be rendered a subjective genitive rather than an objective genitive, as in our text. What exactly is it that is to be brought to light—the things that darkness hides (objective) or the concealing darkness itself (subjective)? Turner answers:

> In a world where decisions are reached by biased judgment, and where motives are mixed, it may be impossible to judge fairly because of an ignorance and prejudice which amounts to blindness. It is not simply that

man falls short of omniscience or some facts are hidden from him when he makes a decision, but the situation is far worse. There is a positive darkness which poisons and misdirects the mind, to be removed only by the brightness of the Lord's *parousia*, not by the mere acquisition of further knowledge. So St. Paul was suggesting that Christ will dispel "the darkness itself which hides," and that was a more radical remedy than the mere dispelling of "the things which darkness hides."[3]

Turner concludes that if the writer was only speaking of setting the record straight about matters concerning which he was being criticized at Corinth, he need not wait until the end of the age. "It did not need the *parousia* to bring new facts to light; yet only the *parousia*, nothing less, could dispel the deep prejudice which is 'the darkness which hides" the truth deliberately."[4]

A Tale of Two Churches (4:6–13)

Using the contrasting examples of the apostles versus those who have usurped the leadership in Corinth, Paul paints two portraits of two very different types of ministry. He says he "figuratively applied" (v. 6; *metaschematizo*, "exchanged the outward fashion") these ideas to himself and Apollos "for your sakes, that in us you might learn not to exceed what is written" (v. 6). One picture is of a ministry built on worldly standards; the other is shaped by apostolic standards. One might be labeled a *worldly* church, the other a *godly* church.

The Worldly Church (4:6–8)

First, in a worldly church, people are more important than God. There is some debate as to what "what is written" (v. 6) signifies. Is it the Old Testament? If so, what text? Is it a previous letter of Paul to this assembly (see introduction)? Probably not. Is it merely a figure of speech for a common standard? Perhaps, but again we have no knowledge of what that would be. A fairly strong case can be made for the suggestion that "what is written" refers here to by-laws—possibly set down by the apostle himself and agreed to by the assembly before his departure. Hanges is even stronger in his assertion: "'That Paul is prohibiting the violation of something written is unanimously held to be the sense of the phrase by interpreters who try to make sense of the present text."[5]

Since these kinds of documents were commonplace among the other religious sects in Corinth, is it possible that the Christian church had such a set of rules dictating their community life?[6] If James C. Hanges is correct, the indictment against the church is even more damning than we imagined. They were not only given to doing things their "own way," but in the process they were running roughshod over their own written constitution—drafted perhaps under the teaching and preaching ministry of the apostle himself. In the very least, whether Hanges is correct or not, they were violating an established rule known to them and the apostle.

In a setting where human opinion and worldly standards abound, God's standards are given short shrift. I often hear pastors speak of "my" church and "my" people. Such talk betrays a distortion of the biblical perspective that understands that the church belongs to God and no one else. Even the founder of their church considers himself to have been nothing more than a hired hand.

Second, in a worldly church, status is more important than service. Paul writes, "that no one of you might become arrogant" (v. 6). God's work is often stymied by people who think they have to get the credit. When ministry becomes a "career" and its success only a leg up to bigger and better opportunities, the church runs the risk of being victimized by status seekers. David K. Lowery speaks to the point: "Paul concluded his address to the problem of division in the church by putting his finger unambiguously on their problem: pride (v. 6)."[7]

Third, in a worldly church privilege produces pride instead of thanksgiving. "And what do you have that you did not receive? But if you did receive it, why do you boast as if you had not received it?" (v. 7). When Paul reflected on the grace of God that brought him to salvation, he was given to expressions of wonder. He said, "Christ Jesus came into the world to save sinners, among whom I am foremost of all" (1 Tim. 1:15). To the Ephesians he writes, "To me, the very least of all saints, this grace was given, to preach to the Gentiles the unfathomable riches of Christ" (3:8). He could never get beyond "the wonder of it all."[8] But these people were on a different planet. They seemed to be working with an entirely different set of standards—and they were not from God. There is no room for pride and self-conceit when all the privileges enjoyed are owing to God. Everything they had—including their ministry gifts—was given by God. To take personal pride in what they had was tantamount to insulting Him.

Finally, in a worldly church, prosperity is the measure of success. "You are already filled, you have already become rich, you have become kings" (v. 8). Material success, political power, intellectual acceptance—all are symptoms of prosperity theology, both ancient and modern. The timely force of this text for the contemporary church is evident. Irony exudes from the apostle in these words. They represent three blessings promised in the coming messianic kingdom. The Corinthians were boasting each with his own party as if he had already arrived in the kingdom. And so Paul says, "*I* would indeed that you had become kings so that we also might reign with you" (v. 8). The Corinthians had already arrived while the apostle was still waiting (cf. vv. 5–6)![9]

The Godly Church (4:9–13)

"For, I think, God has exhibited us apostles last of all" (v. 9). In God's church, the standards of success are counterintuitive to the thinking of the Corinthian believers. It is a place where God is doing the work, where he is getting the glory, and where a cross is more evident than a crown. Those who are "heirs of God and fellow heirs with Christ . . . [will] suffer with *Him* in order that we may also be glorified with *Him*" (Rom. 8:17).

First, the godly church is a ministry of death. "I think" (v. 9; Greek, *dokeo*) is literally "I am of the considered opinion." The apostle is about to level the arrogance of these Corinthians. Considering the suffering and abuse of the apostles, since you are already reigning, God must have placed the apostles "last of all." We have not come into the kingdom yet! To the world, we are a "spectacle" (Greek, *theatron*, "a theater"). The apostles were like exhibits in a sideshow. Notice the verb form of this term in Hebrews 10:33. We appear to have been "condemned to death" (v. 9). Paul knew what it was to die to ambition and pride. Jesus said, "Take up [your] cross, and follow Me" (Matt. 16:24). If Paul was looking for the right "career choice," he would never have gone to Corinth. Paul died on the road to Damascus (Acts 9); nevertheless he lived (Gal. 2:20). When we die to self, we give God the opportunity to infuse us with His life.

A Godly Church . . .

- *Is not in harmony with Satan (Belial) but with Christ (2 Cor. 6:15)*
- *Is a "temple" without idols (2 Cor. 6:16)*
- *Is not defiled by the flesh (2 Cor. 7:1)*
- *Shows forth the proofs of its love (2 Cor. 8:24)*
- *Tests itself to see that it is walking "in the faith" (2 Cor. 13:5)*
- *Has believers who are like-minded and living in peace (2 Cor. 13:11)*
- *Has leaders who will not practice evil (3 John 1:10-11)*

Second, the godly church is a ministry of weakness (v. 10). The series of growing distinctions between Paul and the Corinthians must have been nothing short of embarrassing to his readers. "We are fools for Christ's sake, but you are prudent" (Greek, *phronimos*, "shrewd"). "We are weak, but you are strong; you are distinguished, but we are without honor" (v. 10). "For Christ's sake" indicates that the apostles were considered fools because they knew and preached nothing but Christ. On the other hand, one would suspect that the Corinthians used their Christianity to extend their reputation as wise and enlightened people.

Finally, the godly church is a ministry of rejection (vv. 11–13). The apostles were "hungry and thirsty . . . poorly clothed . . . roughly treated . . . homeless . . . reviled . . . persecuted . . . slandered . . . scum . . . dregs" (vv. 11–13). He is beaten but not broken, bloodied but unbowed—returning blessing for hatred and encouragement for slander. Some find an illusion in the use of *peripsema*, "dregs," to the ancient Athenian custom of throwing certain worthless persons into the sea in case of plague or famine, saying: "Be our offscouring!" in the belief that they would wash away the city's guilt.[10] Jesus said it best: "If the world hates you, you know that it has hated Me before *it hated* you. If you were of the world, the world would love its own; but because you are not of the world, but I chose you out of the world, therefore the world hates you. . . . But all these things they will do to you for My name's sake, because they do not know the One who sent Me" (John 15:18–21).

Dynamics of Discipleship (4:14–21)

The remainder of the chapter contains an exhortation to faithfulness (vv. 14–21). Here Paul's tone changes. He lays aside the irony that characterizes so much of this chapter and now entreats his readers as a loving parent might plead with wayward children. In what follows he offers a wonderful blueprint for discipleship. The English terms *discipline* and *disciple* are from the same root. Discipleship is a call to a disciplined life that involves several key elements, including an expectation (an admonition), submission to authority, a price to pay, and accountability.

Most of us have experienced such relationships or seek to enter into them. Anyone who has ever led a person to Christ knows the importance of discipleship with a new convert. And, as every parent and teacher knows one need not be professionally involved with others in order to disciple them.

The text readily breaks into two broad sections. The first is suggestive of the foundations of discipleship (vv. 14–16), while the second offers several helpful techniques (vv. 17–21).

Foundations of Discipleship (4:14–16)

First, discipleship is rooted in a relationship of love, not fear. "I do not write these things to shame you, but to admonish you as my beloved children" (v. 14). Paul realizes that if all he does is expose his readers to open shame, he will only provoke them to obstinacy. And so, while wishing to expose their sin, he does not wish to exasperate them. With sincere love and affection, the apostle admonishes his children in the faith. He is not interested in making them cringe before him, but in correcting them and offering them a chance to respond and be restored.

Second, discipleship involves a relationship of authority but not authoritarianism. "If you were to have countless tutors in Christ, yet *you would* not *have* many fathers" (v. 15). The term *paidagogos*, "boy leader," is fairly rare in the New Testament. It occurs only in Paul—here and in Galatians 3:24–25. In ancient Greek culture it would refer to a trusted aid (or slave-guardian) who supervised the conduct and morals of a child until he or she became of age. As Paul uses the term, it is almost a pejorative. He applies it in Galatians to the Law, which is useful only to lead us to Christ. After receiving "adoption as sons" (Gal. 4:5), the tutor (the Law) was no long necessary. This is not to say that the Law was no longer valid, but to say that the son no longer needed a slave to tell him how to live. Once the child became a *huios*, or "mature son," it was expected that he would have the character to live in a way that would honor his father without the need for the tutor.

In this context Paul uses the term in much the same way, only it is much more personal. No matter how many tutors you may have had, you have only one father. And, "in Christ Jesus," he adds, "I became your father" (v. 15; *gennao*, "to beget," "to bring forth"). If Paul was just a stranger, he could not have spoken so freely. But he was their father. He was probably the only one who could speak to them in this way. Moreover, he was under obligation to do so. He alone was responsible for the beginning of the Corinthian assembly. The term "begot" does not have in mind so much the conversion of these people, but the fact that it was Paul who laid the foundation (3:10).

One other, rather subtle message is communicated here. If Paul was their father, he was in a class altogether distinct from all others who came into their church usurping authority—whether legitimately or illegitimately. They were mere "tutors." But since Paul was the "father," fidelity to his "laws" takes precedence over the "slave-guardians." But more than this, there is the positive expectation of their spiritual father that they should be mature enough by now to honor him and live by the rules (cf. 4:6 above).

True discipleship recognizes this authority of the spiritual mentor. But authority is a two-edged sword. It cuts both ways, making demands on the mentor and the disciple alike. This is always the case, but when it occurs at the parental level, a price is usually paid. Many would rather be "friends" with their children, when God has called them to a much greater role—*discipl*inarian. When parents settle for merely making friends of their children, they do so for selfish reasons. Parenting is not as hard when the adult lets the child find his or her own way. And if/when the child makes mistakes the parent bears little or no responsibility. By abrogating their parental obligations, such parents ironically make their job easier and at the same time disrespect their children by their neglect.

But when parents set out to build character in their children through discipline and accountability, they do so for the sake of the child—not for their own self-interest. The task is much more difficult and demanding. It requires constant attention on the part of the parent. It requires that the adult be the adult and that the child be the child.[11] It asserts authority and requires accountability. Paul's example here illustrates this point well. He could have just washed his hands of them and gone on. But because he loves them and because he takes his responsibility as their spiritual father seriously, he pays the price to take them to the next level.

Third, discipleship demands integrity on the part of the leader (v. 16). Paul is unafraid to say to them, "Be imitators of me" (v. 16; cf. 11:1, literally, "Continue to imitate me"). No doubt Paul has in mind those characteristics that are common to him and the other apostles, listed in verses 11–13. But his thinking goes further to include his doctrine and his teaching, as shown in the expression "my ways" (v. 17). If they have any questions as to how to follow the apostle, Timothy is on his way and will clarify any problems they have. Personal integrity is absolutely vital to healthy relationships that produce spiritual growth. Nothing is deadlier than hypocrisy and double standards. And no one seems more aware of this than Paul.

Techniques of Discipleship (4:17–21)

Paul understands the importance of having personal integrity and loving relationships with a clear line of authority. These are essential for discipling those whom God has enabled him to "father" in the faith. And he has adopted a methodology designed to foster such vital relationships.

First, Paul knows how to delegate authority. "I have sent to you Timothy, who is my beloved and faithful child in the Lord" (v. 17). Timothy was no neophyte. Timothy was a young man in whom Paul had invested much energy and trust. Paul views Timothy as a child, or "son." Paul knows him to be "beloved and faithful." And Timothy is one who represents the common faith with the same integrity as that known to characterize the great apostle.

Second, Paul is not afraid of confrontation. "Some have become arrogant, as though I were not coming to you. But I will come . . . if the Lord wills, and I shall find out, not the words of those who are arrogant, but their power" (vv. 18–19). Paul was well known for confronting trouble head-on (cf. Gal. 2:11). Lest we misinterpret him here, it is important to continue to see both sides of his humanity. He really does love them and is concerned for their spiritual welfare. But he is also profoundly hurt by their criticism of him, and it is probably not too much to say that he is angry with those who are trying to lead these spiritual children astray. Someone has well said, "Only your friends will tell you." As I noted above, parents who truly love their children will discipline (make disciples of) them (Heb. 12:7).

Third, discipleship is concerned with action, not just words. "For the kingdom of God does not consist in words, but in power" (v. 20). Paul cannot resist the use of irony. He is eager to take on the Corinthians and settle this matter once and for all. The leader *goes to* the problem rather than running from it. As we saw above, Paul understands—and practices—servant leadership. But that clearly does not mean that the pastor must serve as a doormat for everyone in the church. Those called to pastoral leadership would do well to keep this in mind. There are times when people must be called to account. It is not God's will that the church be held hostage by a few ungodly power-mongers. Power without authority is often effectual but illegitimate. Authority without power is legitimate but ineffectual. Authority with power is legitimate and effectual. When we know, with Paul, that we have the authority and God is on our side, then as they used to say in World War II, "Pray and pass the ammunition!"

Finally, discipleship looks for a win-win solution. More often than not, when discipline involving correction is involved, we set it up for a win-lose conclusion. Paul leaves the door ajar for reconciliation. "What do you desire? Shall I come to you with a rod or with love and a spirit of gentleness?" (v. 21). There is no doubt as to what he most desires of them. While he does not fear confronting them with the truth, he would rather see this conflict resolved amicably. When Paul exhorts fathers, "Do not provoke your children to anger; but bring them up in the discipline and instruction of the Lord" (Eph. 6:4), he is there prescribing the same procedure he demonstrates here by personal example.

Reference to "the rod" is a suitable segue for what follows in chapter 5. But it also stands as a symbol used commonly in the ancient world as a sign of authority—precisely the issue at hand. The writer had suffered the sting of the rod on more than one occasion—a point already alluded to in this text and recorded elsewhere (Acts 16:22–23; 2 Cor. 11:25). His preference nonetheless is that he might come with "a spirit of gentleness" (v. 21).

Study Questions

1. Comparing the various terms Paul might have used to designate his relationship with Christ and with this church, what is the significance of his use of the term "servant" in verse 1?

2. Compare and distinguish the terms *servant, steward,* and *trustworthy* as they relate to apostolic ministry.

3. How does Paul characterize the difference between the vision of the church as he conceives it versus that which seems to be developing in Corinth?

4. What practical advice might you draw from verse 5 with respect to "passing judgment before the time"? To what "time" is he referring? Who will be involved in this judgment?

5. Why does Paul describe his ministry as a "ministry of death"? How might his approach to ministry be a helpful corrective to modern methods of church growth?

6. Suggest three foundational principles of discipleship drawn from this chapter.

7. List several methodological principles of Paul's approach to discipleship that are gleaned from this chapter.

SECTION II: CORRECTION

You Have Become Arrogant

1 Corinthians 5—6

CHAPTER 7

Dealing with Immorality
1 Corinthians 5:1-13

Preview:

Because the Corinthians had become arrogant and prideful, they completely overlooked the presence of gross immorality in their assembly. They are obliged to deal with their sin or else it will destroy them. If they don't, Paul will come and deal with it personally.

In coming to this, Paul's second major division of the epistle, it is helpful to remember the vile surroundings out of which the Corinthian converts had come. They had been truly won to Christ. They had broken from their idolatries and formed a local church. They had come out of the corruption of Corinth to form a community of saints. But having brought the church out of Corinth, the question now is whether they can get Corinth out of their church. It is imperative that they learn the dangers of compromise and the dynamics of a life empowered by the Holy Spirit. "The Holy Spirit is grieved and thwarted in the assembly where sin is allowed a footing."[1] There must be a clean break. These are the issues on the table for the next two chapters. And it is precisely these issues on which the Corinthians are in need of *correction*.

The social and theological backdrop of these two chapters is also important. The fabled tale of Sophocles' *Oedipus the King* was without doubt familiar to most Corinthians. Oedipus was said to have been brought to Corinth to be raised by the royal family there. And it was there that the tragic events are said to have unfolded in his life. Certainly the story was known to any lad tutored in the famed city. Accordingly, this story likely provided the justification for

Paul's assertion that the behavior of some in the church was beyond the pale even for a *pagan* ("Gentile") society.[2] But more important, Paul's use of Old Testament texts such as Leviticus 18:8 and Deuteronomy 17:7; 22:22 show us that he is working with an entirely different paradigm than his first readers would have known. Like Israel in its beginnings, the Corinthians were a *new* people (cf. 2 Cor. 5:17–21). Their worldview and the standards according to which they should conduct their lives were established on the basis of that new identity—not by the prevailing mores of "Egypt" behind them or the culture around them. And their ultimate accountability was to conduct their lives in such a way as to honor and build up that new community. The problems of immorality (5:1–13), appeals to Gentile courts (6:1–11), and excessive libertarianism (6:12–20) all reflect a misunderstanding of the nature of this new relationship. Since Christ has died and the believers are joined to Him in a new filial and ecclesial relationship, they need to "clean out the old leaven" (5:7). "His treatment of the issue makes sense only in these terms: just as Israel was to purge itself of the abominations of the inhabitants of the land, so also the church must purge itself of ways of conduct inappropriate to the [people] of God" (cf. 1 Cor. 6:9–11).[3]

One final observation is in order here. The preceding immediate context is *discipleship*. It is not accidental that the dynamics of discipleship upon which the writer focuses his attention in the previous chapter are followed by several practical areas requiring *discipline*. And since it is the heart of the apostle that is most evident, it is clear throughout that his intention is not to break them down, but to build them up—the objective of all true discipleship.

Deliver Such a One to Satan (5:1–5)

Discipline is one of the most difficult assignments for any church. It is difficult for the pastor because it is often contrary to his natural gifting. That is, pastors ordinarily have a special sensitivity and desire to be people helpers. They prefer to negotiate peace rather than to confront potentially hostile situations. And it is difficult for churches because most prefer not to rock the boat. Even when people know things are amiss, they would prefer not to know about it than to disrupt the Pollyanna image they have of their *perfect* church. Often the result is denial—or worse—a whitewash of painfully sinful behaviors that corrode the very soul of the church. In the Corinthian assembly they, like many moderns, reasoned that they should work with the errant couple to bring them to a proper understanding of the nature of their behavior. Perhaps there was, as there is in our own day, a bifurcation of love and discipline. It is often considered that love should be tolerant and accepting—not critical and judgmental. By implication, it is thought that obedience to God's precepts will alienate rather than heal the sinful individual(s).

Paul will come to the matter of Christian love later (chap. 13). For now he wants them to know that their lack of attention to this matter requiring the strictest of discipline is intolerable. Also, from a practical standpoint, Paul affords us a wonderful pattern for *how* to deal with such matters when they come to the attention of the church.

First, he states the reason for discipline. "It is actually reported"—probably from those of Chloe's household (v. 1; cf. 1:11 and introduction). The sad report had come before the apostle concerning immorality practiced by persons associated with the Corinthian assembly. It is entirely appropriate to infer from this that if the matter had not been made public, the disciplinary action may not have required such a public response. The action here is not to be viewed as a contradiction to that given in Matthew 18:15-17. What is evident here is that the offense had gone way beyond a dispute between two individuals. It already involved an offense against the entire assembly.

The word "immorality" (v. 1) is used in a comprehensive way—perhaps implying that the offense in different forms more or less prevailed in the Corinthian assembly. But one case in particular is so gross that it "does not exist even among the Gentiles" (v. 1). Cicero alludes to this type of behavior as "*scelus incredibile, et praeter unum in omni vita inauditum*" (literally, "incredible wickedness, such I never heard of in all my life besides").[4] The crime was "that someone has his father's wife." One of the members of the church had taken his stepmother (cf. Lev. 18:8). (The expression "to have a woman" suggests the binding relationship of marriage; cf. Matt. 14:4; 22:28; John 4:17; 1 Cor. 7:2, 29.) The persons involved were either married or cohabiting as though they were. Since Paul makes no mention of disciplining the woman, it is evident that she was not a Christian. But having said that, it is also difficult not to connect this text with his subsequent discussion regarding the appropriate candidates for marriage of a believer (see the expression "only in the Lord," 1 Cor. 7:39).

Second, he specifies the proper posture. "And you have become arrogant, and have not mourned instead, in order that the one who had done this deed might be removed from your midst" (v. 2). Discipline is done in the attitude of humility. To the Galatian believers his words were similar. "Brethren, even if a man is caught in any trespass, you who are spiritual, restore such a one in a spirit of gentleness; *each one* looking to yourself, lest you too be tempted" (Gal. 6:1). By contrast these people were "arrogant" when they should have been "mourning." There is a penetrating analysis of the dynamics of confrontation here. When sin is allowed to go on in people's lives without the leadership confronting it, the lack of action is neglect, not loving concern for sinners. If allowed to continue, this sin will destroy those who are caught up in it.

If their Christian brethren were not so arrogant and preoccupied with defending their preferred factions or celebrating their liberty and superiority, they would have noticed a brother heading for certain destruction and would have been exercised enough by it to try to "save" him (cf. James 5:19–20). There is also the specter of pharisaism here. The Pharisees were too proud to be honest. They were so busy thanking God for their *holiness* that they forgot to ask for *forgiveness* (Luke 18:10ff.). The problem with the assembly was that they were laden with pride and lacking in discipline. Such an outrageous and detestable sin should have provoked the strongest response from the congregation and its leadership. But because of their pride and carnality, they were immobilized when it came to dealing with the real problem in their midst.

Third, there is a prescribed enablement (vv. 3–4). In these verses, Hughes notes:

> We have an interesting indication of the manner in which discipline was administered in the early church. The congregation would be called together, with an apostle presiding if available, and the person accused would be arraigned before them. After the evidence had been heard, and the accused had said what he had to say in defense of himself, the judgment of the congregation would be pronounced by the president. Paul, though absent in person, yet pictures himself present and presiding in spirit, and he leaves them in no doubt concerning the verdict which ought to be pronounced.[5]

They have (1) *apostolic authority*—Paul. "I, . . . though absent in body but present in spirit, have already judged him" (v. 3). Paul imagines himself presiding over their meeting and as having already passed judgment. They also convene under (2) *divine authority*—it was to be done "in the name of our Lord Jesus" (v. 4). And it was to be done in (3) the *power of Christ*. Reference to "power" responds to the rebuke in 4:19–20. It should be observed in this text that discipline will require obedience and strength. But the authority does not reside in the individual; it resides in our Lord. And the strength required is not from us either; it is from Him. In other words, discipline properly conducted will require and appropriate supernatural enablement.

In the church today, we do not have an apostle physically present, but like the Corinthians, we have Paul and other New Testament apostles and prophets present "in spirit" (v. 4) with the inspired Scriptures of the New Testament. Their teachings, together with the ministry of the indwelling Holy

Spirit, provide to the Church of any age the same guidance, support, and power available to the fledgling assemblies of the early Church. On this issue especially we would do well to give attention to the Word of God over against the excessively tolerant and misguided counsel of others.

Finally, there was a prescribed procedure. "Deliver such a one to Satan" (v. 5). Paul draws from Leviticus 18:29 for precedence in dealing with sexual sins: "For whoever does any of these abominations, those persons who do so shall be cut off from among their people." Specifically, the abomination to which Paul refers is identified in Leviticus 18:8, "You shall not uncover the nakedness of your father's wife." It is not a stretch to suggest that the other "abominations" listed in Leviticus 18 would be equally applicable to Paul should they have occurred. What is important to observe is that the Old Testament principles for personal holiness are not abrogated in the New Testament. They are just as much in force in the New Testament as they were when God gave them to Moses.

To deliver to Satan equates with being "cut off from among their people." Implicit in this association of Paul is that the believing community (the local church) provides a powerful resource for protection against the enemy. And when people are cut off from that, they become vulnerable to all "the schemes of the devil" (Eph. 6:11). We would do well to remember this when we are tempted to absent ourselves from "assembling together, as is the habit of some" (Heb. 10:25). Attempting to live the Christian life apart from other believers is dangerous, for those who do so become prey to the wicked one. But here the sense clearly is that the person identified is to be excommunicated at least until it is evident that he has repented. Today the term *excommunication* tends to be associated with heavy-handed medieval ecclesiasticism. Admittedly, this instrument has been used in rather ungodly ways to further the political ambitions of not a few power-hungry clerics. But as an instrument of correction, it was given to the church as a final solution to discipline problems in the assembly. It has biblical precedent in the Old Testament (Lev. 18), and in the teachings of Jesus (John 15:1–6), Paul (Rom. 11:19–24), and other New Testament writers (Heb. 6:1–8; 2 Pet. 2:1–22).

A final word of caution is in order here. Since this is a discipline associated with one's participation in the local assembly, it does not necessarily address the genuineness of the person's salvation. In the context below, this offender is assumed to be saved; otherwise he would not be contemplated as being present at the "day of the Lord Jesus" (v. 5). And indeed, in most cases of this sort, since they involve members of the local church, this would be the assumption. But salvation is not the issue being addressed here—it is fellowship.

This is not the first-century equivalent to having someone step down from a few church committees. Nor does this resemble a polite request for a letter of resignation. Rather the gist of this passage is that the Corinthians were being told not to associate with him or even eat with him (5:11; 2 Thess. 3:14). Soberly and prayerfully, they were to close ranks and exclude the sinner from their common life, their corporate gatherings and shared meals. No more potlucks. No more prayer breakfasts. No more Holy Communion. The command was, in other words, to banish this man from the one community that provided his spiritual shelter and guidance, and to thrust him out into the world.[6]

One of the outcomes of being delivered to Satan is the "destruction of his flesh" (v. 5). Paul elsewhere perceives affliction, disease, or loss as Satan's work (2 Cor. 12:7; 1 Thess. 2:18; cf. 1 Tim. 1:20). "Destruction" here has the idea of "remedial punishment." (See the use of this term in 1 Thess. 5:3; 2 Thess. 1:9; and 1 Tim. 6:9.) The reference may be to the destruction of the physical appetites that prompted this gross immorality. A more likely possibility is that Paul is saying the same thing James warns about: "When lust has conceived, it gives birth to sin; and when sin is accomplished, it brings forth death" (James 1:15). Recent studies show that in cases involving sexual immorality, there are profound and destructive effects on the body. Twenty-five years ago, at the start of the so-called sexual revolution, the incidence of venereal disease among teens in the United States was about one in thirty. And the specific diseases were rather easily treated. Today among teens the occurrence of sexually transmitted diseases is one in four. And instead of there being a handful of diseases, there are now more than thirty. And these new viruses are often untreatable, incurable, and deadly. The average lifespan for an American male is now about seventy-three years. But the life expectancy of a homosexual without AIDS is forty-two; with AIDS it is thirty-nine. Sin brings about the destruction of the body—regardless of whether it is the body of a believer or an unbeliever.

The ultimate purpose is "that his spirit may be saved in the day of the Lord Jesus" (v. 5). If the flesh is destroyed, that is the worst that Satan can inflict. Calvin rightly observes, "Since, as far as the spirit is concerned, both its salvation and its damnation are eternal, he takes condemnation of the flesh to be temporary. He might have said: 'We will condemn him for a period of time in this world, in order that the Lord may keep him in His Kingdom.'"[7] This is not to say that Satan is God's executioner; rather, it is to say that in the chastisement of God's people, Satan is often used as the unwitting servant of Jehovah.[8] Just as a wicked nation served God's purpose to punish Israel (Is. 10), and by "the predetermined plan and foreknowledge of God

. . . godless men . . . put *Him* [Christ] to death" (Acts 2:23), God will use Satan to teach His own children the folly of sin. Yet, since restoration is in view, the goal is not that this be the "sin leading to death" (1 John 5:16). God does not want the sinner killed; He wants him restored (cf. Matt. 18:15; Gal. 6:1; 2 Cor. 2:1–11).

Purge Out the Leaven (5:6–13)

In what follows this very difficult charge, Paul reveals his pastor's heart once again. He wants them to know that he is not trying to hurt them, but to help them. The price for allowing sin to remain in the church is that the entire body will become infected. He offers four movements of thought to define his continued concerns in the wake of their taking appropriate action against this sin. He offers another Old Testament example to provide a rationale for removing the "leaven" (vv. 6–7). And rather than allowing this to cause further dissension, he encourages them to "celebrate the feast" (v. 8). He then urges them to establish boundaries (vv. 9–11), and finally, he summons them not to be afraid to judge sin (vv. 12–13).

First, Paul introduces another example from the Old Testament with "Your boasting is not good" (v. 6). A more literal translation of this phrase might be "Your proud confidence is not very pretty." Like a cancerous scab on an otherwise beautiful complexion, the spiritual health of the entire assembly is at risk. "Leaven leavens." "Imagine a batch of dough that remains unchanged by 'a little leaven.' We may as well envision a patient unbothered by 'a little cancer' or an arctic explorer scoffing at 'a little gangrene.' Leaven leavens. Infections fester. Sin permeates. To tolerate even one defiantly sinful church member is to contaminate the entire assembly."[9] No sin can be considered an isolated event. Just as with the sin of Achan (Josh. 7:11), the sin had to be purged out or else it would contaminate the whole "lump" (on this see Rom. 12:21). And so Paul adds, "Clean out the old leaven" (v. 7). Here the leaven does not signify the sinful man per se, but evil of any kind in accordance with the more general statement of the leavening power of evil in verse 6. The background for this metaphor is Exodus 12:19 and 13:7.

The larger scope of the apostle's imagery here is that he sees Christ as the fulfillment of the Old Testament Feast of Unleavened Bread. The Passover depicted, typically, Christ's vicarious death. He is "the Lamb of God who takes away the sin of the world" (John 1:29). The feast of unleavened bread accompanied the Passover. It involved a period of seven days during which no leaven was to be found in the homes of the Israelites. This was typical of the holy life that was to accompany the partaking of the Paschal lamb. The expression "you are *in fact* unleavened" (v. 7) denotes a positional truth. Paul is concerned that their practice match their position. "For Christ our Passover also has been sacrificed" (v. 7). Since sin required the sacrifice of the Lamb of God, it is inconceivable that it should ever be tolerated in the assembly of believers. "They are without leaven since some One else removed it, namely Christ, when He redeemed them from their sins. Their obligation to live accordingly is so much greater and their sin, which breaks up the normal relations, is so much worse."[10]

Biblical Teachings on Leaven

Leaven was to be removed from the Jewish house (Ex. 12:15)

Offering cakes are not to be made with leaven (Lev. 6:17)

No leaven was to be eaten for seven days at Passover time (Deut. 16:4)

The sins of the Pharisees and Sadducees is like leaven (Matt. 16:6)

The sins of king Herod is like leaven (Mark 8:15)

Believers are to clean out the sinful leaven in the life (1 Cor. 5:8)

A small piece of leaven ruins the whole lump (Gal. 5:9)

Second, Paul goes on now to say, "Let us therefore celebrate the feast" (v. 8). "Like Israel of old, Paul says, Christians are to "take shelter under the blood. . . . At the center of the feast that Christians celebrate is Christ, whose death, like the death of the unblemished Passover lamb, brings life."[11] They "go on keeping" (present tense) the Passover, not with the "leaven of malice" (chaps. 1—4) or with the leaven of "wickedness" (chap. 5), but with the "unleavened bread of sincerity and truth." *Sincerity* seems to answer to their malicious attitude toward one another. *Truth* answers to their denial of the wickedness that has been festering in their assembly.

As an historical aside, it is not surprising that the apostle uses the Passover as an illustration here. 1 Corinthians was written just before the Passover (cf. 1 Cor. 16:8) and the celebration of the feast is on Paul's mind. This is a good example of how God used the experiences of the Biblical authors in the writing of Scripture.

Third, Paul exhorts them to establish boundaries (vv. 9–11). Reminding them of his previous epistle (discussed in the Introduction above) he begins, "I wrote you in my letter" (v. 9). This letter is now lost but we know that at least one subject discussed in this letter was that they were "not to associate with immoral people" (v. 9). The intent of the apostle in this epistle was evidently misunderstood—or misrepresented, and so he finds it necessary to clarify himself in these verses. "I *did* not at all *mean* with the immoral people of this world" (v. 10). Of course Paul does not intend to say that they are not to have any association with sinful persons. In order to do this one would have to "go out of the world" (v. 10). Such a thought would be nonsense. As long as the believer is "in" the world, it will be necessary to rub shoulders with sinners. The great challenge of these believers to live clean in Corinth is anticipated in our Lord's great High Priestly prayer on their behalf in John 17:15–18: "I do not ask Thee to take them out of the world, but to keep them from the evil *one*. They are not of the world, even as I am not of the world. Sanctify them in the truth; Thy word is truth. As Thou didst send Me into the world, I also have sent them into the world." Believers from Paul's day to the present struggle with this difficult assignment.

While believers rightly desire "to keep . . . unstained by the world" (James 1:27), they have an obligation to be obedient to Christ's commission to follow Him *into* the world. But there is a boundary here: To be *in* the world is not to be *of* the world. Paul will have much more to say about this in the next chapter. For now, he wants his readers to know that his regulation not to keep company with immoral persons is specifically applied to those who claim to be "brothers" (that is, "believers"). The key to Paul's admonition is here. The term translated "to associate with" (v. 11) is found only here and in 2 Thessalonians 3:14. It is a compound of three Greek terms and means "to mingle together with." It has the idea of close, habitual relationships. Paul's instruction relates to those who are in the assembly calling themselves brethren in Christ. If such a person is immoral, covetous, or the like, this person is not to be included in fellowship—"not even to eat with such a one" (v. 11).

The very fact that Paul reacts as he does demonstrates that his vision of the church is not isolationist—as if the local church would have no engagement with the world whatsoever. That is not how Paul saw his task or that of this local church. This is "the church of God which is at Corinth" (cf. 1:2). The church stands as a prophetic countercultural community in the midst of an unbelieving world. It is not indistinguishable from the world.[12] Rather, as Jesus instructed His disciples, the church should stand out as "light" and "salt" (cf. Matt. 5:13–16). In Paul's later word to this church, he writes that they are as a "sweet aroma of the knowledge of Him in every place" and the "fragrance of Christ to God among those who are being saved and among those who are perishing" (2 Cor. 2:14–15). When a church is planted in a community, it brings the very presence and influence of Christ into that community.

Finally, Paul urges the Corinthian believers not to be afraid to judge sin (vv. 12–13). "Outsiders" are those outside the church (cf. Col. 4:5; 1 Thess. 4:12). The command of the apostle had reference only to those who were in the church, but it was not his prerogative to judge those outside. The Corinthians should have understood this. He adds that "those who are outside, God judges" (v. 13). The present tense of this verb fits well with Paul's thoughts in Romans 1:18, written from Corinth and probably inspired by what Paul observed all about him there: "For the wrath of God is revealed [presently] from heaven against all ungodliness." It is true, as the apostle John has said, that "the whole world lies in *the power of* the evil one" (1 John 5:19). But it will not do to simply curse the darkness. It is the task of the believer to proclaim the positive truth of the gospel. The saints are obligated to be faithful stewards; as for the world, God will take care of it.

Paul concludes, "Remove the wicked ["toilsome," "bad"] man from among yourselves" (v. 13). Once again Paul draws upon the authority of the Old Testament to demand action (cf. Deut. 13:5; 17:7). And with this he closes his case against this wicked person. Ironically, in subsequent counsel to them, Paul will be required to ask them to "forgive and comfort" this same person (2 Cor. 2:5–11). Indeed, in the later epistle he will confess that he was, perhaps, going a little overboard to "test" their willingness to be obedient in this matter. But for now, it is critical that they demonstrate their submission to the authority of the apostle and Scripture. Hays has also rightly observed that Paul is not being heavy-handed in order merely to assert himself; rather, "concern for the health and purity of the community remains the constant factor."[13] It is for their spiritual health and well-being that he counsels them.

An important subtext of this passage is the exercise and respect for authority. As we will see in subsequent chapters, there was a layer of libertinism at Corinth, not unlike the spirit of our own age. People had minimal respect for authority and maximal concern for their own personal rights with callous disregard for others. Those who would adopt a "New Testament Christianity" today must, with the Corinthian believers, abandon the radical individualism of modern culture and learn the lifestyle of obedience and submission (cf. Eph. 6:1; 1 Tim. 5:17; Heb. 13:17).

Study Questions

1. How was it that Paul came by the information relating to the immorality in the assembly? Are there any principles to be drawn from this situation with regard to when and if a disciplinary action should be made public? What might these be?

2. What was the "attitude" problem that prevented the Corinthian believers from acting on this situation? In what way(s) could it be said that the church shared some responsibility for the aggravated nature of this sin?

3. In verses 3–5 there is a window into how the early Church might have addressed issues that came up for disciplinary action. Detail this procedure. How might this procedure be appropriated by a contemporary local church?

4. What does it mean to have the "power" of Christ?

5. Explain what it means to be "delivered over to Satan." What are some of the consequences? How would you relate this to an individual's salvation?

6. Discuss the symbolic significance of "leaven" in the Bible. How does Paul appropriate this here?

7. What was the feast Paul was about to celebrate when he was writing this epistle? How did this festive time play a role in what the apostle wrote in this chapter?

8. How does one draw the line between a legitimate relationship with unsaved people and what Paul would view as inappropriate?

9. The matter of exercising judgment in the church plays a significant role in Paul's thinking. How does this anticipate what follows in the next chapter? Relate this function to the role of the church in the messianic kingdom.

10. When and how will God "judge" those who are on the outside of the church?

CHAPTER 8

Taking a Believer to Court
1 Corinthians 6:1–11

Preview:
The citizens of Corinth were accustomed to settling the most frivolous matters before the courts. Christians are challenged to practice the skills necessary for the tasks they will be given when Jesus comes. They should learn how to negotiate and resolve their differences by drawing upon the godly wisdom of those in the church—not the pagan courts.

Should a Christian ever go to court against another Christian? This is the question Paul addresses here. Paul has already addressed the subject of "judging" (cf. 5:12–13), saying simply that it is the obligation to judge those who are within the church. Now we begin to understand why he has brought this up for special attention. It seems that a believer has already "dared" to file a lawsuit against another believer (6:6). Paul's admonition corresponds to the ruling standard in the Jewish community, which held that it was blasphemy against God's law to bring a case before a court of idolaters. We have already observed that Paul draws from the Old Testament as a primary authority when addressing the problem of the immoral person in the assembly. Only as an aside (5:1) does he reference the community standard to say that not even the *Gentiles* sanction such behavior, let alone *God!*

Of course Paul has had his own experiences before these courts. Luke records that Paul was brought before them many times before his eventual martyrdom at their hands. So he has good reasons to be less than sanguine about one's chances of securing justice in such a setting. Yet, as C. K. Barrett observes here, Paul is not necessarily suggesting that "the Roman courts were unjust; for his view of the Roman state and its magistrates see Rom. 13:1–7—and he had special reason for gratitude to Gallio's impartiality in Corinth (Acts 18:12–17); the word is to be taken not in a moral but in a religious sense—not justified, not rightly related with God through Christ."[1] This is further evident in the subsequent arguments he uses to support his case. He shows that matters brought up in the assembly should not be taken outside. They are *family* matters. Beyond that, even if a satisfactory solution evades the offended parties, perhaps it would be better just to "shake it off" (6:7).

The Problem (6:1)

"Does any one of you . . . dare to go to law . . . ?" (v. 1; this is emphatic). "Is anyone so bold as to shock the Christian sense of propriety?"[2] From the language, it is probable that the writer has a specific situation in mind as in the previous chapter. The terms "unrighteous" and "saints" are generic, referring to unbelievers in general as opposed to believers in general. How incredible that the just should go before the unjust for justice! As noted, Paul's sensitivities on this subject are much the same as those that might have been expressed by his Jewish contemporaries. However, his rationale and argument do not proceed from Moses, but from the messianic hope. The principle remains the same, but there is an entirely new paradigm at work for the New Testament believer. Paul has much more to say of this new kind of relationship in Galatians 3:26—4:7. Nevertheless, it is evident here that his thinking proceeds along the same lines. His expectations of the "sons" of God is not that we must be, as it were, obedient children, but that we should begin to behave as adult sons—worthy of those who have received the *huiosthesia* (or "son-placement," "adoption").

It is especially appropriate that Paul would use this analogy here. It seems that these people were already acting as though they had entered into the Millennium (cf. 4:8). The force of the argument here is this: "If you think you are already living in the kingdom, then why don't you act like it? If it were true, you wouldn't need to be seeking legal solutions from others. You would be sitting as judge!" Of course, they had entirely confused the "already" with the "not yet." It is important to observe here as elsewhere in the New Testament that Christ is not yet installed on David's throne and the kingdom will not come until the King arrives. Later Paul reinforces this truth even further by showing that our role in this world is not yet as "reigning kings" but as "ambassadors" (2 Cor. 5:20). We serve our King, not yet in the kingdom, but as His representatives, as it were, in an alien world. Paul will use four arguments here. The first argument turns on the role of the saints in Christ's coming kingdom

(6:2–3). The second argument builds on the first. Considering our role in the kingdom, adjudicating our own issues provides a training ground (6:4–6). The third argument is a pragmatic one. Considering the shamefulness of bringing our petty issues before a pagan court, no solution is to be preferred to one that might be secured there (6:7–8). Finally, he argues that they are deceived. They are forgetting the implications of their position in Christ. These who have been "washed" of their former depravity, "sanctified," and "justified" are now seeking justice from those who have no place in the kingdom to which they have been called (6:9–11).

With Eternity in View (6:2–3)

It is this new status that forms the major premise of his first argument. "Do you not know that the saints will judge the world?" (v. 2). The question seems to suggest that the Corinthians should have known this elementary truth (cf. Dan. 7:22; Matt. 19:28; Rev. 2:26; 3:21; 20:4). Now, if this be the case, Paul goes on to his minor premise—again in the form of a question: "Are you not competent *to constitute* the smallest law courts?" (v. 2; literally, "the lowest tribunals"). You who shall comprise the Supreme Court of the world, do you not feel qualified to sit on some tiny local court? He then goes on to repeat his major premise but kicks it up a notch: "Do you not know that we shall judge angels?" (v. 3; Is. 24:21; 2 Pet. 2:4; Jude 1:6). He then exaggerates the contrast by lowering the minor premise to *biotika*, "common life affairs." The question expects the answer no, and the particle *ge* adds a sharpness to his tone. "For Paul, the assemblies at Corinth and elsewhere, as the eschatological people of God, were set over against 'the world' which stood under God's judgment."[3] As with other writers of the New Testament, this expectation of the imminent return of Christ to establish his kingdom forms an important backdrop behind much of Paul's teaching. (See 1 Cor. 15; 1 Thess 4:13–18; 5:1–10; cf. 1 Pet. 5:1–4; 2 Pet. 3:9–14; 1 John 3:1–3.)

Practice What We Preach (6:4–6)

Paul's second argument builds on his first. Given our future participation in Christ's kingdom, can we not find one qualified person to arbitrate these matters? In repeating the term *biotika*, "common life affairs," in verse 4, Paul connects what is to follow with the preceding context. "So" (v. 4) is inferential. "Courts" may mean "legal causes," or it may simply mean "trials." The latter is more consistent with the normal usage of the term. "Do you appoint them as judges who are of no account in the church?" (v. 4). This may be taken either as indicative or interrogative. If it is the latter, then Paul is being sarcastic. That is, if you are going to go to a civil court, you might just as well choose your least qualified members as jurors. If it is a question, then it is emphatic: "Are you actually setting them to judge who are of no account in the church?" (that is, "the heathen"). This would render a statement of shock and surprise that they were doing such a thing. The latter seems more in keeping with the context. In other words, Paul is addressing a specific instance of one believer taking another believer to court.

Here Paul suggests the nature of the issues that are being brought before the civil magistrates and which are the focus of this chapter. They do not seem to be criminal matters nor matters that would ordinarily require a civil court's decision. Jesus said to "render to Caesar the things that are Caesar's" (Matt. 22:21). When necessary, Paul, himself, "appealed to Caesar" (Acts 25:11–12). We know that Paul had great respect for "rulers" and those who "bear the sword" (Rom. 13:3–4). Furthermore, it is unlikely that Paul is establishing a standard that would forbid a believer from seeking legal counsel or even from filing a legal suit on an issue that requires a formal judgment in a court of law. This is important when one attempts to appropriate the teaching of this chapter. There are numerous issues—for example, insurance claims, criminal cases, and property issues—that require formal legal "due process." Such may well entail a judgment by secular courts. It is not necessary to legalistically interpret these verses to forbid all such due process. F. W. Grosheide adds: "To deduce from verse 1 that any going to court is forbidden to Christians is unwarranted. . . . [J]urisprudence is a blessing from God if it reckons with the laws given by the Lord. From verse 5 we learn that Corinth did not yet possess any Christian judges."[4]

The kinds of issues that the writer seems to be addressing are frivolous disputes that have pitted one believer against another and should never have been taken to court. It is not unlikely that the cultural climate is a major factor here as well. If the Jews considered it entirely inappropriate to ever submit to pagan law courts for anything, the Greeks were a litigious lot and seemed rather to enjoy, as with their sports, the opportunity to spar with one another in court.[5] Paul finds it necessary to put a stop to this and to challenge them to arbitrate their differences within the family and not before the watching world. And so he says, "I say this to your shame" (literally, "I say this to move you to shame"). Paul's purpose in speaking as he does is to move them to right action.

"*Is it* so, *that* there is not among you one wise man . . . ?" (v. 5). There is irony in the question when asked of these who boasted in their wisdom. What is shameful is that "brother goes to law with brother, and that before unbelievers" (v. 6). The apostle is incensed for at least two reasons: (1) that they went to law and (2) that they went to law before heathen judges. In what follows, the apostle offers a third argument while probing some of the underlying causes for this situation.

You Win—You Lose (6:7–8)

They are defeated. "It is already a defeat [*ettema*] for you" (v. 7). Paul uses the language of the courts here: *Nike* was victory; *etta* was defeat. This is Paul's third argument. They have already lost the case before they begin! Something was already wrong if they would even consider taking a petty problem between themselves before a heathen judge. The apostle says it would be better to "rather be defrauded" (v. 7). Instead of following the correct course when they were wronged, they were defrauding one another. It would be better to accept the wrong committed than to pursue it and inflict further injury on anyone else. The implication here is that when two believers seek a solution to their differences with appeals to those who are unbelievers and incapable of comprehending the will of God in such matters, the outcome is worse than no solution at all.

A case was recently brought before the courts in our small community involving a dispute among a group of factious church members. They became so enraged against one another that the police had to be called into the church sanctuary to disburse the angry crowd with tear gas. The case was subsequently brought before the courts with the media eager to report every delicious morsel of the scandal. The outcome was an additional black eye on the face of the church before those who were already skeptical of the "hypocrites in the church." One side *won* that day in court, but in reality they all were *losers*. "The existence of contention that calls for decision by a third party (whoever he may be) proves that love . . . has been overthrown and replaced by selfish desire, either to acquire or to retain. So far as this is true, the Christians involved have ceased to be Christian; they have suffered defeat."[6]

To seek out "one wise" who will be able to bring about a solution to the problem by contrast provides an opportunity for the "wisdom of the cross" to be applied. And when that happens, in contrast to the civil court, there are no losers—only winners. The church wins because it identifies one in their assembly who has the maturity and wisdom to "be able to decide" in this way. And the decision that is made "between brethren" appropriates the principles of chapter 13 as love is applied that "does not seek its own, is not provoked, does not take into account a wrong *suffered*, does not rejoice in unrighteousness, but rejoices with the truth" (1 Cor. 13:5–6).[7]

Unrighteous Shall Not Inherit (6:9–11)

Paul's final argument is that these church members are deceived. The force of his argument is that such persons who fall outside the company of those who are to inherit the "kingdom of God" (v. 9) are in no position to stand in judgment upon those of us who are heirs of God's kingdom. Paul is not suggesting that these are the kinds of issues that ordinarily should be decided in the "ecclesial court." He is referring to those who stand in judgment on the issues about which he is speaking. Those whose character is defined by unrighteousness do not qualify to serve as judges over the saints of God. Several additional thoughts suggest the practical importance of this teaching.

Those who would accuse the apostle Paul of bifurcating works and faith should take a closer look at these verses. "The unrighteous shall not inherit the kingdom of God" (v. 9). Those who profess Christianity as a system of doctrine but not as a rule of life are mistaken. "Do not be deceived." No one who can allow himself the indulgence of known sin in his life can be assured of salvation. This passage proves that "Paul and James are in agreement on this crucial question. Both affirm that genuine faith produces works (cf. Eph. 2:8–10), and that the absence of good works indicates the lack of faith (James 2:14–26)."[8]

Additionally, in his appeal Paul assures the Corinthian believers that they have been delivered. "Such were some of you" (v. 11). Here Paul cites the fact that there were some in the assembly who were formerly characterized in the catalog of sins listed in verse 10. "But you were washed, but you were sanctified, but you were justified in the name of the Lord Jesus Christ, and in the Spirit of our God" (v. 11). Logically, one would expect to find these words in inverse order. That is, they are first justified, then they are sanctified, then they experience daily cleansing. Paul placed them in this order for emphasis. Now you are washed; indeed, you have been sanctified, or set apart, to do God's special service. Indeed, you stand before God declared righteous. In such an exalted position, it seems incredible that such people would find it necessary to go before an inferior human court to have personal disputes arbitrated.

"The quite unconscious Trinitarianism of the concluding words should be noted: 'the Lord Jesus Christ, the Spirit, our God' (v. 11). Trinitarian theology, at least in its New Testament form, did not arise out of speculation, but out of the fact that when Christians spoke of what God had done for them and in them they often found themselves obliged to use threefold language of this kind."[9]

The catalog of sins listed in verses 9–10 is also instructive at another level. These who are now called "saints" were once fornicators, idolaters, adulterers, effeminate (passive homosexuals), homosexuals (the passive and active partners of male homosexual relationships),[10] thieves, covetous, drunkards, revilers, and swindlers. The writer not only says that persons such as these are not properly understood as belonging to the kingdom of God. He also says that such characterizations were once true of many who are now part of this assembly of called-out ones. There are two extremes to avoid here. On the one hand are those who pharisaically define their Christian experience by their performance. We might call this "performance-based" Christianity. It leads to legalism, hypocrisy, and denial. Paul reminded these of the pit from which they had been dug (cf. Is. 51:1).

Paul's Doctrine of Sanctification

Positional Sanctification

Salvation results in sanctification (Rom. 6:22).

Through the gospel Gentiles are sanctified by the Holy Spirit (Rom. 15:16).

Salvation sanctification comes through Jesus Christ (1 Cor. 1:2).

Christ becomes sanctification to believers (1 Cor. 1:30).

Believers are "washed" and sanctified in the name of the Lord Jesus Christ (1 Cor. 6:11).

Christ sanctifies His bride the church by "the washing of water with the word" (Eph. 5:26).

Salvation comes through positional sanctification (2 Thess. 2:13).

Experiential Sanctification

The believer's body is presented as a slave to righteousness, resulting in sanctification (Rom. 6:19).

Husbands and wives provide for each other a marriage sanctification (1 Cor. 7:14).

Children likewise have a kind of "sanctification" in a Christian home (1 Cor. 7:14).

Sanctification means abstaining from immorality (1 Thess. 4:3).

Sanctification means for marriage possessing one's "own vessel" (1 Thess. 4:4).

God has called believers to live a sanctified life (1 Thess. 4:7).

Paul prays that believers be sanctified "entirely" (1 Thess. 5:23).

Women are to be kept secure and blessed "in faith and love and sanctity" (1 Tim. 2:15).

Everything God makes is good and is sanctified by His Word and by prayer (1 Tim. 4:4–5).

The other extreme is that of libertinism. There are those—apparently many in this assembly—who think the gospel has nothing to say about their lifestyle or their actions and that "all things are lawful" (6:12). Paul reminded these, "such were some of you." But now that they are "washed," these behaviors should no longer characterize their lives. Between these two extremes of legalism and libertinism, Paul threads the needle. "He who is spiritual" is characterized neither by one's ability to live righteously in the flesh, nor by one's free abandonment to the works of the flesh. Such people are known as those in whom the Holy Spirit dwells, who have the mind of Christ, and who belong to a community that is knit together in the "Spirit of our God" (v. 11). This anticipates our next chapter.

Study Questions

1. Compare and contrast the Jewish attitude toward going to a secular court with that presented by Paul to New Testament believers.

2. How would you characterize Paul's attitude toward these believers who have taken one another to court? Why is it that this behavior is unbecoming of them as members of the church of Christ?

3. Why does Paul suggest that when believers take their issues before civil courts, they have already "lost" the case?

4. In what way(s) would you limit the instruction in this chapter? In what way(s) would you apply it to a modern setting?

5. How would you characterize the attitude of legalism in today's church?

6. How would you characterize the influence of libertinism in today's church? Which of these two worldviews is the most dominant in our culture? How should churches address this?

7. Is it possible to be a homosexual and be truly saved? How do you interpret verse 9 in relation to the gospel? How should the church deal with homosexuals who come for church membership?

8. Look up the terms *sanctify* and *justify* in a Bible or theological dictionary. Define and distinguish these two terms. Why does Paul appeal to these doctrines in this chapter? What practical impact is he hoping to have?

CHAPTER 9

Are All Things Lawful?
1 Corinthians 6:12–20

Preview:

Having established that the church is a holy assembly, Paul further has shown that this has practical and legal implications. Now he focuses on the ethical implications, underscoring that the church cannot allow the world to define its standards. The believers are not their own; they have been bought with a price. They are indwelt by God's Spirit, and it is to His glory that they are to conduct their lives.

The writer of Hebrews tells us "the word of God is living and active and sharper than any two-edged sword" (Heb. 4:12). Paul enforces this same truth in his instruction to Timothy. Scripture, he says, is God-breathed and "profitable for teaching, for reproof, for correction, for training in righteousness; that the man of God may be adequate, equipped for every good work" (2 Tim. 3:16–17). Because of neglect (5:1–13) and arrogance (6:1–11), the believers in Corinth failed to appropriate the Word of God as they should in matters of practical Christian living. But to make things worse, they also underestimated the value and importance of their own spiritual community—the church. In the preceding portion of Paul's letter, he made it abundantly clear that the assembly was to be independent and autonomous; that it should not resort to the established courts for justice or the surrounding culture for its ethical standards.[1] The prevailing world was politically corrupt, spiritually diverse, economically distressed, and culturally degraded. Paul was quite convinced that it should not be to that world that these believers should look to find the wisdom and resources for life and godliness.

It is difficult not to draw parallels with our own culture. American culture is inebriated with materialism, narcissism, and moral relativity. Our heroes are athletes—who drop off the scene by the time they reach thirty-five years of age. Our philosophers are musicians whose lyrics belie the depravity of our culture. Justice eludes the poor but is somehow more accessible to those with great wealth. Dare we think we can find our help or direction in such a world? I think not! In the previous verses (9–11), Paul has established two vital principles: (1) There is a moral absolute, for God hates sin. God as judge will not be interested in whether we were politically correct or well received by our peers. (2) God has cleansed believers of those very sins He hates. In an ultimate sense, they have received "justice" before the courts of heaven in having been declared righteous ("justified") on the merits of Jesus Christ. As such, even the least of them stands in a position vastly superior to even the elites of the surrounding society.

The unity of chapters 5 and 6 has been variously debated. Some argue that the structure of these chapters is only accidental—moving from one crisis issue to another.[2] Others have seen a more reasoned development throughout. Some suggest that the issue of immorality introduced in chapter 5 remains the topic throughout. In this view, the lawsuit in 6:1–11 relates to the previous case of immorality, and apparently those who brought it to court lost the case. Chapter 6 then picks this back up to say that it never should have been handled in the courts in the first place. The church has both the resources and the standards by which to adjudicate such matters. Although this view has been rigorously argued[3] and contains many points with which I agree, I remain unconvinced that Paul is still discussing that particular issue.

In my view, Paul focuses on the same message (cf. 1:9) throughout these chapters, and the continuity of his argument is seen in the logical flow—not in a singular issue. In chapter 5, Paul addresses the issue of a specific case of immorality that had been exposed but not treated. He instructs the church to deal with this "in house." This portion of the letter serves as a segue to the legal aspects of his instruction (6:1–11)—his point being that the believing community should be able to take care of their own affairs without resorting to the Roman courts, as apparently some were doing.[4] In the remainder of chapter 6 Paul examines the *ethical* implications of his teaching (6:12–20). Here his burden is to distinguish between proper Christian liberty and unbridled license. Some were presuming that all physical passions and appetites were as lawful as eating and drinking and were to be freely gratified.[5] In the social context, prostitution was accepted as normal. In my view, Bruce Winter and Brian Rosner have argued convincingly that while there is little evidence that temple prostitution of the "old city" was any longer practiced in the first century, there was a general climate of moral degeneracy associated with temple feasts and in the culture that included prostitution (cf. also Acts 15:20, where the prohibition of certain foods is joined with the prohibition against fornication). This situation forms the background for the remainder of chapter 6.[6] It was apparently not difficult for some of the Christians to justify themselves with the argument that such behavior involved only the body and not the soul. Since the believing community was a called-out assembly, those principles that separated them from dependence on the Roman legal establishment also differentiated them from the pagan social and ethical establishment. The instruction to the Corinthians was simply: Others may, but you cannot!

In developing this theme, Paul lays out a series of principles by which ethical issues may be evaluated and according to which the believers may be able to judge for themselves on questionable matters.

The Principle of Law (6:12)

"All things are lawful for me" (v. 12). This expression, *panta moi exestin*, occurs only here, where it is associated with fornication, and in 10:7, where it is associated with idolatry and temple feasts. Rosner notes, "With the words, 'all things are lawful,' it is conceivable that they defended both the use of prostitutes in the temple and the consumption of temple food."[7] Concerning the latter reference, Ben Witherington adds, "1 Cor. 10:7 is a meaningful warning only if Paul had good reason to assume that sexual play was a regular part of some meals in one or more of the pagan temples in Corinth."[8] While it is possible, as some argue, to suggest that this aphorism was a Pauline expression, misunderstood and misapplied by the believers in Corinth, in light of the evidence of an "ascetic element" (7:1) and its converse here, Barrett is probably correct when he observes:

> The most probable view (in view of their recurrence at x. 23 where the whole context, including viii. 7–13, should be noted) is that they were the watchword of a gnostic party in Corinth. . . . We know that developed gnosticism in the second century moved sometimes in the direction of asceticism, sometimes in that of libertinism. Its disparagement of the material (see verses 13, 18 f. below) could already have led to the moral indifferentism of "all things are permitted me"—nothing done in the body really matters, and therefore anything may be done.[9]

Of course, "all things" in this saying was never understood in an absolute sense.[10] Nor was Paul teaching this. As appropriated here for purposes of discussion, Paul shows that the principle of law is only good so far as it goes. In most cultures it would suggest a basic agreement on matters with which Christian (and biblical) teachings would agree. In keeping with Paul's other instruction in Romans 13, it does not bear the sword (have the power of capital punishment) in vain. But in the Roman courts before which these believers would potentially stand, it is not likely that it would proscribe Paul's entire list of 6:9–10 above. Certainly matters related to moral and spiritual inclinations, such as fornication, idolatry, adultery, homosexuality, covetousness, drunkenness, and reviling would be considered outside the legal jurisdiction of any Roman court. In our own time, the attitude of libertinism supports a growing sentiment to legalize drugs, prostitution, gambling, and the like. It is evident that the principle of law is inadequate on its own to sufficiently guide the believer in matters of personal conduct and holiness. Continuing on, Paul shows that the principle of Law must be tempered with a higher principle— the principle of expediency.

Law versus expedience (6:12b). The term *sumphero*, "profitable," translated "expedient" in the KJV, occurs frequently in this letter and elsewhere in Paul. But most significant for our reflection is 12:7, where it is translated "common good" to describe the purpose for spiritual gifts. They are given for the common good, or for the profitability of the various members of the body. When Paul offers this corrective to the saying "all things are lawful," he does so by suggesting that even if this were one's guiding principle for life, it does not legitimate every possible action. By appropriating a consequentialist ethic, Paul shows the practical limits of libertinism. For the Christian, this principle would already be bordered by that which Scripture forbids. But what about those issues Scripture does not explicitly address? Such matters would be left to the Christian's own judgment. Without vitiating the principle of Christian liberty—about which Paul will have more to say—the principle of expedience suggests that there is a standard that overrides liberty. Not everything is beneficial. Whether a law of prohibition exists or not, it is simply wrong to do something to ourselves or others just because it is *adiaphorous* (cf. Rom. 14:15–23; 1 Cor. 8:7–13; 10:23–33). An additional corrective is also needed.

Law versus control (6:12c). Paul limits libertinism further with "I will not be mastered by anything." This is the principle of control. Certain forms of indulgence become wrong when they bring the person into bondage. One of the character qualities of the believer is self-control (cf. Gal. 5:22–23). The spiritual person of 1 Corinthians 2:15 is not in subjection to any appetite or habit but is under the control of the Holy Spirit. That Paul has in mind bodily appetites is evident in the following verses where he isolates eating and sexual activity for special attention.

The Teleological Principle (6:13–15)

The biblical term *iniquity* (*avon*, in the Old Testament, and *adikia*, in the New Testament) communicates the idea of "twisting" something to use for purposes alien to its proper intent. A related term is "perversion," used in our text to translate a cluster of biblical terms to convey a similar idea. One of these terms is *skolios*, used by Peter in his stinging indictment of the Jerusalem crowd in Acts 2:40: "Be saved, from this perverse generation!" The term is used in our contemporary medical vocabulary to describe scoliosis, the condition of having a twisted spine.

Biblical Terms for Iniquity and Perversion

Avon

Punishment is due the workers of <u>iniquity</u> (Job 31:3).

God's anger casts forth workers of wickedness (Psa. 56:7).

The Lord hates the heart that devises <u>wicked</u> plans (Prov. 6:18).

When the <u>wicked</u> man perishes his wishes perish with him (Prov. 11:7).

The fool's heart inclines toward <u>wickedness</u> (Isa. 32:6).

For the idolater the idols speak <u>iniquity</u> (Zech. 10:2).

Adikia

<u>Unrighteousness</u> men suppress the truth in <u>unrighteousness</u> (Rom. 1:18).

Believers are not to use the members of their bodies as instruments of <u>unrighteousness</u> (Rom. 6:13).

Believers are not to rejoice in <u>iniquity</u> (1 Cor. 13:6).

The lost who take pleasure in <u>iniquity</u> will be judged (2 Thess. 2:12).

Those who name the name of Christ are to depart from <u>iniquity</u> (2 Thess. 2:19).

The tongue is a fire, a world of <u>iniquity</u> (James 3:6).

By confession of sin believers are cleansed from <u>unrighteousness</u> (1 John 1:9).

All <u>unrighteousness</u> is sin (1 John 5:17).

Skolios

By the ministry of John the Baptist the <u>crooked</u> was made straight (Luke 3:5).

The generation of Christ was a <u>crooked</u> generation (Acts 2:40).

Believers live in a <u>crooked</u> and perverse generation (Phil. 2:15).

Christian servants are to pay respect even to their <u>perverse</u> masters (1 Pet. 2:18).

The teleological principle denotes purpose and design. As applied here in our text, Paul is saying that bodily appetites and natural drives are not ends in themselves. They are given for specific purposes. They are means to great ends. And when these are used for purposes not intended, they may be said to be "perverted." A person can continue to get around with a twisted spine, but because the spine is twisted, it fails to offer the body the support for which the spine was designed.[11] Likewise, the "twisting" of God-given appetites and drives results in a weakened spiritual life.

"Food is for the stomach, and the stomach is for food; but God will do away with both of them" (v. 13). Nature demonstrates the law of design. The stomach and food are mutually adapted for each other. Yet even this physical process, so necessary for physical life, is only temporary. God will eventually replace the body and even, for that matter, the physical universe as we know it.

The second illustration is by way of contrast, and so Paul begins with, "Yet"—a mild adversative, better "but"—"the body is not for immorality" (v. 13). Contrary to the natural law of adaptation, the body is not designed for fornication, "but for the Lord" (v. 13). The body is intended to be a member of Christ (v. 15) and the dwelling place of His Holy Spirit (v. 19). This is striking, because Paul moves from the natural to the supernatural—from the physical to the metaphysical—without warning. We would have expected him to say something here—to follow the parallel—about the body not being for fornication, but for procreation or (as it is developed in chapter 7) the mutual pleasure of a married couple. Instead, he suggests that the body, in its ultimate sense, has a purpose far beyond the "functions" with which we identify. And he knows this because Christ has been "raised" and God intends to "also raise us up through His power" (v. 14). The writer will have much more to say about this later (chap. 15), but for now he teases the reader with the thought that the ultimate purpose of the human transcends the limits of form and function as we experience them.

Bodily functions designed to sustain life here will be replaced in the resurrection. They all have a temporary function associated with this life. But what is the ultimate design for the body? For what purpose(s) is it created? Paul's use of the pronoun "us" (v. 14) shows that his use of the term "body" goes beyond its normal usage to signify the whole person (note also its connection with the second person pronoun in v. 19, below). (On the destiny of the body, see also 1 Cor. 15:15, 20, 35–54; Phil. 3:21; Rom. 8:11; 2 Cor. 4:14; 1 Thess. 4:14). Paul's argument here runs something like this: It was an uncommon honor that God should raise up the body of Jesus Christ. It will be an undue honor when our bodies are also raised by His power. Therefore, let us not abuse our bodies through fleshly lusts. All of this is given in order

to take the reader to the next level. The real purpose of the body is to participate in the body of Christ.

Final Principles (6:16–20)

The Corinthian believers seemed to be unaware of the implications of their
relationship to Christ. Perhaps, like many today, they compartmentalized
their spirituality. They engaged the believing community and religious obser-
vances with only a part of their lives. Outside was the other world, to which
they belonged and which operated by a different set of rules. In Paul's view,
when the body, which is "for the Lord" (v. 13), is used for any other purpose,
it is perverted. Adding to these primary directives for biblical morality, the
writer offers several additional principles that provide practical insights for
those who would be obedient to God in this crucial area.

First, there is the principle of intimacy. "Do you not know that your bodies
are members of Christ? Shall I then take away the members of Christ and
make them members of a harlot? May it never be!" (v. 15). The body is not
only for the Lord (v. 13), but it belongs to Him by virtue of His redemptive
work, and because of this it participates in a spiritual union with Him. This
pertains not only to the soul, but also to the body (cf. 1 Cor. 12:12–27; Rom.
8:6–11; Eph. 2:6–7; 5:30). It is this fact, above all else, that makes fornication
such a wicked and malicious sin. It takes away (v. 15) what belongs to Christ
and joins it to a harlot. To this Paul recoils with the strongest language available to him, "*Me genoito!*"

"Or do you not know that the one who joins himself to a harlot is one
body *with her?*" (v. 16). The verb "joined" is used in Genesis 2:24 of the relationship of husband and wife (it is also used of man's relationship to God;
see Deut. 10:20; 11:22; Jer. 13:11). When fornication is committed, the parties involved share a common life. In the same sense, one cannot serve God
and mammon or share in the life of Christ and in the life of Belial. It is
inconceivable that one can be simultaneously joined to Christ and to the
body of a harlot. (On the phrase "The two will become one flesh," v. 16, cf.
Eph. 2:15.)

"But the one who joins himself to the Lord is one spirit *with Him*" (v. 17).
As if Paul's mundane analogies were not enough, he lays them aside to express
in brief a concept that suggests to us the highest possible unity between the
believer and the Lord. Many other forms are used to express this identification,
but none approach this in the conception of inseparable oneness. "The sheep
may wander from the shepherd, the branch may be cut off from the vine, the
member may be severed from the body, the child alienated from the father, and

even the wife from the husband, but when two spirits blend in one, what shall part them? No outward connection of unity, even of wedlock, is so emphatically expressive of the perfect merging of two lives in one."[12] This intends to impose the highest conceivable obligation to refrain from fornication.

Second, there is the principle of consequences. "Flee immorality" (v. 18; literally, "Make it your habit to flee"). We cannot help but reflect on Joseph and his response to the temptation to participate in sexual sin with his master's wife (Gen. 39:1–12). Few experiences common to human beings compare with this. People who testify to the results of committing sexual immorality speak of something in their soul that is subsequently broken. Solomon said it this way: "Whoso committeth adultery with a woman lacketh understanding: he that doeth it destroyeth his own soul" (Prov. 6:32 KJV). Every other sin may be committed "outside the body" (as subject). When a person commits fornication the sin is "against his own body" (as object). The most severe consequence of this sin is the violation against one's own person—body and soul.

Third, there is the temple principle. "Your body is a temple of the Holy Spirit who is in you" (v. 19). Earlier Paul taught that the local church is a "temple" of the Holy Spirit (cf. 3:16). Here the truth is related to the individual believer. As with many issues raised in this letter, Paul will have much more to say of this before he finishes (cf. chaps. 12—14). For now he wants them to see this as significant incentive to avoid immoral and compromising situations. The Holy Spirit, as Jesus taught in the upper room, is a companion with whom we share the very presence of Christ in everything we do and in every place we go. Of the Holy Spirit he adds, "whom you have from God" (v. 19). This is indicative, not imperative. Paul is not telling them that they can become more spiritual by receiving the Holy Spirit, for they have already received the Holy Spirit. He dwells within them. Instead, Paul is introducing the imperative of verse 20. Given the fact that the believers to whom this teaching is directed are participating in such sinful behavior, it is instructive that such behavior does not necessarily obviate the truth of which Paul is speaking—namely, that as believers they all share in the presence and ministries of the Holy Spirit.

Fourth, there is the ownership principle. "You are not your own . . . you have been bought with a price" (vv. 19–20). The blessed fact that our body is the temple of the Holy Spirit has two sides—He is ours and we are His. The believer was purchased on Golgotha's hill by the blood of God's only Son (Acts 20:28). While this truth is applicable to all people, even those who deny the Lord (2 Pet. 2:1), it has a unique significance for the believer (cf. 1 Pet. 2:9; 1 Tim. 4:10).

Finally, there is the glorification principle. Paul concludes with the imperative, "Therefore glorify God in your body" (v. 20). In stark contrast to the libertines who considered the body to be useless for spiritual matters, Paul asserts that the body is suited for the highest of possible spiritual activities—that is, to glorify God. This is so because God, in the person of the Holy Spirit, actually indwells each believer, rendering the body a "temple." The challenge is not to transform our bodies in such a way that we replicate God in our lives. Rather, we are to recognize that our bodies are the instruments through which God can shine and be seen by others. Paul develops this thought much further in his letter to the Romans (chap. 6). The glory of a temple is not in the building per se; it is in the divine presence residing within.

Concluding thoughts. Paul has established that there are two kingdoms—the kingdom of God and the kingdom of the world. The world is dying, but God's kingdom is eternal. Thus, our first priority is our relationship with God. Some people spend their entire lives trying to attain wealth, power, status, or acceptance. The reality is that all of these are already theirs in Christ. They have wealth—God's riches at Christ's expense. They have power, for greater is He who is in them than He who is in the world (1 John 4:4). They have status, for they are seated in the heavenlies. And they have acceptance, for they are accepted in the Beloved One.

Study Questions

1. Explain the problem associated with the issue developed in the latter half of 1 Corinthians 6. What is the issue being addressed and of what practical importance is it for these believers?

2. How does this section relate to the issues raised in chapter 10 of this letter? What influences in the culture were creating a stumbling block for these believers?

3. What is the significance of the expression "All things are lawful for me?" Who were the people saying this? Does Paul agree? Why does he raise this issue?

4. How is it that some things may be lawful but not profitable? Suggest some examples of this in your own life and church.

5. Explain the "control principle" in this chapter. Are there areas in your own life that fall under this injunction? What are you doing to eliminate that "control" from your life?

6. What does the doctrine of the resurrection say about the purpose of the body from God's point of view?

7. In what way(s) is the reality of the indwelling Holy Spirit an incentive to moral purity?

8. Sin is always a terrible thing. But for Paul the sin of immorality was especially heinous. Why?

9. When faced with the temptation to commit sexual sin, in a word, what is the best response?

10. Suggest some practical ways that you can demonstrate to the world that you are "owned" by God.

SECTION III: INSTRUCTION

I Do Not Want You to Be Ignorant

1 Corinthians 7—14

CHAPTER 10

Concerning Marriage
1 Corinthians 7:1-40

Preview:

Christian marriage requires a break with the standards current in the surrounding culture. It also requires some creative understanding of how to apply Old Testament biblical truth to New Testament situations. Unlike Israel, the church is composed of people from various ethnic and religious backgrounds, so new situations abounded. The Corinthians raised a variety of questions relating to unsaved spouses marital ethics, and divorce. Paul responded to each question with pastoral sensitivity and godly wisdom.

Until now the main thrust of Paul's first letter to the Corinthians has been on reproof and correction. Here he turns his attention to matters of instruction. The Corinthians had written to Paul concerning several matters that had perplexed them. Paul now deals with each of these in order. The first concerns Christian marriage. It is not surprising, in light of the prevalence of immorality in Corinth, that there were problems in this area. Some were evidently influenced by incipient gnostic asceticism, and to these Paul demonstrates the appropriateness and sanctity of marriage. Some who were unmarried sought guidance regarding their situation. Others were married but to spouses who did not share their faith. These presented unique problems not confronted until the gospel spilled over into the Gentile world. There apparently was an especially distressful situation—perhaps related to the famine that occurred during this time—that seems to have raised some anxiety and practical concerns requiring pastoral advice to young couples seeking to be married. Chapter 7 is another clear window in this epistle into the pastoral heart of

Paul, who takes on their questions with sincerity and sensitivity—adding his own directives where necessary. Paul's advice may be broken into three broad categories: (1) the *precept* of marriage (vv. 1–7), (2) the *permanence* and place of marriage (vv. 8–24), and (3) the *priorities* of marriage (vv. 25–40).

Marriage Is for Keeps (7:1–7)

In the opening section Paul discusses the general principle of marriage. Succinctly, he lays down five vital principles that should govern all Christian understanding of the ordinance of marriage.

First principle: Abstinence is good (v. 1). Paul begins, "Now concerning" (Greek, *peri de*; see also 7:25; 8:1; 12:1; 16:1). This recurring formula indicates that he is dealing in turn with the points the Corinthians had raised in their letter.[1] "It is good for a man not to touch a woman" (v. 1). The manner in which the apostle introduces this subject suggests that there was a reactionary element in the church to the libertines dealt with in chapter 6. It is likely that they were recommending celibacy as desirable if not obligatory for all believers. Paul says such a practice is "good" ("expedient" or "profitable"; cf. 9:15; Matt. 17:4). This not only suggests moral propriety, but it also underscores the positive benefits of a clean lifestyle. The person is free from worry, mistakes, accidents, disease, and regrets. That the apostle does not intend to teach that marriage is morally wrong as compared with celibacy is clear from verses 2, 7, 9, and 26 (see also Gen. 2:18; Rom. 7:4; 2 Cor. 11:2; Eph. 5:28–33; 1 Tim. 4:3; Heb. 13:4). Here and throughout this passage, Paul demonstrates balance. More important, he confronts the moral laxity prevalent in the culture to say that *virgin* is not a four-letter word. This was not the norm in Corinth, and Paul knows that it will take character and strength to live up to this standard.

Second principle: Sex is for one man and one woman within the bonds of marriage (v. 2). On the one hand, there is a principle established to be applied in extenuating circumstances (such as those in which the apostle finds himself). But, on the other hand, there is the more general rule to be applied to the majority of cases. Paul overrides his principle of expedience (v. 1) with the principle of necessity: "But because of immoralities" (v. 2). Because of the prevalence of immorality in Corinth, Paul's advice to these believers is that every man is to have his own wife and every wife her own husband. To those who might object that such a position degrades the noble estate of marriage, Calvin responds: "What it comes to is this: What is at question here is not the reasons for which marriage has been instituted, but the persons for whom it is necessary."[2]

Third principle: Marriage is a relationship of mutual ownership (vv. 3–4). The precept of marriage is further viewed by the apostle as a pledge of persons. Each is, first of all, to "fulfill [his/her] duty" (v. 3). Paul clarifies what he means by this when he says, "The wife does not have authority over her own body, but the husband *does*; and likewise also the husband does not have authority over his own body, but the wife *does*" (v. 4). Marriage partners no longer have the right to autonomous existence (cf. vv. 32–33). The sexual bond that exists between a husband and wife is not a form of recreation—optional for any individual or group of individuals. It is an obligation (a *duty*). It is monogamous (*one* man, *one* woman) and heterosexual (one *man*, one *woman*). Furthermore, it is sacred (his *own* wife—her *own* husband). In this respect, it is a sanctuary of mutual giving and receiving and a fortress against immoralities.

Fourth principle: Physical intimacy may not be abandoned as a test of spirituality (v. 5). "Stop depriving one another." The biblical precept of marriage implies that conjugal rights should be regularly exercised. The only exception to this rule will be "for a time," and then only for "devot[ing] yourselves to prayer." Again the apostle's advice is practical in nature. It is given "lest Satan tempt you." Cultures, such as ours, that emphasize rights over responsibilities tend to chafe under this teaching. Ownership means that your spouse has certain "rights" over your body. Loving mutual relationships of affection involve giving the other person the key to your heart. This first happens between husband and wife and then spreads to their children. The word for failure in this area is "abuse."

Fifth principle: Marriage is a matter of permission, not command (vv. 6–7). "But this I say by way of concession, not of command" (v. 6). The apostle does not take sides with the extreme Jewish view that held that it was a sin if a man reached age twenty without being married. Instead, he regards the matter as optional. "Even as I myself" (v. 7) may refer to Paul's being *content*, not necessarily *single*. As to Paul's marital status, he was probably a widower.[3] But that is not the point here. The point is that "each man has his own gift from God" (v. 7; cf. vv. 17, 20, 24, 27). Both marriage and celibacy are considered gifts of the Holy Spirit.

It is important to observe in the structure of the language here that the direction of this verse is forward, not backward. That is to say, Paul's "concession" (v. 6) relates to what follows, not what has gone before. The mutually supportive roles established for husbands and wives are not optional. On the other hand, there are issues that may or may not relate to every person—married or unmarried—about which Paul wishes to speak. This anticipates the discussion that follows regarding marriage, divorce, singleness, and the married state in general.[4] Bruce Winter concludes: "Its role is certainly crucial in 1 Corinthians 7:6–7, for it occupies a pivotal place as Paul turns from the

Corinthian request for an apostolic ruling in 7:2–5 to the apostolic and dominical sayings in 7:8ff., inserting his own 'concession' in 7:6–7a. He then proceeds in 7:7b to provide the framework for the discussion of Christian conduct in relation to the different gifts and callings of God."[5]

Marriage, Divorce, and Remarriage (7:8–24)

In this second major section of the chapter, the author discusses the permanence and place of marriage. Here he offers a series of practical guidelines for three categories of individuals—the unmarried and widows (vv. 8–9); married believers (vv. 10–11); and mixed marriages (vv. 12–16). Then he gives counsel to all concerning the importance of contentment in whatever estate one finds himself or herself—in or out of marriage (vv. 17–24).

Counsel to the Unmarried and Widows (7:8–9)

"But I say to the unmarried and to widows" (v. 8). The apostle is not being redundant when he singles out widows for special mention along with the unmarried. No doubt they would have special cause to consider their situation a sad one and therefore desire to have it changed. Hence he gives the directive, "Remain even as I" (v. 8). The personal reference here is not identical with that given in verse 7. The point of verse 7 has to do with being content with the gift God gives you. This verse instructs the formerly married that if they find themselves single again, they should endeavor to remain as such. Nevertheless, he adds, "It is better to marry than to burn" (v. 9). This expression does not indicate that the apostle conceives of marriage in mere physical, brute terms. Rather, it is to be understood in light of the preceding. That is, if a person's gift is to be married, then let that person not try to exercise a gift he or she does not possess.

Counsel to Married Believers (7:10–11)

"But to the married I give instructions" (v. 10). Notice that Paul's advice to the unmarried is given as optional; his advice to the married is given as a command. In case his readers miss this point, he reinforces it with the words, "not I, but the Lord" (v. 10). No doubt, the apostle has in mind explicit instructions our Lord had given—which are recorded in Matthew 5:32; 19:3–9; Mark 10:2–12; and Luke 16:18. "The wife should not leave" (v. 10). Paul's command here is in opposition to Greek and Roman law, which permitted a woman to divorce her husband. The command is unequivocal; let not the wife leave her husband, but "if she does leave, let her remain unmarried, or else be reconciled to her husband" (v. 11). While Paul disapproves of separation on any grounds, he recognizes that there will be cases of unapproved separation. In these cases, the former spouses are to "remain unmarried" (v. 11). The present tense emphasizes a permanent state. The only other option is reconciliation. "The husband should not send his wife away" (v. 11). This is tantamount to saying, "and the same thing goes for husbands." There is no double standard in Paul's teaching on this sensitive subject.

Counsel to Those in Mixed Marriages (7:12–16)

"But to the rest I say, not the Lord" (v. 12) When Paul says "I, not the Lord," he is not making a contrast between inspired Scripture and what he is about to say. On the contrary, while on the earth, the Lord explicitly gave instructions about marriage and divorce. However, He did not make any special reference to the case of a mixed marriage—that is, a marriage involving both a believer and an unbeliever. Thus, it is incumbent on the apostle Paul, under inspiration of the Holy Spirit, to give additional instructions regarding this kind of situation. It may have come as a surprise to some that the instruction is essentially the same for the believing couple. If a Christian person is married to an unbelieving spouse and the unbeliever "consents to live" (v. 12) with the believer, then divorce or separation is prohibited. Paul's advice here is intended to answer any of his Jewish converts who might be inclined to make an unwarranted application of the situation recorded in Ezra 10:3.

In the event that his readers should have any misgivings, the apostle shows why his advice is sound. "The unbelieving . . . is sanctified" (v. 14). And the children are "holy" (v. 14). This does not mean that the children or the spouse of a believer are automatically born into the family of God. The words "holy" and "unclean" in this text are equivalent to "sacred" and "profane." Again, the apostle's thought has Old Testament antecedents.[6] The unbeliever and the children are considered holy in a positional sense. Hence, the principle of the communication of uncleanness given in the Old Testament does not apply here (cf. also Rom. 11:16). Together with the believer, they share in God's blessings and are under the direct influence of the Holy Spirit.

"Yet if the unbelieving one leaves" (v. 15; in the middle voice, almost a technical term for "divorce"[7]). In the foregoing instruction, the apostle presumes that the unbeliever is content to remain with the believer. But what if the unbeliever takes the initiative in dissolving the marriage? In such a case, Paul's advice is that the believer is "not under bondage" (v. 15). There is no conflict here between Paul's advice and that of our Lord in Matthew 5:32. The point is that the divine standard cannot be imposed upon the unregenerate. There is nothing the believer can do but submit to the divorce. The overriding principle is that "God has called us to peace" (v. 15). The mild adversative gives us a clue to Paul's meaning in the use of this principle. He does not herein justify the divorce, even though the believing partner is free. Rather, the believer should make every effort to avoid the separation if possible. This understanding fits well with the previous context and also helps us understand the intent of the next verse. "For how do you know, O wife, whether you will save your husband?" (v. 16). The reason why every means should be taken to induce the unbeliever to fulfill his marriage covenant is that the unbeliever might be saved.

Counsel Concerning the Place of Marriage (7:17–24)

Now Paul offers a range of practical suggestions for cultivating contentment at all levels in the place God assigns to each individual. Marriage, like everything else, is determined by the selection of God (vv. 17–20) and is directed to the service of God (21–24). "As the Lord has assigned to each one, . . . in this manner let him walk" (v. 17). The apostle now builds on the principle stated in verse 7, that is, "Each man has his own gift from God, one in this manner, and another in that." Assuming one is not engaged in an unethical or illegal activity, there is no special reason why a believer should change his or her occupation or position in life subsequent to being saved. When applied to marriage, this simply means that there is no reason why a believer should put away an unbelieving spouse. Paul illustrates his point with the rite of circumcision. There is no need for a Gentile convert to be circumcised. On the other hand, there is no obligation incumbent upon a Jewish convert to be uncircumcised. In the New Testament, this rite had no direct impact on the life of faith (cf. Rom. 2:25, 29; Gal. 5:6). Therefore, even though it may mean living with an unbeliever, Paul is able to say, "Let each man remain in that condition in which he was called" (v. 20).

Paul closes this section with one final illustration to show that, properly understood, marriage should be viewed as directed to the service of God. "For he who was called in the Lord while a slave, is the Lord's freedman; likewise he who was called while free, is Christ's slave" (v. 22). As to one's social status at salvation, it matters little whether one is a slave or free. In reality, this person has been set free from the bondage of sin to serve the living and true God. Thus, the horizontal relationships have little significance when compared to the vertical. The writer does not legitimate the practice of slavery; rather, he wants the reader to know that although one's earthly circumstances might be unpleasant, they must not be used as an excuse to try to escape from a situation, however difficult. When applied to the question of marriage, there is no reason why the believer cannot remain faithful to his or her obligation to God, whether single, widowed, married in the Lord, or married to an unbeliever. The overriding principle is again repeated. "Let each man remain with God in that *condition* in which he was called" (v. 24). The prescription for peace and holiness is to embrace our situation and in that very place to know and live the will and purpose of God.

Should We Be Married? (7:25–40)

Next Paul advises young people contemplating marriage and instructs the parents of young people who are of marriageable age. Without being dogmatic, the apostle begins by giving his personal judgment in the form of a maxim (vv. 25–26). Then he reminds them of the likely prospect of tribulations (vv. 27–28), the passing away of worldly fashions (vv. 29–31), and the problem of divided allegiance (vv. 32–35). He follows this with suggestions for advising dependent/single daughters (vv. 36–38). Finally, Paul gives a summary and a final admonition (vv. 39–40).

Again Paul begins with *"peri de,"* which indicates that he is responding to yet another question addressed to him (cf. 7:1). "Now concerning virgins I have no command of the Lord" (v. 25). In our Lord's instruction regarding marriage and divorce recorded in the Gospels, there is no record of Him speaking to this issue. And so the apostle says, "But I give an opinion" (v. 25; *gnome*, "consent," "judgment"). Again, this is not to say that Paul's advice is less inspired than something he may quote from the sayings of Jesus. Rather, Paul gives advice under the inspiration of the Holy Spirit in order to fulfill this obligation to the Lord "as one who by the mercy of the Lord is trustworthy" (v. 25). Both the form and function of Paul's counsel here indicates that he is employing the language ordinarily associated with the "Greco-Roman rhetorical maxim and not merely an opinion. It provides not only a key to the shape and purpose of the argument in 1 Corinthians 7 but also a window on the give-and-take of moral persuasion taking place between Paul and members of the Corinthian community."[8] It is for this reason that he also underscores the matter of his own trustworthiness, since that too was an important element in establishing the authority of a maxim given. As a maxim, the instruction takes on much more force than it would if merely understood as a personal opinion—even though it is given by an apostle.

"It is good for a man to remain as he is" (v. 26). There is a temptation to consider this to be a generic use of "man" (Greek, *anthropos*), but the context forbids. Paul is talking to the men here. He will get to the matter of single women in turn. He tells the men that it is good to remain single. In Paul's judgment, celibacy is to be preferred "in view of the present distress" (v. 26). This expression may be understood in light of 1 Corinthians 15:30–31 and 2 Corinthians 11:21–33. The apostle Paul had already experienced intense persecution and no doubt anticipated it would get worse. If so, history records all too well that he would have been correct. However, a more likely probability is that he is referring to a specific local distress (Greek, *anagke*, "dislocation," "hardship"). Bruce Winter has shown that there is firm evidence for the presence of social unrest due to grain shortages occurring in the city during this time. What seems to have been happening is related to general anxiety and "threats of rioting that accompanied grain shortages."[9]

In this present "distress," Paul advises that there are good reasons to be cautious about entering into a life together until things settle down. Because of the situation, Paul's advice is, "Are you bound to a wife? Do not seek to be released. Are you released from a wife? Do not seek a wife" (v. 27). Although what Paul has said can never justify the dissolution of a marriage, hopefully it will discourage some from getting married. To those who are married, Paul says, "You have not sinned" (v. 28). There is nothing morally wrong with getting married. "Yet such will have trouble in this life, and I am trying to spare you" (v. 28). The Greek term *thlipsis* indicates that Paul understands this trouble will not come from within, as though marriage would necessarily be accompanied by turmoil and distress; rather, this trouble would come from without. Again, this fits well with his emphasis on the trouble confronting the church at that time.

The essence of all worldly relationships constitutes an additional reason why one may not wish to marry. "Brethren, the time has been shortened" (v. 29). Life, at best, is exceedingly brief. Furthermore, the relationships contracted during this life are only transient. Indeed, it will be all too soon for all of us that marrying and weeping and rejoicing and buying (and every other earthly activity) will be over and it will be as though they never occurred. Paul is not asking his readers to give up anything of eternal value, only temporal things: "the form of this world [which] is passing away" (v. 31).

What emerges in this discussion is a worldview entirely juxtaposed against that of prevailing attitudes. In the Corinthian culture, marriage was everything. The pursuit of happiness, condemned in the New Testament (Luke 8:14; Titus 3:3; James 4:1, 3; 2 Pet. 2:13) was an obsession among the Corinthians. Following Plato and other philosophers, they believed that nature offered them only this life to enjoy all that could be secured of human experience and accomplishments. Such joys and satisfaction were not available to the unborn or to the dead—only to those living here and now. The result was a worldview not unlike the prevailing one in modern Western society. People lived for the moment. What Paul shows is that the Christian lives his or her life in light of eternity. This earth is not all there is. There is a blessed hope toward which the believer orients all of life—its joys and its sorrows—which are just as real as those about them. But in light of the eschatological hope of the believer, the day-to-day exigencies of life are relativized (cf. 1 Thess. 4:13–18). "Paul is certainly not suggesting that marriage is nothing, [rather] in contrast to the young people who in secular society regarded it as 'everything' because it gave important signals concerning social class."[10] Winter adds, "What Paul is saying is that even one of the most important creation ordinances, and in many ways, a major relationship of life (Gen. 2:20–25), cannot be judged to be everything in the light of the eschatological factor."[11]

In his timely challenge to the common evangelical distortion of the biblical worldview, Winter observes that the groups who preach a prosperity gospel have fallen prey to the Greek way of thinking. They have collapsed the future hope, which is unique to the Christian perspective, into the present (much as the Corinthians did—cf. 4:8ff.). "All too often such teaching is garbed in Christian terminology of prosperity based on a full exploitation of the opportunities and resources that this world provides, and among its more high profile exponents it has assumed 'gospel proportions.'"[12] Winter contends correctly that the church needs to return to this eschatological perspective—to "provide a crucial paradigm for life's goals and expectations and an awareness of a proper use of the present world."[13] When we adopt the Greek worldview, we "gravely distort the Christian's perception of the seasons of life."[14] Such a reorientation of their thinking and proprieties is especially appropriate for young people contemplating marriage.

Paul goes on. A person who is married has a problem with divided allegiance. The unmarried man is "concerned about the things of the Lord," but the married man is "concerned about the things of the world" (v. 33). It is only natural for the married man to be concerned about the welfare of his wife and family. But as noted above, these issues have only passing significance. The same problem also exists for the woman. If the woman is a virgin, she is unencumbered by worldly necessities, and her only concern is for "the things of the Lord" (v. 34). On the other hand, she "who is married is concerned about the things of the world, how she may please her husband" (v. 34). One must take care not to misconstrue the force of Paul's argument here. It is not that he views the married life as less spiritual than the celibate life, but that the celibate life is less distracted by worldly cares. Hence, the single man or woman enjoying greater freedom also enjoys greater potential in terms of service. And so Paul is able to add, "This I say for your own benefit" (v. 35). It is not that the apostle is trying to ensnare them, nor much less that he is trying to mislead them. He does not impugn the divine ordinance. Rather, he is concerned about the distress that will surely accompany them should they be married, and he wishes to encourage "undistracted devotion to the Lord" (v. 35). The focal point of Paul's advice throughout this chapter is here—undistracted devotion to the Lord.

So how then how does a father advise his single daughter? To understand this passage, keep in mind the control the father had over the marriage of his daughter in ancient times. The apostle's advice is first to the man who thinks "he is acting unbecomingly toward his virgin *daughter*" (v. 36)—in other words, the father who thinks that he is being unreasonable. In this case, his daughter is "of full age" (v. 36). This is a euphemism for "full sexual maturity." On the other hand, "if it must be so" (v. 36), his advice is softened. If there be some reason why marriage is necessary—perhaps the daughter's happiness is involved (Paul does not elaborate)—then he suggests, "let him do what he wishes, he does not sin; let her marry" (v. 36). In other words, in spite of Paul's foregoing advice, he does not intend to discourage marriage, especially in situations where it becomes necessary for the happiness of the individuals involved.

Where there is no "constraint" and the father "has decided this in his own heart, to keep his own virgin *daughter*" (v. 37)—again, there is no hard, fast rule. And so Paul is able to say of this man, "He will do well" (v. 37). But all things being equal, the one "who does not give her in marriage will do better" (v. 38). While there is no sin in marriage and no superior virtue in celibacy, in light of the "present distress," Paul still maintains that singleness, for now, is better.

The practical value of this text is enormous. We live, as did the Corinthians, in a culture that glamorizes sex and is biased toward married couples. This is especially true in the church. Single people often feel ostracized from the normal activities of the church, which include programs for children, teens, young adults, and married couples. Often nothing is specifically offered for single adults who don't happen to be divorced. Paul offers these people several encouraging words. You will be spared trouble (v. 28). You will have extra time (vv. 29–31). You will have a friend who sticks closer than a brother (v. 32). And you will be able to serve God without distraction (v. 35).

In summary, marriage is for life, broken only by death. In that event, a woman "is free to be married to whom she wishes, only in the Lord" (v. 39). But in Paul's personal judgment, "she is happier if she remains as she is" (v. 40). The expression "I think that I also have the Spirit of God" (v. 40) has sometimes been taken to suggest that Paul did not know for sure if he was writing under inspiration. Some have even used this verse to suggest that everything Paul ever said about the relationships of men and women fell under this umbrella. And with that they have classed them with the advice of Job's three friends as *interesting* but not necessarily *true*. Others,[15] in recent years, follow similar reasoning to say that all of Paul's statements in this regard are colored by his Jewishness—reflecting more rabbinic prejudice than divine truth.

Such a case cannot be established on the basis of the language of this verse. The verb "think" (Greek, *dokeo*) does not suggest doubt in any way (cf. 12:22 Gal. 2:6). The phrase is better translated, "and I consider also that I have the Spirit of God." It cannot be disputed that many of the matters to which Paul gives his attention are local—and related especially to the peculiar *sitz im leben*. It is a mistake to relativize his counsel to them on this account. My former professor Charles Ryrie often cautioned us that all of Scripture can be relativized if its significance is limited to the historical setting. If we did that, we could relativize the entire Bible into the dustbins of history. In this case, the very fact that Paul asserts the unction of the Holy Spirit argues not only for the authority of what he says, but for its normativity for instruction to the Church of all ages.

Study Questions

1. Explain the significance of the expression "Now concerning," which appears for the first time in this epistle in 7:1.

2. Suggest some practical ways Paul's teaching on the mutual obligations of a husband and wife toward one another (vv. 1–5) might be creatively applied in a marriage counseling setting.

3. What is Paul referring to when he says, "I say by way of concession, not of command" (v. 6)?

4. Write down some of the reasons why Paul advocates singleness at the time of this writing. Are there situations in a modern setting where this advice might still be appropriate? What might they be?

5. What positive reasons would Paul suggest for believing spouses remaining faithful to their unbelieving partners rather than divorcing them?

6. Is Paul advocating slavery in verse 22? If not, what exactly is he talking about and how does slavery relate? Suggest another New Testament passage that teaches the same truth.

7. Explain the nature of the "present distress" referenced here in relation to young couples wishing to marry.

8. What is the meaning of "the time is shortened" in verse 29? How does this suggest Paul's worldview? Why is this important to his first-century readers?

9. Some believe that Paul teaches celibacy in this text. Do you agree? If this is not so, what *is* he saying about the life of singleness that commends it to the believers of this early church?

10. Explain the significance of verse 39 for the question of the divorce and remarriage of a believing couple. How might you relate this teaching to that of Jesus in the Gospels? To Paul's teaching elsewhere?

CHAPTER 11

Concerning Christian Liberty: The Principle
1 Corinthians 8:1-13

Preview:

The subject of Christian liberty occupies three chapters in this epistle as Paul undertakes to present the principle, illustrate it, and explain how to apply it. In his opening discussion, he addresses the problem of meat offered to idols as a way to respond to libertarians who wanted to take Christian liberty to an extreme. While Paul agrees in part with their logic, he challenges their lack of love as symptomatic of a problem far more serious than eating meat offered to idols.

The next issue concerning which the Corinthian believers had solicited Paul's advice had to do with whether it was going to be possible for them now, as members of the body of Christ, to continue to participate in festive community events. Reference to "meats sacrificed to idols" seems to contemplate more than a question of diet. It has to do with their new identity as "God's church" as opposed to their former citizenship "in Corinth." The question was a serious one, for there were many pagan temple rituals, state occasions, and festivals in which they were obligated to participate. Those who did not participate were segregated from society as outsiders. Generally at such events a part of an animal was burned at the sacrifice and the rest was prepared for the feast that followed. Sometimes portions were taken home and eaten there. Unused meat was sold in butcher shops.

The Jerusalem Council had been determined earlier that the Gentile converts should "abstain from things sacrificed to idols" (Acts 15:29). Although the apostle does not allude to this decision in this text, it is possible that it constituted a legal precedent at least for the Jewish converts in the assembly. The exact occasion of the problem cannot be known for certain. That it centered on a misunderstanding of the principles of Christian liberty is evident and that it created a serious challenge to the unity of this church is obvious. Many scholars now consider the entire section (chaps. 8—11) to be a unit. In our analysis, however, we will examine the first three chapters as a unit and the last separately.[1]

The Greek term *exousia*, "authority" (v. 9), is translated "liberty" in our text. The term, in various forms, has already been used in 6:12; 7:4, 28, and it will be used repeatedly throughout these chapters (cf. 9:4, 5, 6, 12, 18; 11:10). The term even shows up in 15:24 to designate a time when authorities will be abolished altogether, when Christ "has abolished all rule and all authority and power." The general context of the question relates to an issue concerning certain people in the church who were asserting their "rights" to continue to network with their former pagan associates and friends as they had always done. They even seem to have contrived "theological" grounds for their position. Paul spends fully three chapters dealing with this subject (actually four chapters before he leaves the subject altogether), which tells us that it was a matter of highest concern to him. If we would be as faithful to the force of this epistle as to its teachings, we must also give serious attention to both the issue at stake and to Paul's final resolve.

Paul introduces the principle of liberty (8:1–13) then uses his own experience to show what real Christian liberty actually looks like and to demonstrate some surprising ways it will be expressed—especially when there are consequences involved for others besides the individual who happens to be exercising it (9:1–27). Finally, Paul demonstrates to the Corinthians how they should appropriate this liberty in reference to the specific issues that have been placed before him—with some added nuances for which they may not have asked (10:1–11:1). As will be seen, each of these units functions to cause Paul's readers to listen carefully to his instruction and then to follow him willingly to its conclusion. The writer seems to employ a full range of rhetorical devices to bring this about. Chapter 8 focuses on the first of these—the *principle* of liberty.

Now Concerning . . .

"Now concerning" (see 7:1, 25; 8:4; 12:1; 16:1, 12 and comments on the expression *peri de* as used here and elsewhere in this epistle). Here again Paul signals that he is responding to questions the Corinthians have raised. *Eidolothuton*, "sacrificed to idols," refers to the flesh offered to heathen idols.

The same term is used in verses 4, 7, and 10. (See also 10:19, 28.) Here is one way that the Hellenistic and the Hebrew cultures clashed radically. Greek fellowship that centered on their sacrificial feasts was very important to them. But these occasions were an offense to the Jews. Considering the way Paul develops his argument, however, it is entirely possible that the problem, ironically, came from another direction—that is, from an overemphasis or misuse of Jewish monotheism—that is, Jewish-Christian libertines. This would explain Paul's reference to Deuteronomy 6:4 in verse 6. Nevertheless, it may well have come about from a misunderstanding of the implications of this truth for practical Christian living among the Gentile converts. In either scenario the so-called "wise" ones were the Christian Jews and the so-called "weak" ones were probably Gentile converts.[2]

A third possibility is discussed by S. K. Stowers, who

> maintains that the wise Corinthians regarded the Christians who refused to eat idol sacrifices as suffering from an *astheneia*, interpreted as a moral deficiency or illness, in analogy with the sickness of the soul ascribed to the person who joined a philosophical school. The Corinthian wise consequently entered into a campaign to rid the weak of their false beliefs by making them participate in pagan cultic meals to achieve *gnosis* by praxis.[3]

If we follow this analysis, we will conclude that the problem arose from within the context of the Corinthian philosophical environment.

Just how this problem presented itself to the Corinthian believers is difficult to know for certain. It is likely that many were highly networked in the matrix of urban Corinthian life before they were saved. In today's world this might be akin to holding membership in the country club, or perhaps, membership in a secret society, such as the Masons. Membership in secret societies is considered by those who have "come out from among them" to be tantamount to pagan idolatry. Or perhaps a new believer was formerly a part of a musical group that traveled about performing in dance halls and honkytonks. I know a person who gave up playing his musical instrument—even in the church—because he couldn't get the old associations out of his mind. I also know a man who loved stock car racing before God saved him, but after he received Christ, his associations and interests changed. For many people, these old associations are reminders of the old life—the one they turned from when they turned "to serve a living and true God" (1 Thess. 1:9). For my friend who loved to race his car on Sundays, his old interest just dropped off. Today he doesn't even watch the races on TV.

Those who have been saved out of a life of abandon and alcohol or substance abuse are unable to imagine how alcohol or worldly amusements can have any place in the life of a Christian. In such situations, it is easy for those whose consciences have been sensitized in these areas, to become confused—or worse, when they see others whose lifestyle contradicts their claim to having a relationship with Christ, they are encouraged to abandon some of their "scruples" as silly or immature. And in a worst-case scenario, they may abandon their Christian principles altogether.

For the Corinthians the problem centered on the fact that idolatry had been so insinuated into their daily lives that it was difficult, if not impossible, to eat a meal, attend a public festival, or even join a neighborhood block party without compromising their testimony. Some who seem to have adopted a radical monotheism, had rationalized this problem and decided it was *adiaphora*, that is, it didn't really matter. At the other end of the spectrum were those who for various reasons were offended by this thinking as an unacceptable compromise of the principles of godly separation. In what follows, Paul will accept the reasons of those who have "knowledge." But he will reject their "solution." At the same time, he will resist identifying with those who are labeled "weaker" brothers while defending their need for understanding.

Recent analysis of these chapters has recognized the rhetorical structure of the text in keeping with a style of argumentation with which the readers would have been familiar. Paul seems not only to be familiar with this, but to have made use of it with a high degree of skill.[4] Accordingly, the chapter breaks rather neatly into two divisions. There is first of all an opening paragraph in which Paul states the situation, anticipates his subsequent argument, and establishes a common ground of agreement (vv. 1–6). He follows this with a discussion and refutation of the libertine position based on the foundation of truth concerning which they all agree (vv. 7–13).[5]

Knowledge versus Christian Love (8:1–6)

"We know that we all have knowledge" (v. 1). Paul uses irony here. To paraphrase: "We both know that you consider yourself to be thoroughly informed about this matter." Apparently in their question to Paul they implied that they felt adequate to deal with the problem. Perhaps some in the assembly were disputing their approach. One should recall that it is this arrogance in regard to their knowledge that Paul confronts repeatedly in this epistle. But knowledge alone will not suffice when dealing with Christian liberty. Paul is about to introduce a much higher principle: "Knowledge makes arrogant, but love edifies" (v. 1). Mere theoretical or speculative knowledge acquired in a vacuum has the effect of inflating a person and rendering him or her vain and conceited (*phusioo*, from *physa*, "bellows"). On the other hand, love (*agape*) edifies (*oikodomeo*, "builds"). And it is this incomparably higher principle that the apostle applies to this case. Paul often employs this same metaphor, as in 14:3–4, where, in a similar context, edification is viewed as a vital criterion for evaluating the relative value of the exercise of spiritual gifts. Some driven by pride vaunt themselves even in the latter case. Paul advocates that we build on the bedrock of love to establish one another in the faith. Ralph Earle observes:

> The picture here is a striking contrast. Intellectualism often inflates a person with pride. We can blow up a balloon in a minute or two, and collapse it in a second with a pin prick. So it is with self-important intellectuals. They can be deflated with a single remark.

> But building up with love is something else. Just as one has to lay stone on stone or brick on brick in order to construct a solid building, so we must lay one loving deed on another if we would build a solid life that will last.[6]

"If anyone supposes that he knows [*oida*] anything" (v. 2) sets up a wordplay. If knowledge is simply a cognitive process, then Paul says of such a one, "he has not yet known [*ginosko*] as he ought to know" (v. 2). A person who has simply accumulated information is a seriously defective person. The wordplay is lost to the English reader. Paul deliberately plays on the term *oida*, which has in mind the investigative process, and *ginosko*, a deeper and more personal and experiential understanding that leads to moral wisdom. This unity between ideas and experience has been lost to modernity in Western culture and requires explanation and emphasis in our contemporary world.

In true knowledge, intellect and emotions go hand in hand. "But if anyone loves God, he is known by Him" (v. 3). The true knowledge of God does not come about through the acquisition of information concerning Him; it comes through *loving* Him. A more important reality underscored in this language is that this person is not only in possession of true knowledge of God, but is *known of God* Himself. A personal relationship exists between the true believer and God (cf. Paul's use of God's foreknowledge in Rom. 11:2 to denote a "prior relationship"). It is this kind of relationship that is here appropriated by the apostle for application to his Gentile converts.

"Therefore concerning the eating of things sacrificed to idols" (v. 4). Paul returns now to the main subject. First, he wishes to establish a common ground from which to argue his case. He does this by agreeing with the libertines that "there is no such thing as an idol in the world" (v. 4), as any thinking person knows. More important, there is a "confessional" agreement on this, so he adds, "and that [*kai hoti*][7] there is no God but one." If a person offers a sacrifice to an idol, he is, in fact, sacrificing to a nonentity. Second, having alluded to their common faith, Paul notes that while we know of "so-called gods" (v. 5) in the pagan world, "for us" who are Christians "there is *but* one God, the Father, . . . and one Lord, Jesus Christ" (v. 6). Here he stands in agreement with the rationalizations of those who share his "knowledge" on these matters, and he appeals to the common core of their Christian faith. On these matters Paul can be assured that there will be no disagreement with him. He will have more to say, but for now he wishes to go on record as giving them their argument.

The effect of this statement is to subtly establish Paul's authority by slipping behind the truth concerning which they all agree. Then, with the use of *hemin* and *hemeis*, "for us," and "*we* exist for Him . . . and through Him" (v. 6), he draws his audience into his rhetorical embrace by acknowledging a shared experience and a common faith.[8] Those who are following his argument cannot help but stand with him.

The "double *eis*" (*eis theos* and *eis kurios*, "one God . . . one Lord") exclamation is a powerful adaptation of Deuteronomy 6:4. The *Shema*, the central teaching of Jewish monotheism, was taken over by early Christians and "contained the central tenets of the missionary preaching that the Corinthian Christians had previous listened to and which led to their conversion."[9] In fact, the "'wise' Corinthians' radical monotheism, which gave them permission to eat idol sacrifices even in a temple setting, could be seen as a logical development of the formula's monotheism." It may provide a clue as to how their argument was derived. It may also suggest that the real source of the problem related to a misunderstanding or a misapplication of a biblical truth—one that was most certainly preached by Paul on his first visit to their city.

As a side note, it is important to observe the content of this common core of faith. One of the scandals of Christianity was and remains the equation between God and the Lord Jesus. If the early Christians had abandoned the idea that Jesus is God, they would have had no problem fitting in. But then, if they had done so, there never would have been a Christian movement to be granted acceptance! Christianity is Christ. In a pluralistic culture where all gods are given equal hearing, Christians stand out because they worship the only God who is real; who has something to say, and whose voice has truly been heard (cf. Rom. 10:13–18). This is not triumphalism—just the truth.

An additional offense in today's gender-sensitive world is that God is "Father." Then as now, the ultimate test of orthodoxy is faithfulness to the Scriptures as revealed by the living God. Perhaps it was the goddess worship that compelled Paul to underscore this point. Or perhaps Paul did so simply because Christ taught it and it was so impressed on Paul's mind and heart that he never seemed to tire of celebrating its significance (cf. Rom. 8:12–17). Those today who recline at meat "in the temple of the goddess are depriving themselves of the most intimate of all spiritual experiences—that of being parented by their *Father* God. They rob every man of the opportunity to explore the meaning of being an earthly father by following his heavenly Father's example. They impoverish every woman by failing to show her the ultimate standard by which she should evaluate her future husband and the father of her children. And they deprive every child of a mom and dad who know what it means to follow the Lord in a life and relationship modeled after the Christian God who, as a holy triangle of love, is the Father, the Son, and the Holy Spirit—and none other! Most important in this context, Paul is detailing material with which both he and his readers agree. Unfortunately, in our modern world, we cannot always be certain of the same consensus by those who claim to be followers of Jesus Christ.

And there is "one Lord, Jesus Christ, by whom are all things" (v. 6). When Paul, as John (cf. John 1:1ff.), links the lordship/deity of Christ to His work in creation—and, of course, all things owe their existence to Him—the impact is the same as Jesus' claim in John 8:58, "Before Abraham was born, I am." But beyond this, since all things owe their existence to Him, the same must be said of the meat sacrificed to the idol. "However not all men have this knowledge" (v. 7; *pas*, "all")—the sense is generic. Many are still without a correct understanding of who Jesus Christ is and what that means in terms of the power and influence of false gods. For such a person to eat meat sacrificed to idols, "their conscience being weak is defiled" (v. 7; *asthenes*, "infirm, feeble;" *moluno*, "to pollute, stain, contaminate, defile"). For a condition caused by "nothing" (cf. v. 4), the apostle uses rather strong language here. However phantom may be the enemy, the outcome is deadly.

The "Weaker" versus the "Wise" (8:7–13)

Since we know that our relationship with God is not affected by whether or not we eat meat, it ought not to be offensive to the "wise" Christian to limit himself or herself for the sake of the weak. Here is where the principle of love is most conspicuously applied. "But take care lest this liberty of yours somehow become a stumbling block to the weak" (v. 9). The term *exousia* may be translated "authority" or "lawful right." It has in mind the power of choice, or the liberty to do as one pleases. As noted, it helps us to understand that the essential context of this issue had to do with those who were asserting their "rights" over against those who might take offense with their exercise of them. The reader is called upon to interrupt their logic of choice with loving discernment. The availability of an option does not necessitate its exercise, especially when love and concern for someone else come into play. The most serious danger of an unbridled latitudinarian approach to Christian liberty is the possibility of causing sin in another. "For if someone sees you, who have knowledge, dining in an idol's temple, will not his conscience, if he is weak, be strengthened to eat things sacrificed to idols?" (v. 10; *katakeimai*, "to lie prostrate, to recline, as at a meal"). In the writings of Aristotle and Thucydides, such sacrificial feasts constituted one of the chief means of social enjoyment. This term shows that the offense is more than just *eating* the meat. They were reclining at the table. They were in attendance at the feast and participating in the pagan celebration. That this is in view is supported by the later rebuke in 10:1–8 where the apostle has to instruct his readers to refrain from such events because they are antithetic to participation in the Table of the Lord. The Corinthians' indifference compromised their witness and undermined their ministry. When Paul reflects on what really happens at these events (in chap. 10), it will be abundantly clear why these are places where Christians should never be found. Their rationalizations were entirely misguided. Throughout this epistle Paul makes it clear that the "world" as a source of wisdom (1:20–21) is out of touch with the "hidden *wisdom*, which God predestined" (2:7). The world, before which we are made spectacles (4:9) and "scum" (4:13), is not a place where we should seek to keep company (5:10–11).

If the brother with this "knowledge" publicly exercises his right to join the pagan feast, he in effect encourages the weaker brother to violate his conscience. The problem in so doing is that he causes the brother to sin. The expression "be strengthened" is *oikodomeo*, "be edified." The sense is ironic; edification should build up to righteousness. Here one is edified, or built up, to sin.

"For through your knowledge he who is weak is ruined" (v. 11). Is Paul implying that the weak brother could lose his salvation? Paul explains this elsewhere when he says, for example, in Romans 14:23, "He who doubts is condemned if he eats." In other words, he is to be brought under the sure judgment (or chastening) of God for his sin. The most extreme application of this principle would involve sinning unto death (cf. 5:5; 11:30; 1 John 5:16–17). There is also a kind of irony here. The offended brother or sister is described as "weak." The "knowledgeable" one is often understood, by implication, as the "strong" one. But in truth, this person is not strong; he or she is merely "puffed up" to appear larger than they really are. Real men and women of God care about the weak "for whose sake Christ died" (v. 11). The force of this expression is practical, not soteriological. That is, Paul is not suggesting that the weaker brother's salvation hangs in the balance. Rather, he is saying that there is an inherent incongruity with the gospel when my behavior causes sin in someone else. It is true that Christ died to secure salvation, but speaking more to the point; He did so to put away sin. Hence, Paul says that if you should entice another brother to sin, then in effect, "you sin against Christ" (v. 12). This truth is derived from two facts. First, and most immediate, is that the one brother has enticed another brother or sister to sin against the Savior who died for them both. Second, in application of Matthew 25:40, "to the extent that you did it to . . . *even* the least *of them*, you did it to Me." The sin is ultimately against Christ. This raises the question of who is really the superior in the analogy here. It would seem that Paul uses this contrast for sake of argument to point up the *weakness* of their case. Many repeat the mistake of the Corinthians by assuming that liberality in matters of personal conduct is a sign of spiritual maturity and strength, while scrupulosity is a sign of weakness. I have known people to participate in questionable practices just to "prove" they are strong. This misses Paul's point entirely. He paints these insensitive worldly minded intellectuals into a corner of their own making. And then he shows them that they are not as smart as they pretend to be. They have *knowledge* but have no idea how to use it *(wisdom)*.

"Therefore" (v. 13) directs us to the conclusion of the matter. It is not knowledge that forms the basis of the conclusion, but love. Hence, Paul says, "If food causes my brother to stumble, I will never eat meat again, that I might not cause my brother to stumble" (v. 13). The hyperbole is intended for emphasis. The apostle does not qualify this. He does not say he will refrain in public and exercise his liberty in private. In order to avoid offending a brother, he would permanently exclude the eating of meat from his diet. He of course also anticipates his eventual conclusion to this matter in chapter 10. Here we need only emphasize that he does not have two different standards. He remains consistent throughout this section. S. L. Johnson offers two final words of caution regarding this text:

> In the first place, the passage does not refer to legalists desirous of imposing their narrow-minded scruples on others. Such are not weak brethren but willful brethren desirous of glorying in the subjection of others to their tenets (cf. Gal. 6:11–13). This is tyranny, and Christianity must always be on guard against this. In the second place, it should be noted in this verse that the decision to follow the path of love rests with Paul, not with the weak. The strong are to yield to love's appeal voluntarily, not because the weak demand it (legalists always demand subjection to their laws).[10]

Christian liberty is not a principle that affords certain privileges thought to be off-limits by some believers. Christian liberty (in Paul's mind) brings the elect of God into a new kind of relationship with their heavenly Father and gives them rights and privileges hereto unknown before the coming of Christ (Gal. 3:23 4:7). It is not about the petty issues to which they had reduced it.

In fact, when Christian liberty is rightly understood, it may "cost" them more than they can imagine before they realize the unimaginable blessings that it will one day bring. To illustrate the point, Paul draws from his own experience.

Study Questions

1. What is the weakness of having knowledge?

2. In verse 2, what is Paul saying about the limitation of knowledge?

3. Why was the issue of eating meat offered to idols such a problem in the Corinthian church?

4. In verses 4–6, why is eating things sacrificed to idols such an abomination?

5. In verse 7 is Paul speaking of Christians who are still eating food sacrificed to idols? Or is he describing the practices of the pagan Corinthians?

6. In the issue of eating, does the consuming of foods or the abstaining from certain foods have anything to do with true spirituality?

7. What is the role of conscience in the conviction about eating or not eating food offered to idols?

8. In Paul's teaching, what is more important—Christian freedom or offending the weaker brother? Explain.

9. What is Paul's practical resolve if he offends a brother or causes him to stumble?

CHAPTER 12

Concerning Christian Liberty: The Portrait
1 Corinthians 9:1-27

Preview:

Christian liberty is not to be used as an opportunity to behave in ways that will bring disrepute to Christ or injury to His children. In fact, true Christian liberty, if exercised properly, will cause people to place the spiritual welfare of others over and above their own personal rights. Paul and the other apostles are examples of servant leadership, which is characterized by concern for others and personal discipline.

At first glance, it may seem that the writer is introducing an entirely new topic. For this reason, as Leon Morris observes, many have speculated that this may have been an insertion—perhaps from one of the missing letters of Paul to the Corinthians (see introduction). I agree with Morris that there is no reason to do this.[1] Upon closer inspection it is evident that Paul is still developing the subject introduced at the beginning of the previous chapter and continued through the next—Christian liberty. "Paul has been dealing with people who asserted their rights to the detriment of others. He has told them that this is wrong. He now proceeds to show how he himself has consistently applied this principle. He practices what he preaches."[2]

The principle rightly applied cuts across every layer of the Christian's life. Paul appeals to his own experience to show how complex Christian liberty is. He does this to offer more direct evidence of his authority and at the same time to encourage them to follow his example. There are two expressions around which the two dominant themes of this chapter turn. The first is found in verse 16: "Woe is me if I do not preach the gospel." The second is in verse 22: "I have become all things to all men, so that I may by all means save some." These in turn define Paul's dominating *ideological* principle and then his dominating *methodological* principle. We have organized our exposition around these two themes. The first is contained in verses 1–18. The second comprises the remainder of the chapter (vv. 19–27).

Paul's Dominating Ideological Principle (9:1–18)

An ideological principle represents how we view the universe and our place in it. Paul has already introduced his eschatological worldview in previous chapters to show the contingency of human life experience compared to the glory to follow. Now he opens his heart to enable his readers to see what "makes him tick." Worldviews can be discovered by listening to people talk. Someone says, "I'm a self-made man, but I think if I had it to do over again, I'd call in someone else." Another person might say, "America's ideals are all great so far as they go, but it is financial success that really counts." It's not difficult to recognize a cynical worldview in such comments. In the opening section of this chapter, Paul tells us something of himself, his worldview, and what motivates him to do what he does. While none of us today is an apostle, anyone in church leadership will resonate with the compelling drive to serve Christ and the ambivalent response of his or her contemporaries.

The Exhibition of Paul's Authority (9:1–6)

Paul begins by defining his relationship with the people. Earlier (8:4–6) Paul hid his authority behind the common body of faith shared by himself and his audience.[3] Now he asserts this authority in a still subtle, but more explicit and personal way. The "seal" of his authority is the very existence of the Corinthian church itself. Whenever he speaks, he can do so with authority—at least in Corinth—because of his relationship to the Corinthian assembly. In verse 1 he opens with two questions: "Am I not free? Am I not an apostle?" (Greek, *eleutheros*, "not a slave, not under restraint"). The first question has to do with his freedom and liberty in Christ. "Am I not just as free as any other believer to regulate my conduct according to my own convictions? Yet more, I am an apostle as well." "Have I not seen Jesus our Lord?" (v. 1). Paul asks this question to substantiate his claim to apostleship (cf. Acts 1:21–22; 9:3–9, 17). "Are you not my work in the Lord?" (v. 1). If Paul is an apostle, then one would expect to see evidence of his ministry. The Corinthian assembly itself was that evidence. Whether anyone else considered Paul an apostle, there was absolutely no ground for doubt among the Corinthians. Conversion of souls is a divine work performed through the agency of God's ministers. The fact that people were saved at Corinth and formed an assembly of believers validates Paul's commission. As he puts it, "You are the seal of my apostleship in the Lord" (v. 2).

"My defense to those who examine me is this" (v. 3). His answer to those who are questioning his authority is another question: "Do we not have a right to eat and drink?" (v. 4). In the list of those options over which Paul had discretionary power, he includes "to take along a believing wife" (v. 5); that is, he had the authority to take a wife and bring her on his journeys with him as "the rest of the apostles" (v. 5). The inclusion of "the brothers of the Lord, and Cephas" (v. 5) shows the fallacy of those who promote celibacy among the clergy by citing the example of the apostles (cf. Matt. 8:14). More important in this context is the obvious reinforcement of his instruction in the previous chapter. Some matters take precedence over the comforts of this life. This was a radical worldview change for the reader.

The irony of Paul's next question had to be apparent to his audience: "Or do only Barnabas and I not have a right to refrain from working?" (v. 6). To paraphrase, "Are Barnabas and I the only exceptions to the rule that ministers should be supported by their respective churches?" At the beginning of his ministry in Corinth, the apostle supported himself. Then, when financial aid did come, it did not come from the Corinthian assembly. This should have been an embarrassment to the Corinthians and appears to have been something Paul has waited long to get off his chest. But the opportunity is timely and works in his favor. In no way is he indebted to them.

The criticism leveled against Paul by these people may be compared to a person who has been saved from choking to death by the efforts of a doctor in the house. Later, when following up on the patient's condition, the doctor even waives her fees. But as the patient is leaving the office, he criticizes the helpful medic for what he considers the outrageous fees normally charged to her regular patients. This may sound far-fetched, but any pastor who has been subjected to the proverbial "Sunday roast" by critical members of the church knows the pain it inflicts and the discouragement it can cause.

Expectations of Paul's Work (9:7–14)

That Paul has the right to expect remuneration for his labors is supported by common experience. Whoever heard of a soldier who went to war "at any time . . . at his own expense"? (v. 7). The same is true of the owner of a vineyard or of a flock of sheep. Such laborers have the right to expect to be supported by the vocation to which they devote themselves.

What Paul says is further supported by the Mosaic Law (v. 8). "I am not speaking these things according to human judgment, am I? Or does not the Law also say these things?" Is this simply a secular principle, or can we expect to find biblical precedence? "For" introduces Paul's quotation of Deuteronomy 25:4: "You shall not muzzle the ox while he is threshing" (v. 9). Even the ox has the right to expect to be fed for his labors. "God is not concerned about oxen, is He?" (v. 9). This question is no longer spoken in irony, nor is the writer being contemptuous. A better translation might be "Is not God concerned about oxen?" The implied answer is yes. God does care for His creation (cf. Job 38:41; Ps. 147:9; Matt. 6:26; Luke 12:24). So he adds, "Yes, for our sake it was written" (v. 10). Certainly if this principle should apply to brute beasts, much more, it should apply to humankind in general. "The plowman ought to plow in hope, and the thresher *to thresh* in hope of sharing *the crops*" (v. 10), that is, of being rewarded. It is only natural and right, but more than that, it is scriptural that one should expect profit from his or her labors.

In verses 10 and 11 Paul expands on this principle and reminds the Corinthians that his service to them was just another area where his liberty in Christ was voluntarily restricted by his love for them. "We sowed spiritual things . . . we should reap material things" (v. 11). The contrast here is not of a moral sense, but of a qualitative sense. Paul as their minister and teacher imparted to them spiritual things. Was it any great thing if he should expect remuneration to sustain the body? The former connoted things of infinite value, the latter, only of temporal value. Paul is not through with this argument yet, but he pauses here to interject a reminder: "Nevertheless, we did not use this right . . . that we may cause no hindrance to the gospel of Christ" (v. 12). The apostle continues to "endure all things" (v. 12). He is not justifying something he did, but something that he has the right to do—a right he did not exercise. He continues.

Not only is Paul's position supported by common experience and by Scripture; it is also supported by the temple law: "Those who perform sacred services eat the *food* of the temple" (v. 13). Every sacrifice made at the altar included a portion for the priest. This was an institution ordained by God Himself in the Old Testament. "So also," Paul concludes, "the Lord directed those who proclaim the gospel to get their living from the gospel" (v. 14). The ministers of the gospel in the New Testament have no less holy a vocation than the priests of the Old Testament.

In conclusion, Paul had a right to the Corinthians' support (vv. 7–9), and he had a right to expect to see spiritual growth from his efforts (vv. 10–14). People called of God to full-time ministry connect all too well with the frustration of this man driven by the "love of Christ" (2 Cor. 5:14), who poured his energies into the lives of people, sowing the good seed of the Word of God, only to see thorns and weeds at the harvest. That he did not give up in the face of such discouragement is also a powerful example to all who follow his footsteps in ministry.

To strengthen his argument, Paul does two things here. He reminds his readers of his right to their support, which he has waived for their sakes. He also reminds them of his right to see spiritual growth in their lives as a product of his labor. These rights he will claim from them. Such an argument provides a powerful inducement for the so-called "wise" to follow his example and put aside their own personal rights in favor of giving attention to the spiritual growth of others in their assembly—the so-called weak.

Explanation for Paul's Zeal (9:15–18)

"But I have used none of these things" (v. 15). Paul asserts that he has never exercised that right. And he is quick to add that he is not mentioning these things now to get retroactive pay. He would rather "die than have any man make my boast an empty one" (v. 15) (or, "that any man should pay me now for my labors in Corinth"). The reason for this is simply that his policy of self-denial enabled the apostle to face his enemies squarely. He could never be accused of self-interest, nor could his integrity ever be legitimately questioned. So why does he do it? He answers, "For if I preach the gospel, I have nothing to boast of" (v. 16). Here is the answer to his original questions. "Am I not free? Am I not an apostle?" The implied answer to the first question is no. He answers the second, "Yes, but that is no cause for glorying." "For I am under compulsion; for woe is me if I do not preach the gospel" (v. 16). Paul, like Jeremiah (in Jer. 20:7–9), had a difficult assignment, but knew that in the final analysis he didn't really have a choice in the matter. He could never hold his peace.

> O Lord, Thou hast deceived me and I was deceived;
> Thou hast overcome me and prevailed.
> I have become a laughingstock all day long;
> Everyone mocks me.
> For each time I speak, I cry aloud;
> I proclaim violence and destruction,
> Because for me the word of the Lord has resulted
> In reproach and derision all day long.
> But if I say, "I will not remember Him
> Or speak anymore of His name,"
> Then in my heart it becomes like a burning fire

Shut up in my bones;
And I am weary of holding *it* in,
And I cannot endure *it*.

For Paul there are no grounds for boasting. "For if I do this voluntarily, I have a reward" (v. 17). If it was optional for him to preach the gospel, then he would deserve remuneration. "But if against my will, I have a stewardship entrusted to me" (v. 17). By this, the apostle is not implying that he was an *unwilling* servant of the Lord (cf. 15:9–10; Rom. 1:5; 11:13; 15:15–16; Gal. 1:15–16; Eph. 3:8). Rather, he draws a distinction between what was optional for him and what was obligatory upon him. Paul was given a "stewardship" to preach. That was enough (cf. 4:1–2; Luke 17:10). A steward received no pay. Such a one was merely a slave doing an assigned task.

So why does he do it? "What then is my reward?" The answer to this question is twofold. First, "that . . . I may offer the gospel without charge" (v. 18) and, second, "not to make full use of my right in the gospel" (v. 18). The former discharges Paul's obligation to God. The latter discharges his obligation to man. In the context, it is important to note that Paul is not laying this down as a general principle for all ministers of the gospel to follow. He had the authority to do many things, yet he did not "make full use of [his] right in the gospel" (v. 18). In the calculus of Christian liberty, the fact that one has the right to do something does not, on that basis, suggest that it is the appropriate thing to do.

Paul's Dominating Methodological Principle (9:19–27)

In the opening section of chapter 9, the writer explains his dominating ideological principle. There he made clear what it is that really drives him. In so doing, he articulates a world and life view that offers a radical alternative to that which was commonplace in Corinth. In what follows, he draws upon this perspective and reflects on his methodological principles as an apostle and church planter. He is careful to demonstrate that his methods match his message. This text is especially instructive to those who struggle, as most of us do in our churches, to discern the relationship between the two. We often hear it simplistically stated: The *message* must remain the same, but *methods* must change. Often this rationale is used to justify methods that are considered avante garde. However, it is naïve to consider that there is no relation between the two.[4] Paul's methodology was driven by his message. And this should be true in our ministries today. While we remain *in* the world, we are not *of* it. It is this principle throughout that offers the most practical and sustaining value of this text for our own situation.

One can imagine, in this context, that some might argue for the priority of Christian liberty in deciding whether to eat meat sacrificed to idols—indeed, pagan feasts might be great places to witness. It is not difficult to imagine people today going to places of worldly amusement on the pretext of doing the same. It is important to remember that it is precisely to the issue of how to draw the line in Christian conduct that the writer still speaks. Paul resolves the problem by integrating truth and life, not bifurcating them. What drove Paul is the truth of the gospel. What directed him are the implications of that truth for his own life and those to whom God had sent him. D. L. Moody used to liken the world to a dying ship. We are called to rescue as many as we can from the icy waters.[5] It was this perspective that drove Moody. Likewise, it is Paul's theological perspective that defined his strategies and methods.

What Paul does here is differentiate himself on the one hand from the professional peripatetic sophists who make a living by giving motivational speeches. On the other hand, he distances himself from the Jewish legalists (the *Judaizers* of his letter to the Galatians) who would bring the church back under the Law of Moses. As we have seen, there were influences from both of these factions in the Corinthian assembly. And because of their divisiveness, they were pulling from one extreme to the other, both in terms of the correct teaching on these matters and in terms of practical guidelines for their lives. So the foundation for his methodology is the gospel. It is here that he secures the perspective required to understand the nature of the human predicament and what God has done about it. In the light of this truth, he goes on to tell his readers what he is doing about it.

Paul Was a Servant to All (9:19–21)

"I am free from all *men*" (v. 19). When understood in the context of his Christian liberty, Paul was indeed free. But when understood in light of his Christian responsibility, he adds, "I have made myself a slave to all" (v. 19; Greek, *douloo*, "brought myself under bondage"). With all the freedom in the world open to him, why did the apostle restrict himself so severely? The answer is "that I might win the more" (v. 19). His foremost interest was to preach the gospel and win the lost to Jesus Christ. Whatever it took in terms of personal freedom, he was prepared to pay the price. It is only fair to point out here that the apostle is not preaching the utilitarian doctrine that the end justifies the means. Nor is he suggesting compromise. If anyone was prepared to stand rigidly upon matters of principle, it was Paul (cf. Gal. 2:5). But as for matters of indifference, they are viewed as luxuries, and therefore, in Paul's view, dispensable. It is with reference to these lower-tier issues of conscience and preference that he speaks.

"To the Jews I became as a Jew" (v. 20). How far Paul was willing to go in this regard is recorded in Acts 21:18–27. Again, he did not accommodate himself to sin or error, but to social custom. Likewise, he accommodated himself "to those who are under the Law, as under the Law" (v. 20). He goes on to explain that he does not intend to subscribe to antinomianism. He is still "under the law of Christ" (v. 21).

Paul Was a Seeker of All (9:22–23)

Paul summarizes his guiding principle in the words "I have become all things to all men, that I may by all means save some" (v. 22). He is willing to concede Christian liberties at all points if the gospel is preached and the lost are won to Christ. And make no mistake, his reference to the "weak" (v. 22) along with his identification with them was explicitly linked to his previous discussion of the so-called weak and wise.

"To the weak I became weak" (v. 22). Since this is given in the context of his word concerning the "weak" ones, it is fair to say that this also provides a key to understanding his point. He is identifying—not with the "power-pockets" (whether legalistic or intellectual), for he will not be their champion to support a private agenda—but with people whose hearts are tender toward Christ and who are looking for a deliverer from their sins. Our culture has abandoned such concepts as duty and responsibility as antiquated Victorianism. But these are the virtues our text extols against an emphasis on "demands" and "rights." Those who would use this passage to support libertarianism miss his point entirely. It is precisely because he was "all things to all men" that he would not participate with the pagans in their temples.

Some might argue that Paul contradicts himself. If he was truly "all things" to the Gentile, he would attend the pagan festivals, not avoid them! It is here that the interface of the message and the method is seen. He does not attend because it would entail the compromise of his message (a point he will expand in the next chapter). The festival was a place of "fellowship" with demons. And it is entirely incompatible with the believer's association with the Table of the Lord and the body of Christ. Paul refuses to mingle godlessness with the things of Christ (10:14–23). By the same token, he will approach the Jew with a keen sensitivity to those matters of religious observance that might cause offense and stand as stumbling blocks to their response to the gospel. But here too he will draw the line where he might compromise the law of Christ. In such cases, he will take his stand and let the chips fall where they may.

The contemporary Church struggles with this today. Many fail to recognize the line Paul draws between communication and compromise. In our

efforts to be "all things to all," is it possible that we have forgotten the message for which we have sacrificially abandoned all rights to personal liberty?
New Testament believers "came out from among them" when they "turned to
God from idols." Today it is not uncommon to invite the idols (be they musical or media figures) into our feasts in order to "identify" with the lost. One
wonders what we think we are supposed to do with our unsuspecting guests
after we have put the idols on the platform and hidden the gospel, like a door
prize, under the tables.

Compromising Truth Versus Communicating Truth

Instruction for a good conscience and sincere faith (1 Tim. 1:4).
Instruct not to teach "strange" doctrines (1 Tim. 1:3)

Have nothing to do with worldly fables (1 Tim. 4:7)
Strive to fix the hope on the living God who is our Savior (1 Tim. 4:10)

Flee from evil things; pursue righteousness (1 Tim. 6:11)
Fight the good fight of faith (1 Tim. 6:12)

Suffer hardship as a good soldier of Christ Jesus (2 Tim. 2:3)
No soldier entangles himself with everyday affairs (2 Tim. 2:4)

Be diligent to present yourself approved to God as a workman (2 Tim. 2:15)
Avoid worldly and empty chatter that spreads like gangrene (2 Tim. 2:17)

Silence those who upset whole families, teachings things they should not (Titus 1:11)
But as for you, speak the things which are fitting for sound doctrine (Titus 2:1)

Be careful to engage in good deeds (Titus 3:8)
But shun foolish controversies (Titus 3:9)

We are no longer under the law as a tutor (Gal. 3:25)
For we are all sons of God through faith in Christ Jesus (Gal. 3:26)

The naysayer turns away and will not endure sound doctrine (2 Tim. 4:3)
But you, be sober in all things, endure hardship (2 Tim. 4:5)

"I do all things" (v. 23), that is, all the things mentioned above, I do "for
the sake of the gospel" (v. 23). Paul's ultimate criterion is not the prejudice of
culture, but the gospel. This is so much more than simply preaching the
gospel. It is *living* the gospel. Whether one is talking about the message or the
means by which it is communicated, in Paul's mind both are governed by the
"treasure in earthen vessels" (cf. 2 Cor. 4:7). It is the precious gift of God conveyed to believers that is ours to communicate.

Paul Strove for Mastery (9:24–27)

Paul now draws upon a familiar scene to his Corinthian readers in order to drive home his point. The Isthmian games were an athletic event known to all of his readers and held on alternate summers within the vicinity of Corinth. The games were an event not to be missed by anyone of importance in all parts of Greece. As a national institution, it was as familiar to his readers as football in Dallas or baseball in Boston. He calls attention to the competitive edge required of those who participate. He says, "Do you not know . . . ?" (v. 24). He takes for granted that his readers understand the game rules. The most important rule is that while all run, only "one receives the prize" (v. 24). Paul's desire for his readers is that they receive the prize. He encourages them, "Run in such a way that you may win" (v. 24). No law demands that the runners strive to attain the crown. Why, then, do they run? They run because they are athletes. That is why they came there in the first place. And achieving their ultimate objective takes great sacrifice, dedication, and commitment.

"Everyone who competes in the games exercises self-control in all things" (v. 25). During the long days of preparation, the athlete is free in every respect, but if his intent is to win the crown (a celery wreath), he must restrict diet, activities, associations, and probably even friendships. The dedicated athlete "laid aside every weight"—for nothing more than temporal glory. But, counters the apostle, the "wreath" for which we strive is "imperishable." If temperance and self-discipline are important in the temporal realm, they are much more so in the spiritual.

"Therefore I run in such a way"—that is, like the athletes in verse 25—"as not without aim" (v. 26; this term, *adelos*, appears only here in the New Testament). Paul does not run as one who has no specific objective. Then as now, there was an appreciation for the importance of *mission*. Someone has well said that if you aim at nothing you will hit it every time! If we are to accomplish anything in life, we will have to use goals and strategies to get us there. We saw this kind of preplanning in 2:1–5, where Paul explained that the content and style of his preaching were crafted in keeping with his objective to see to it that their "faith should not rest on the wisdom of men, but on the power of God."

Paul now changes his metaphor to that of a boxer. "I box in such a way, as not beating the air" (v. 26). He does not swing wildly without hitting his target. To reach this level of proficiency in the gospel ministry he explains, "I buffet my body and make it my slave" (v. 27). Paul's Corinthian readers knew that in the Isthmian games, the boxers wore gloves made of ox-hide bands covered with knots and nails and loaded with lead and iron. To prepare for such an event, a man would have to steel himself against all forms of physical abuse.

In his final reflection on this extended analogy, Paul expresses a chilling concern: "lest possibly, after I have preached to others, I myself should be disqualified." It is unlikely that the apostle intends to associate himself here with the herald at the Grecian games whose task it is to proclaim the rules and to summon the competitors to their places. It is more likely that he drops the metaphor now and applies it to the main subject at hand. The reason he, in effect, restrains himself so—sacrificing even his essential Christian liberties— is that he might never reach the point where he is disqualified to run. Again, this expression must not be construed to suggest that Paul was afraid of losing his salvation. His subject is still Christian liberty, and his point is that sometimes the mature Christian will have to restrict himself for the sake of the work. And the fearful reality is that if one is not careful and does not commit to a disciplined lifestyle, he or she could be taken out of the game. For a true athlete, the only thing worse than losing is not being able to play at all. This anticipates the next chapter.

Study Questions

1. In Paul's running series of questions (vv. 1–10), is he bragging and swinging his weight around, or is he making a legitimate point that the Corinthian church needs to hear?

2. In this series of questions, what kind of problem do you think the Corinthians had with the apostle?

3. Is Paul, the servant of the Lord, being materialistic in verse 11? Why or why not?

4. Explain how Paul summarizes his point in verses 12–14.

5. In verses 15–17, list the ways Paul shows he is sold out to giving forth the gospel.

6. In verses 19–21, for what reason does the apostle "adjust" himself down to where people are living?

7. Would Paul place himself back under the Law to please the Jews? Explain what he means by verse 20.

8. In verse 22 is Paul referring to moral weakness? Why or why not?

9. What drove Paul to be so committed to the gospel, as he explains in verses 24–27?

10. In verse 27 is the apostle speaking of the loss of personal salvation?

CHAPTER 13

Concerning Christian Liberty: The Practice
1 Corinthians 10:1–11:1

Preview:

Drawing from the negative example of the Israelites who fell into idolatry and were eventually banished to the wilderness because of their sin, Paul challenges the Corinthian believers to better things. The Table of the Lord is a sacred place where believers enter into communion with Christ and one another. Participation with the festivals of idols is communion with demons and is disallowed. Association with idols does not contaminate the meat, but we must be careful in the exercise of our liberty that we not offend Jews, Greeks, or the Church.

Paul concludes his discourse on Christian liberty with an admonition to beware of temptation and unbelief (vv. 1–13), to be conscious of the association of pagan feasts with demons and idolatry (vv. 14–22), and to be guided by the principles of thankfulness and expediency (10:23—11:1). Throughout this discussion (8:1—11:1), the writer has threaded together two distinct arguments. The first is his *theological* argument. The second is a *social* and ecclesiological one. The theological argument is found in 8:4–6 and 10:1–22. The social argument is presented in 8:1–3 and 8:7—9:27. It is then rounded out in 10:23—11:1. The present chapter has two distinct sections. The first, contained in verses 1–22, brings Paul's theological argument to closure, while the second section anticipates potential objections from his readers. Paul answers these in a way that shows his agreement with their understanding of the principle of Christian liberty while at the same time showing that the principle of love will always override the exercise of one's liberty when another's spiritual welfare is at stake.[1]

The Theological Argument (10:1–22)

"For" (v. 1) connects what follows with what has gone before. Here it conveys the sense of "for this reason." Paul concluded chapter 9 with reference to the athlete as an example of the need for self-discipline. Like an athlete—even more so—the serious believer is characterized by self-denial, discipline, and commitment. Paul's use of "For" here leads to a reflection on a classic case of what happened in the experience of Israel when self-control was absent.

Life, Liberty, and the Pursuit of Happiness (10:1–13)

In America, the right to "life, liberty, and the pursuit of happiness" is a birthright bequeathed to us by our forefathers. Any challenge to the free exercise of these rights is generally viewed as an attack on our way of life and prerogatives as American citizens. It is probable that some of this same attitude prevailed in Corinth as seen in the emphasis throughout this section on the appropriate use of our Christian *exousia*. While Paul has many reasons (only some of which are developed here) for agreeing with this slogan in principle, he shows that it needs to be tempered by love and exercised with discretion. In this first section, he cites an example from the experience of Israel in the wilderness to show how the failure to understand this truth brought great calamity upon the nation.

The immediate connection is with the word, *adokimos* "disqualified," the next to last word of 9:27 in the Greek text. Israel refused to deny self, demanding the luxuries of Egypt, and so became a castaway in the desert. "I do not want you to be unaware" is one of Paul's favorite expressions introducing a matter of great importance (cf. Rom. 1:13; 11:25). "That matter is that our fathers were all under the cloud." The five "alls" in verses 1–4 emphasize the five downward moral steps of verses 5–10. The very same people who enjoyed great privilege from God also fell into serious apostasy from God. This also ties in with 9:24, "those who run in a race *all* run" (italics mine). Historically, in the case of Israel, all ran, but only Caleb and Joshua received the prize. The five privileges are enumerated as follows. (1) "Under the cloud" speaks of divine guidance and protection (cf. Num. 9:15–23; 14:14; Deut. 1:33; Ps. 78:14; Matt. 28:20). (2) "Passed through the sea" has reference to divine deliverance (cf. Ex. 14:15–22; 1 Pet. 1:18–20). (3) "All were baptized into Moses" (v. 2) is a nontechnical use of the term *baptism*. The people were immersed in Moses' authority. Thus, the expression speaks of divine leadership (cf. Ex. 14:31). (4) They "all ate the same spiritual food" (v. 3) refers to manna, spoken of in Psalm 78:25 as "the bread of angels." This evidenced divine provision. By employing the term "spiritual," Paul does not intend to imply that the manna was not literal food. It was clearly designed for physical nourishment (cf. Neh. 9:15; John 6:49). It was spiritual in the sense that it was supernaturally provided by the Spirit of God. (5) Likewise, "all drank the same spiritual drink" (v. 4). The water that was received from the rock was real water. It was spiritual in the sense that it was given through the divine intervention of God. They drank of the spiritual rock that followed them, and "The rock was Christ" (v. 4). Here Paul does not intend to advance an old Jewish fable that the rock that Moses smote actually was not part of the mountain but rolled after them during their journeys. The rock was not a theophany; rather, it was a "type" of Christ. It prefigured the provision that Christ would ultimately make for His people. But it also is intended to mean that the ultimate supply was Christ, not the rock. This spiritual Rock, even Christ, remained with them and followed them.

This passage is an impressive affirmation of the preexistence of Christ (cf. also v. 9; John 8:58; 12:41; Jude 1:5). In light of what follows, it is most probable that the expressions "spiritual meat" and "spiritual drink" are intended to be parallel with the elements employed in the Lord's Supper. "Nevertheless, with most of them God was not well-pleased" (v. 5). Divine privilege does not guarantee divine success. The evidence of this is that "they were laid low in the wilderness" (v. 5). Paul draws a pathetic picture of people, sated with providential privilege, paving the wilderness trail with their dead bodies (cf. Num. 14:29).

The five successive backward steps are now enumerated. "Now" (v. 6) introduces Paul's application of the preceding to the experience of his readers. "Examples" is the Greek *typoi*, meaning "type" or "example." Unless we are careful, the history of Israel will be duplicated in our own experience. The first step was that they "crave[d] evil things" (v. 6). Not satisfied with the manna supplied by the Lord, the people lusted after the fleshpots of Egypt. Because of their inordinate desire, while the meat was yet in their mouths, God struck them with a plague (cf. Num. 11:4, 33–34). The specific application to the Corinthians' situation is hard to miss. The pot roasts of Egypt were no more unclean than the prime ribs of Corinth. But what a terrible thought that meat could become an obstacle between God and His people.

The second step down is to substitute a graven image for the holy God. "Do not be idolaters, as some of them were" (v. 7). The illusion is to Exodus 32. Just as the Israelites considered that their golden calf was made in honor of Jehovah, many of the Corinthians considered the inordinate exercise of Christian liberty to be a celebration of their freedom in Christ.

The third step is "act immorally" (vv. 7–8). The evidence of idolatry was seen in that "the people sat down to eat and drink, and stood up to play." Sensual amusement was frequently associated in the pagan world with their feasts and idolatrous practices (see my comments on chapter 6). The association of immorality with idolatry is suitable here for another reason. Idolatry committed by Israel in the Old Testament is frequently viewed as "spiritual harlotry" (cf. Hosea). Spiritual defection always leads to moral defection. If this was symptomatic of the spiritual decay in Israel, it was more so in Corinth (cf. 5:1–5). Allowing immorality to persist in their assembly, they were no different than their neighbors who worshiped the goddess. Again, the same truth holds today. When people, even Christians, substitute anything for God, the results are the same. "Twenty-three thousand fell in one day" (v. 8) is not a mistake. In Numbers 25:9, the total number of people who died is given as "24,000." The discrepancy may be accounted for in at least two ways. The actual figure may be midway between 23,000 and 24,000; hence, in each case the figure is rounded off. Or it could simply be that Paul refers to the number slain in one day while Numbers refers to the total number of those who died. In any case, the precise number is only given in approximate terms.

The fourth step down is to "try the Lord" (v. 9; cf. Num. 21:4–9; Ps. 78:19). This, in effect, is having an attitude of skepticism toward the possibility that God would discipline them for their sins. The exhortation is that we should not provoke the forbearance of God. If it comes as especially obnoxious that some of the Corinthians had to give up their better cuts of meat for the cause of the gospel, let them remember from whence they were delivered. To become overly concerned about temporal desires is to forget the great spiritual blessings they enjoy. Anyone who doubts that God can and will exercise His option to punish sin should remember Israel and the fiery serpents.

The fifth step down is to "grumble" (v. 10), which implies a total rejection of divine leadership. The reference is to Numbers 16:41–50, but the attitude that prompted the situation is expressed in Numbers 14:4. The results are that they "were destroyed" (v. 10). The parallel situation and obvious admonition is seen in the Corinthians' attitude toward their leadership (that is, Paul). Nothing provokes the anger of God more than to chafe under the yoke that we share with Christ (cf. Matt. 11:29–30; 1 Cor. 3:9).

Paul summarizes with both an admonition and an encouragement. "Now these things happened to them as an example" (v. 11) emphasizes God's providential control over all the affairs of humans (cf. Gen. 50:20; Prov. 21:1). Even though the Israelites rebelled against God and subsequently received judgment because of their rebellion, God intended to use their experience for His own good. "And they were written for our instruction" (v. 11). The reason

God had Moses record the experiences of the children of Israel was because he had Paul and the Corinthian believers in mind. He knew that the future believers were going to face a similar crisis situation. And when that time came, the example of the children of Israel would provide a deterrent to sin and lead them to spiritual victory. "Ends of the ages" ("consummation of the ages") is for those living in the end times. The entire church age is contemplated in this expression. It was to be the final age before Christ's coming to establish His kingdom on earth.

Danger enters by way of two sinful attitudes: pride and presumption. "Therefore let him who thinks he stands [that is, the one who thinks himself to be the "wise" Christian who can exercise his Christian liberty at the expense of weaker brethren], take heed lest he fall" (v. 12). The fall is not a fall from salvation nor yet from a position of superiority over the supposed weak ones. Rather, it refers to falling as the Israelites fell "in the wilderness"—that is, the allusion is clearly to God's judgment.

"No temptation has overtaken you" (v. 13). The force of this word of encouragement is to help the readers see that the issues about which Paul is speaking are not as large as they make them out to be. The temptations they are facing are "common to man" (in the New Testament *anthropinos* occurs almost exclusively in this epistle). The trials we face are only normal problems (cf. also 2:4, 13; 4:3; Rom. 4:19 James 3:7; 1 Pet. 2:13). "And" (a mild adversative) in the context of those temptations "God is faithful." What great comfort Paul provides for his readers. If all around us are false, God is true. He is faithful, and our strength and security are in Him. "Beyond what you are able" (v. 13) may be read as a slight or simply as a truism. If the Corinthian believers are so taken up with their "right to choose," then Paul is saying to them, "You are perfectly capable of doing this—it is not that difficult!" Or, perhaps he is merely speaking the obvious. In any event, Paul is encouraged for two reasons. First, his readers can rely on the wisdom of God. And second, God will "provide the way of escape" (v. 13). In early Greek, this was a nautical term that had the sense of a landing place. The idea is not that God will enable us to escape temptation, but that He will enable us to land safely on the other side victorious. Often the only escape is "to endure" (cf. James 1:12 but also 1 Cor. 6:7).

Ordinarily we interpret this verse to have reference to temptations that test our limits in the extreme. We make the verse say something that is not really there. We use it to create an illusion that the war against Satan and temptation is no problem at all. God, we are told, will never cause us to go up against something that we are not eminently qualified to face. And when life throws things at us that are overwhelming, we wonder why our experience doesn't seem to match our understanding of this verse. Some even lose heart.

The truth is that "our struggle is not against flesh and blood, but against the rulers, against the powers, against the world forces of this darkness, against the spiritual *forces* of wickedness in the heavenly *places*" (Eph. 6:12). And it is not the case that God will prevent us from having to go up against these enemies. Rather, He has resourced us for just such an engagement:

> Stand firm therefore, having girded your loins with truth, and having put on the breastplate of righteousness, and having shod your feet with the preparation of the gospel of peace; in addition to all, taking up the shield of faith with which you will be able to extinguish all the flaming missiles of the evil *one*. And take the helmet of salvation, and the sword of the Spirit, which is the word of God. With all prayer and petition pray at all times in the Spirit, and with this in view, be on the alert with all perseverance and petition for all the saints. (Eph. 6:14–18)

Paul never trivializes our warfare with wickedness. What he has in mind in this text, however, has to do with the petty issues that often split churches—indeed, that have split this one. We know what these are because we deal with them every day. They are what he has called things that are "common to man." For the Corinthian believers it had to do with idol meat; for some churches we know, it has to do with the color of the carpet in the new sanctuary. These issues involve personal preferences that pit one believer against another. Concerning these, the writer says, you will not be tempted beyond "what you are able" (*dunamai*, "power"). The use of "power" suggests that it is within a believer's power to decide this. And if these conflicting believers will determine to find God's way through their trial, God will provide a "way of escape." Those who put aside their own personal agenda and seek the Lord will know how to find the way out of any dilemma posed by such conflicts.

Koinonia *without Compromise (10:14–22)*

Having shown the seriousness of abusing one's Christian liberty, the apostle now goes on to inform his readers that there is a direct correlation between heathen feasts and demonic activity. What follows in this paragraph is intended to bring Paul's theological argument to final expression. The instance of greatest contrast between Christ and Corinth may be seen in comparing their pagan feasts with the Table of the Lord. The flow of his argument may be seen in four principles.

Principle one: The greatest danger in the exercise of Christian liberty is the danger of falling into idolatry (vv. 14–15). "Therefore" (*dioper*, "for which very reason") appears only here and 1 Corinthians 8:13 (14:13 in some manuscripts). In light of God's judgment upon Israel, the writer warns, "flee from idolatry" (v. 14). These words have a triple significance. They contain a *concern*, because they are addressed to people whom Paul loved. They express a *command*. And they hint of a *consequence*, because in the exercise of their Christian liberty, the Corinthians are edging dangerously close to idolatry. The writer no doubt has in mind such texts as Exodus 32 and Judges 17. And he is able to recall, from the experience of the Jewish nation, all too painfully how easy it was for them to drift from the proper worship of God to the worship of the true God with idols and then to the worship of false gods.

"Wise men" (v. 15) is not intended to be read as irony. Not wishing to be authoritarian or dogmatic on this issue, Paul appeals to his readers' intelligence: "You judge what I say," that is, "Consider for a moment the logic of my argument."

Principle two: Participation in the Lord's Supper involves a mutual sharing of Christ (vv. 16–17). This is both a personal and a corporate reality. "Is not the cup . . . a sharing in the blood of Christ? Is not the bread which we break a sharing in the body of Christ?" (v. 16). Consider the Lord's Table. When a believer participates, he or she partakes of Christ's blood and His body, signifying a sharing in the benefits of Christ's saving work on Calvary. Thus, all those who come to the Lord's Supper enter into communion with one another. They form one body in virtue of their joint participation of Christ. And so Paul adds, "Since there is one bread, we who are many are one body; for we all partake of the one bread" (v. 17).

Principle three: Participation in a fellowship meal involves a mutual sharing of the altar (vv. 18–20). "Are not those who eat the sacrifices sharers in the altar?" (v. 18). When a sacrifice was brought to the altar, it was not entirely consumed. Rather, what was left was divided between the priest and the one who brought the offering (cf. Lev. 7:15; 8:31; Deut. 12:18). Thus, it became an act of mutual sharing and worship of God. Non-Jews therefore were forbidden to attend the sacrificial feasts of the Jews, for they involved mutual sharing and a joint worship of Jehovah. This passage must not be construed to indicate that the Lord's Supper is a sacrifice. The point of correspondence is not sacrifice, but communion.

"What do I mean then? That a thing sacrificed to idols is anything . . . ?" (v. 19). Paul anticipates the obvious rejoinder: "But Paul, you just said an idol was, in reality, nothing. Therefore, to worship an idol is to worship nothing. If one participates in fellowship with an idol, he would, in fact, participate in nothing. Paul's response is in effect: Yes, it is very true; an idol is nothing. But the demons behind the idol are very real. "The things which the Gentiles sacrifice, they sacrifice to demons, and not to God" (v. 20). What is of grave concern to the apostle is that behind the idols are fallen angels—evil spirits. This is in keeping with Deuteronomy 32:17 and Psalm 95:5. Since Paul has already established that these religious feasts involve fellowship with the altar, should the believers attend a heathen feast, they will be become "sharers in demons" (v. 20). And this was the last thing Paul hoped for his young converts at Corinth.

Principle four: It is not possible to participate simultaneously with the Table of the Lord and the table of demons (vv. 21–22). "You cannot drink the cup of the Lord and the cup of demons" (v. 21). It is not possible to be simultaneously related to the Lord and to demons. Paul does not merely suggest that this constitutes a logical contradiction; rather, it is as impossible as it is for a "house divided against itself" to stand (see Luke 11:14–23). We cannot expect that the Lord will allow this to continue. The consequences of this behavior have already been amply illustrated in the case of Israel. As a concluding statement, for those who have been following the progression of Paul's argument, Paul need not do more than ask a simple question: "Do we provoke the Lord to jealousy?" (v. 22). Unless they intend to provoke the greatest displeasure from the Lord, the Corinthians must be careful not to attend the heathen feasts. And imbedded in this argument is that they should do all they can to avoid mingling their newfound faith in Christ with the "fleshpots of Egypt." The libertarians in the church were already dangerously close to doing just this and, consequently, bringing upon themselves the sure judgment of God.

The Social Argument (10:23–11:1)

As noted above, the argument presented by Paul throughout this extended section (8:1—11:1) has a theological dimension and a social dimension. These two threads are woven into a fabric in which the writer presents his case, establishes his authority, appeals to the Corinthians' common faith and understanding, and calls them to a standard of action that paradoxically rises above the demand for rights and bows to the spiritual welfare of others. This standard is exemplified in Christ and the apostles and will be enjoined upon the Corinthian believers once again before Paul is finished.

In this concluding paragraph, Paul seems to introduce an entirely new situation. He established at the beginning in fairly general terms that he would address the matter of meat offered to idols. As the discussion unfolds, however, he seems to focus primarily on one rather egregious example of believers exercising their liberty to their own detriment and that of the believing body at large. Now he seems to switch gears and almost contradict what has gone before with the statement: "eat anything . . . without asking questions" (v. 25). Expositors have struggled to align this text properly with the earlier discussion. Some resolve the issue by simply suggesting that the writer is introducing a new topic.[2] This strategy bypasses the problem but does not eliminate it. We then have to bracket these verses from everything Paul has said about idol meat in the preceding section. And we create an even more serious problem with respect to the unity of the epistle as a whole. I have argued that these chapters must all be taken as a unit. Paul's message is cohesive from start to finish, and each chapter plays a crucial role in demonstrating why and how to correct misconceptions about the practice of Christian liberty.

Biblical Teachings on Idolatry
God's people are forbidden from making idols (Ex. 20:4).
God's people are not to make idols to the form of "anything" (Deut. 4:25).
God's people are not to make idols for "themselves" (Deut. 5:8).
God was angry with the idols of Israel (1 Kgs. 16:13).
There were to be no idols in the house (temple) of God (2 Chr. 33:15).
God "hates" those who give regard to meaningless idols (Ps. 31:6).
Idols are the gods of the nations (Ps. 96:5).
Idolatry is an issue of the heart (Ezek. 14:7).
Believers are to abstain from things contaminated by idols (Acts 15:20).
In reality, there is no such thing as an idol in this world (1 Cor. 8:4).
An idolater is as sinful as the most evil of sinners (1 Cor. 5:10; 6:9).
Believers are to flee from idolatry (1 Cor. 10:14).
Believers can be led astray by "dumb" idols (1 Cor. 12:2).
Greed is the same as lusting after idols (Col. 3:5).
Believers must guard themselves against idols (1 John 5:21).

I believe that the correct approach is to view these last few verses as a final statement of the matter. On the strength of his extended discussion, Paul now anticipates a range of possible objections to his admonition. These relate primarily to situations in which his guidelines do not seem to fit. The ethics of attending pagan feasts is a black and white issue. But what about the gray areas? Wouldn't eating idol meat in the privacy of my own home be permitted? And what about my obligations to a (theoretically) unsaved host who invites me to dinner? If these represent situations where Paul's general principle does not apply, then the force of Paul's argument throughout this section will be weakened. Since he anticipates these questions, he is compelled to respond. His approach, as he demonstrated earlier, is to "take the wind out of their sails"[3] by agreeing with the general principle of Christian liberty as it is defended by the "wise." But in his final denouement, he will show that the principle must always be tempered by our overriding obligations to "give no offense either to Jews or to Greeks or to the church of God" (v. 32). Here of course, he anticipates his classic soliloquy on love (chap. 13).

The section breaks into three units: the regulation (vv. 23–24), the application (vv. 25–30), and finally, the recapitulation (10:31—11:1).[4]

The Regulation (10:23-24)

In brief, the regulation is "All things are lawful" (v. 23). The reader should recognize this from 6:12, where the same general principle was established. The regulation has not changed. Everything is permitted, but it is still qualified by the caveat, "but not all things are profitable . . . not all things edify." This is inserted to regulate those cases in which the free exercise of the principle causes harm to others. In such cases, "Let no one seek his own *good*, but that of his neighbor" (v. 24). In cases where one law conflicts with the other, the rule is that "obligation outweighs permission."[5]

The Application (10:25-30)

Two types of situation are discussed in applying the principle. Verses 25–27 establish that if a believer purchases food in the marketplace, where it is probable that it comes from the temple, there is no reason on that account to ask questions "for conscience' sake." If all things are lawful, then to concede that idol meat has been somehow contaminated by the association with idols is to concede that the idol has properties that we all know it does not have. The same principle holds true when the believer is invited to a meal at the home of an unbeliever. There is absolutely no reason "for conscience' sake" to ask any questions.

"Meat market" (*makello*, a Latin term used only here in the New Testament, refers to the "market"). Usually only part of the animal used for sacrifice was consumed. The rest was given to the priest or sold again in the market. Anyone might therefore unknowingly purchase meat offered to idols. Concerning such purchases, Paul's advice is to "eat anything that is sold . . . without asking questions for conscience' sake" (v. 25). Your conscience need not be exercised on this account. Going back to the original discussion, the idol is nothing; therefore, it can have no intrinsic effect upon the meat. While it is wrong to go to the heathen feast and to participate with demons in idolatrous worship, once the meat has been disassociated from that gathering, there is no reason why it cannot be eaten without scruples.

The second type of situation, however, yields a different response (vv. 28–30). If a believer is sharing a meal with someone and that person or someone else ("for conscience' sake") raises the concern of whether the meat has been sacrificed to an idol, then the response must be sensitive to the possibility of causing harm to that one who raised the question. The correct response is to relinquish one's right to eat, not because the act is thereby deemed to be wrong, but because the act of knowingly doing something that injures another person is wrong.

The question naturally arises, "Why is my freedom judged by another's conscience?" (v. 29). This is a legitimate question. The answer is: "I partake with thankfulness" (v. 30; KJV "grace"). "Thankfulness" here is used in the sense of thanksgiving. We use it today when we speak of "saying grace" before a meal. It is illogical to give thanks to God for something that will cause slander. His point here is that even my eating (or not eating) is an act of worship. I receive (with thanksgiving) from God's good hand. And I respond in appropriate ways to demonstrate a right attitude toward God for His supply—hence the admonition that follows.

The Recapitulation (10:31–11:1)

Here Paul summarizes his entire discussion on idol meat and related issues in three concise exhortations.[6] The first admonition is "Whatever you do, do all to the glory of God" (v. 31). We fail in the proper exercise of Christian liberty if in the process we do not bring glory to God (see also Col. 3:17; 1 Pet. 4:11).

Then Paul exhorts, "Give no offense either to Jews or to Greeks or to the church of God" (v. 32). This quite adequately covers everyone on the earth. The reason for this is the same as that for which Paul earlier said he was all things to all people: "That they may be saved" (v. 33). "Why should I go about offending people in the name of Christian liberty and unnecessarily causing them to repudiate the gospel?" (cf. also 9:22). While it is incidental to his argument here, it is important to note that in Paul's thinking there are distinctions to be made between the lost (Greeks), Israel (Jews), and the believers of this age (the Church of God). We will do well to maintain this distinction in evaluating the New Testament teaching regarding the present and future destinies of each.

The final admonition is "Be imitators of me, just as I also am of Christ" (11:1). The bottom line on the discussion of Christian liberty is the example of Christ as He is reflected in the Apostle Paul. The ultimate standard is Christ, and insofar as Paul is following Him, Paul is able to say to the Corinthian believers, "Be imitators of me."

To summarize then, in this section on Christian liberty, Paul is eager to lead his assembly to maturity under grace. The Christian life is not governed by legalism, yet this does not justify license. The best example of how Christian liberty works is Jesus Christ. In Him we see ultimate sacrifice and supernatural love. And every act is to be judged by His standard.

Study Questions

1. Why does Paul bring up the story of the Jewish fathers passing through the sea by God's leading?

2. How does that Old Testament generation stand as an example for us today?

3. What lessons is Paul trying to get across to the Corinthian church?

4. By what Paul says in verses 1–12, what can we learn about the morality of this assembly?

5. From verse 14, could Paul's exhortation indicate that some of the Corinthian believers were flirting with idolatry?

6. In the context of writing about idolatry, why does the apostle bring up the issue of the Lord's Supper?

7. What would cause us to believe that the Corinthian Christians were confused about the Lord's Supper in relation to some of their pagan idolatrous practices in the past?

8. What does Paul have in mind when he writes that he pleases "all men" (v. 33)?

CHAPTER 14

Concerning Worship
1 Corinthians 11:2–34

Preview:

Having introduced the matter of Christian worship in the previous chapter, Paul now expands on this to address two major concerns. The first has to do with the reverent recognition of the order of authority as God has established it. The second has to do with the proper observance of the Lord's Supper. In the context of worldliness, Paul warns his readers of the seriousness of violating this sacred meal.

Having established that Christian worship is sacred and that its practice is not to be confused or mingled with pagan rites, the apostle now turns his attention to a number of issues related to what Christian worship entails and how it is to be conducted.[1] This chapter is pivotal because it establishes the main topic of conversation for the next several chapters. While we will be dealing with them separately, the issues of gender, the Lord's Supper, spiritual gifts, love, tongues, and prophecy are all grouped by Paul under a general discussion of worship.[2]

There is much to commend this discussion to those assigned to leadership in our contemporary churches. That the passage is relevant today is evident by the very fact that the reader is already charged with predispositions about what I mean by *contemporary*. In recent years, most churches have had to make a choice as to which "worship style" they were going to adopt—traditional or contemporary. It reminds me of the question servers at our local chicken restaurant ask: "Do you want traditional or crispy?" In our family we always want both. And most church families want both kinds of worship—

not just one or the other. We would rather have people focus on what binds us together in Christ than to insist on a mode of expression—whether it be labled new or old—that separates us. We intuitively understand that there is something wrong if and when worship divides God's people.

Since Paul does not begin with his characteristic expression, "Now concerning" (*peri de*), it is possible that this chapter falls into the category of unsolicited advice. Perhaps in their letter to Paul the Corinthian believers alluded to some of their public worship practices. Or perhaps Paul's discussion of worship practices in the previous chapter prompted him to speak directly to the issue. If his instruction here flows from what has gone before, then he would be expressing concerns about pagan practices creeping into the worship of the church. In that regard we may well wonder if some of the meat sacrificed to idols was being brought to their eucharistic meals. If so, it is no wonder some were offended. And is it possible that the rulings regarding women in the worship service are largely due to inordinate associations they might bring with fertility cults and immoral practices associated with the pagan feasts? If this were the case, then a modern appropriation of Paul's counsel would lead us in the direction of modesty, respect for biblical authority, and the exclusion of worldly influences in our communal worship.

If what Paul offers in this chapter links to what follows, then we would view chapter 11 as the foundation for Paul's subsequent teaching regarding the practice of spiritual gifts, the exercise of love, and the discernment of the Holy Spirit. Deference to Christian tradition and reverent observance of the Lord's Supper would be seen as inducements to unity and loving participation with one another in the giving and receiving of diverse ministries associated with the gifts of the Spirit. If this were the case, then a proper application of this important teaching would lead us in a slightly different direction. We would want to maintain a high sensitivity to those influences that would disrespect the central expression of worship or that would tend to divide the body by failure to respect or appreciate *all* the gifts of the body—regardless of one's gender, generation, or socioeconomic status.

A third way of thinking about this text is to see both a backward reference *and* a forward look as forming a "full court press." That is, Paul is not simply drawing from previous discussion to wrap it up. Nor is he beginning a new topic merely to lay a foundation for what follows. Rather, the inclusion of this discussion in the middle of his epistle already tells us that it is rooted in the first ten chapters and serves to form a vital link to what follows. This is my preference, because it honors the unity of the epistle and it offers the greatest help to those who would attempt to understand and apply these teachings in a local setting. It becomes incumbent on the modern interpreter, then, to consider all of the imbedded challenges to our contemporary situation in attempting to resolve these and similar issues today.

The discussion breaks naturally into two related paragraphs. The first is contained in verses 2–16, dealing with appropriate behavior in the worship service. Specifically, Paul raises the issue of gender and the need for proper recognition and display of God's order of authority. The second section is contained in verses 17–34, with instruction concerning the ordinance of the Lord's Supper and worship. Here Paul expresses his dismay at their inordinate behavior and challenges them to do better.

Respect for Authority (11:2–16)

The very concept of authority structures is alien to many modern societies. Those in our own culture who attempt to apply biblical standards for home, church, and the workplace often find themselves under severe attack from the PC-police for daring to defy their secular ideals. In this challenging time, with Paul, we are called upon to destroy "speculations and every lofty thing raised up against the knowledge of God, and *we* [must take] every thought captive to the obedience of Christ" (2 Cor. 10:5). We must be careful to avoid the temptation to interpret Scripture according to cultural bias. Every thought must be subjected to the objective teaching of God's Word. Today we live in a technological age that has abandoned traditional and biblical values for family, vocation, and morality. Most people in our culture uncritically accept a litany of modern myths—birthed in secularism, atheism, Darwinism, and materialism—according to which this age is directed.

These include, first, *the myth of equality*. Any thought that is viewed as being in noncompliance with accepted egalitarian doctrine is attacked and styled as paternalism, bigotry, or sexism. When the Bible is understood to teach specific social roles within a cohesive social structure (such as family, church, and community), its teachings are abandoned in favor of the principles of radical individualism and socialism. The *myth of freedom* is another modern myth. For many in the twenty-first century, freedom means that each person is responsible only to himself or herself. Virtue, duty, and responsibility to God, family, country and established authorities have been abandoned. The *myth of self-fulfillment* teaches us to begin with the *self* as the center of the universe. Each person is obligated to find his or her fulfillment in self-expression. Such radical egocentrism runs roughshod over the biblical principles of servanthood and sacrifice. The *myth of authenticity* emphasizes the importance of each person acting out and upon his or her personal feelings: "If it feels good," we are instructed, "do it." On the contrary, the Bible teaches that we must do what is right, regardless of how we feel about it. Finally, there is the *myth of personhood*. This has come to be used in recent decades to define the very essence of humanity. Those who have limited or no ability to express themselves or who are unwanted and thus have no chance of achieving their potential are defined as nonpersons. This doctrine is being used to justify policies of euthanasia, abortion, and selective breeding.

Due to these and other faulty ideas propagated by the "worldly wise" of our age, people are living in lonely isolation, frustrated by the failure of the world to make good on its promises. Emotional support structures of family and community are gone. Relationships between parents and children have been stretched to the breaking point. Fathers are increasingly marginalized in their families while wives and mothers are seduced into a workforce evermore driven by marketplace demands. Children are shuffled off to day care and dependent parents are tucked away in nursing homes. All the while the propaganda machine pumps out slogans to the weary workers to convince them that they will be successful and happy so long as they continue to support the system and consume its products.

While these myths abound in our modern world, in many ways they are reflective of ideas at least as old as Paul and the text of 1 Corinthians. The names on some of the idols may have changed, but the idols of sex, materialism, and self-indulgence have been around since long before the writing of this epistle. As we unpack this chapter, we will see that it is as relevant today as it was to its first readers.

Central to Paul's response to these issues is recognition of divine authority along with the structures and dynamics God has established to guide believers on a broad range of issues. The structures are developed in reference to the home, church, worship (chap. 11), relationships, and ministry (chaps. 12—14). The dynamics of all of these are quantified by love in action (chap. 13). As noted above, Paul uses this discussion to draw his instruction regarding the church and the outside world to a close, and to open the topic of internal church matters. We could say that the earlier section of this letter was Paul's *critical* phase, while the latter section is his *constructive* phase. He begins by showing that God's authority has a structure to it that is rooted in the very character of God and His creative work. This structure needs to be recognized in both the church and in human relationships in general.

A General Introduction (11:2)

"Now" (v. 2) indicates the transition to a new subject. "I praise you." It is always a good practice to use a compliment to soften the blow of a rebuke.

And so it is that Paul explains, "because you . . . hold firmly to the traditions, just as I delivered them to you" (v. 2). Earlier, Paul used this device to introduce critical concerns in much the same way (cf. 1:4–5). There is a play on the words "traditions" (*paradosis*) and "delivered" (*paradidomi*). Both are derived from the Greek term meaning "to give over." The sense is this: "What has been handed down has been given over to you." In saying this, the writer is letting them know that his teaching is not a novelty—it is the same thing he received (from the other apostles and from Christ; Acts 9). This body of truth has been hand-delivered without modification.[3]

"But" (v. 3) is adversative. "I want you to understand" is probably not intended as ironic, but it is difficult not to miss the irony of the situation. The Corinthians prided themselves in their knowledge, yet it is their knowledge that Paul repeatedly finds deficient. Harold Holmyard III correctly notes that Paul's "praise functions as a preface more than an integral part of 11:3–34, because both verses 3–16 and verses 17–34 negatively qualify it."[4] So Paul is not complimenting the Corinthians on their observance of either of these issues. Rather, he is likely complimenting them on their attention to the traditions, but having said that, there are still some problems. The first issue requiring a corrective relates to the principle of headship governing the structure of authority in the believing community. The second relates to the observance of the Lord's Supper. Both appear to relate to situations that have come up when the church was gathered for prayer, exhortation, and worship.[5]

The Principle of Headship Established (11:3–6)

Paul develops this subject in two ways. First, he states the principle of headship (vv. 2–6). Then be defends the principle from Scripture and nature (vv. 7–16).

"Christ is the head of every man" (v. 3). In later epistles, Paul defends this truth by showing that Christ is the head of the body, which is the church (Eph. 1:22–23; Col. 1:18). "Man" is not to be taken as generic here, since it is followed with "The man is the head of a woman" (v. 3). This constitutes the fundamental order in the race. That this is absolute, rather than culturally contingent, is evident by its correspondence to the Godhead. "God is the head of Christ" (v. 3). This concept of headship cannot suggest qualitative or essential difference, since the prototype is seen in the Persons of the Trinity. It connotes a functional responsibility, not inferiority and/or superiority. The Father and Christ are coequal, yet the Son is obedient to the Father (cf. John 6:38–40; 10:29–30; 14:9; 1 Cor. 15:28; Phil. 2:6). It is unfortunate that Paul has been so misunderstood on this. Those who would challenge the appropriateness of his injunction are forced to challenge the nature of God Himself. What is in view here has to do with function, not essence.[6] For example, the Son, who is coequal with God the Father, was uniquely called to be "obedient to the point of death" (Phil. 2:8).

Having established that there is an inherent continuity between the relationships of the persons of the Trinity and between men and women, Paul considers that it is appropriate for some recognition of this to be given. And when this is done properly, there will be a difference between a man and a woman in the way it is expressed. Since it constitutes the order of authority, the symbol should show how this authority flows from the Creator God to those with whom it is shared.

The use of the term "head" (v. 3) signals that the writer is talking about hierarchical relationships. Christ answers to God, the man answers to Christ, and the woman answers to the man. Those who argue for the notion that the Greek term *kephale* denotes "source" and not "subordination" introduce a linguistic innovation unknown to the use of this term in ancient literature.[7] We do not argue that the notion of source is absent from Paul's argument (cf. vv. 7–10). Rather, source (in creation) becomes an argument for subordinate relations on which he then elaborates. C. K. Barrett, who recognizes the idea of "origin" in the text, notes in relation to God and Christ that "the Son is what he is in relation to the Father. There can be no doubt that Paul taught a form of . . . subordinationism; see further iii. 23; xv. 28. . . . The Son would no longer be the kind of Son we know him to be if he ceased to be obedient to and dependent on the Father."[8] Paul wants them to know that this same kind of authority structure exists between the man and his wife.

We limit the discussion here to husbands and wives since there is no evidence that the ancient cultures of the Mediterranean imposed this obligation on young unmarried girls.[9] Paul certainly could not be saying that all these girls should be shaved if they don't wear the covering. It is also unlikely that this covering compares to the full veil of contemporary Muslim cultures. This appears not to have been required in the Roman Empire. Some see the Greek term *peribolaion* (v. 15; "that which is thrown around," "shawl"), as indicative of the kind of covering that was expected (see also this term in 1 Tim. 6:8).[10]

In verse 4 the apostle builds on his basic axiom of headship and shows how it relates to the custom of wearing a head covering. What he shows is that the head covering is appropriate for a woman but not for a man. The writer's rhetorical skill emerges once again as he elaborates on this truth with a "running pun":[11] "Every man that prays or prophesies while having (something) on (his) head [literal] shames his 'head' [figurative, i.e., Christ]; but every (married) woman that prays or prophesies with head [literal] uncovered (*akatakalupto*) shames her 'head' [figurative, i.e., her husband], for it is the same thing as her being shaved."[12]

The observance is crucial to Paul because the "disgrace" is directed upward. The man who would violate this (perhaps in following the practice of men covering their heads in pagan worship settings)[13] would disgrace their Head, namely, Christ. To fail to observe this proper order would be tantamount to challenging the Trinitarian relation in the Godhead. Women failing to do so would disgrace their husbands. It is wrong for precisely the opposite reason that it is wrong for the man. The covering is symbolic, indicating the authority that exists above the woman yet still under Christ—the authority of the man. Whether used by the woman or not used by the man, the significance is the same. It is a concrete and culturally acceptable recognition of the authority structures established by God according to which He directs His will and receives worship from His spiritual children. The covering would seem to represent the authority standing above the individual on the way *toward* addressing God in prayer or communicating truth *from* God in prophecy.

A further assertion of this verse is that women prophesied and prayed in public worship. Since Paul does not qualify this in any special way, it may be assumed that the ministry of these women involved the revelatory gift[14] appropriate to a prophet in the technical sense. Apparently this did not constitute a point of contention, since the apostle does not feel obligated to speak directly to it. The only point to be noted here is that when a woman did so, she was to have her head covered. (Regarding women with the gift of prophecy, see also Joel 2:28–32; Luke 2:36; Acts 2:17–18; 21:9.) It is important here to distinguish this important function from that which is ordinarily associated with pastoral authority and ministry. The reference here is to a genuine prophetic gift ("prophetess").

This is an issue that often takes on the aspect of Jesus' contention with the Pharisees when they caught Him and the disciples picking and eating grain on the Sabbath day (Mark 2:23–28). The Pharisees were so tangled up in their effort to keep the letter of the Law that they missed the point—that "the Sabbath was made for man, and not man for the Sabbath." The point here is the deference to authority and the appropriate symbolic (or concrete) recognition of that. In the ancient world, this covering was rather substantial. Today it may be associated with a little cap or perhaps a more elaborate head covering prescribed by some. It has, unfortunately, been totally trivialized in most Protestant churches as no longer having any obligatory significance to women in modern society. The proper biblical approach is somewhere between the two extremes of legalism and neglect. The covering is not a legal prescription. It represents an outward voluntary demonstration of respect for God's order and authority. When it is said to include those who "prophesy," it refers to those women who have a direct role in the service. When it speaks of those who only "pray," it designates all the rest of the women in the service. There are only two types of participants in the worship service—those (men and women) who exercise their various gifts of proclamation, exhortation, and so on, and those (men and women) who pray. It is important with respect to the "prophetess" that she speak with authority that is *not usurped* (cf. 2 Tim. 2:12), but *delegated* by Christ through the man—her husband and/or the elders of the church. By wearing the covering she shows that she is not taking the place of the male leadership—she is simply (and reverently) exercising her spiritual gift. We need to qualify this with one additional caveat. The delegation of this authority must not be taken to suggest that a person (man or woman) may be delegated to ministry forbidden by God (for example, when someone does not meet the qualifications of 1 Tim. 3). This is not a backdoor access to legitimate what God has not also ordained.

On this point, one must also be careful not to create a contradiction with 1 Corinthians 14:34–37. As noted above, I disagree with those who suggest that the context of this chapter does not apply to a formal worship service in contrast to that of chapter 14.[15] Here the context is public worship in general and the protocol for those gifted and directed to speak. The context of 1 Corinthians 14 is less clear. It may have to do with disruptive behavior, or it may be that the latter text is given to limit the exercise of the gift of tongues. At any rate, it is important to observe that the injunction that women are to "keep silence in the churches" must be interpreted in balance with other texts, such as this one, that legitimated their speaking out—even authoritatively—when it was done according to correct order (see also 1 Tim. 2:9–15; 5:2–16; and related passages). More will be said of this later.

The writer continues, "For if a woman does not cover her head, let her also have her hair cut off; but if it is disgraceful for a woman to have her hair cut off or her head shaved, let her cover her head" (v. 6). Perhaps the argument here is a *reductio ad absurdum*,[16] that is, the uncovering of the woman in the context being discussed might as well, in the extreme, be put in the category of shaving one's head entirely. If this is the case, the verses that follow would fit well with his argument. That is to say, it is only "natural" that women cover their heads.[17]

This is not a point of indifference to the apostle; it is a serious matter. A woman participating in the worship of the church with her head uncovered is tantamount to going out in public with her head shaven. In Corinth it was not uncommon for prostitutes and loose women to shave their heads—sometimes this might have been done as punishment. These would often wear elaborate wigs and could be easily identified in a crowd. So Paul is suggesting shamefulness in the extreme. The force of his words is poignant. Just as no respectable Christian woman would go out in public with the appearance of a prostitute, it is important that she not participate in public worship unless she wear a covering to show respect for her husband who is understood to be her authority under Christ.

The Principle of Headship Defended (11:7–16)

Having established the principle of headship, Paul then goes on to validate this teaching from Scripture (vv. 7–12) and from nature (vv. 13–16). It is evident too that as he develops his argument further, he moves away from "husbands" and "wives" in particular to a more general reference to men and women in general. He also draws a distinction between the principle and the custom by which it is expressed. This will become important as we consider its application to the church today.

"For a man ought [*opheilo*] not to have his head covered, since he is the image and glory of God; but the woman is the glory of man" (v. 7). The point here is not that the man is "less than" God (although that is true) and therefore obligated to observe this practice, but rather that he stands in God's image as a display of His "glory." The same must be said of the related expression for the woman. It is not that she is "less than" the man, but that having come "from" him, she is a display of his "glory." Of course, as Genesis 1:26–27 teaches, just as the original (man), so the copy (woman)—both are understood as being in God's image.

The order of creation also supports Paul's position. "For man does not originate from woman, but woman from man; for indeed man was not created for the woman's sake, but woman for the man's sake" (vv. 8–9)—chronologically, she comes after. Constitutionally, she was made "for the man's sake" (cf. Gen. 2:20–24). The only time God said of his creation that it was "not good" (Gen. 2:18) was when the man existed "alone." It was for his sake that she was brought forth to complement and complete him. Paul begins with reference to Genesis 1:26 but then moves to Genesis 2. It is noteworthy that he does not draw from Genesis 3 or 6. The order of which he speaks was established at the very beginning. There are some today who suggest that the so-called authority of the man is part of the curse upon the woman. This cannot be sustained since the truth is derived from the account of creation, not the fall. So Barrett concludes, "Thus as Adam was brought forth directly from God, and was made for his sole service, so the woman was brought forth from man, and was intended from the beginning to be his helper. In that sense therefore in which man is the glory of God, she is the glory of man, deriving her being from man, and finding her fulfillment in serving him."[18]

"Therefore the woman ought *[opheilo]* to have *a symbol of* authority on her head" (v. 10). The language of obligation (cf. v. 7) is once again employed to speak to the woman. This is significant since the term bespeaks the responsibility or moral duty of the person to act freely (see Rom. 1:14; 4:4; 8:12; 13:7; 1 Cor. 7:3; Gal. 5:3). This does not mean that the injunction to wear a covering is relativized, but that those who do so are enjoined to obedience as moral *agents*. "Symbol" is in italics indicating that it is supplied by the translators. The result, however, in taking the expression this way is that the ordinary meaning of *exousia* is reversed. That is, the symbol becomes not one of authority but of submission. For this reason I do not consider this to be the proper sense of the text. The language here simply asserts that "the woman has authority over her head." This seems to me to be fairly unambiguous. Having already said that she "ought" to wear a covering, he now instructs that this is a matter over which she has personal control. It is an opportunity for her to demonstrate "her faithfulness to her husband or . . . her status."[19] Submission comes from the heart and is reflected in a person's behavior. Peter understood this when he instructed the women to concentrate on the display of the "hidden person of the heart, with the imperishable quality of a gentle and quiet spirit, which is precious in the sight of God" (1 Pet. 3:4). So this is not merely a perfunctory observance that is instructed. It is obligatory upon the woman as *agent* to exercise her will in a free demonstration of godly submission.

"Therefore" (*dia touto*) in verse 10 indicates that the writer is now drawing a conclusion from the preceding discussion. The reason for this injunction is "because of the angels." To those of us who are outside of Paul's context, the reference has caused no small amount of confusion and speculation. Yet, to the readers, it seems to have been clearly understood. We know they were still confused on a number of points in this first epistle—requiring the writer to come back in subsequent letter(s) to give further explanation (see introduction). But this does not appear to have been one of the questions on their list—or his. Explanations of this text range from speculations about the need to protect women from evil angels lusting after their beauty, to gnostic influences,[20] to guardian angels who are actively worshiping together with the saints.

In fact, the significance of the expression may be little more than a circumlocution for the "presence of God." The reference is clearly not to evil spirits, but to the holy angels who elsewhere in the New Testament are spoken of as "ministering spirits" (cf. Heb. 1:14). Paul was conditioned by his Jewish roots and, as any devout Hebrew to this day, he was scrupulous about taking God's name in vain. This cultural practice is seen in the Gospels where the "kingdom of *God*" (cf. Luke) in a Gentile context comes to be labeled the "kingdom of *Heaven*" in a Jewish setting (cf. Matthew). Understood in this way, it becomes an additional argument for the fact that he is talking about a formal gathering of the church here—not some other type of gathering.[21] In the "presence of God," there should be a sacred recognition of the order God has established for His creation. Here in the presence of the angels there is no place for insubordination. Of course one can still imagine that the angels would have an interest in this (cf. 1 Pet. 1:12). The angels who have their very existence in God's presence are also present whenever the congregation meets together to worship the Lord (cf. 1 Cor. 4:9; Eph. 3:10; 1 Tim. 5:21). The failure of women to cover their heads would be an offense committed in the very presence of God.

Finally, Paul closes his argument with an appeal for balance and understanding. Lest his readers understand this distinction in a qualitative sense, he adds, "However, in the Lord, neither is woman independent of man, nor is man independent of woman" (v. 11). Both are mutually dependent upon each other. The expression "in the Lord" has the sense of "according to the will and purpose of the Lord." Neither can exist without the other. We consider the suggestion by some to associate this with so-called "mutual subordination" drawn from a misunderstanding of Ephesians 5:21, to be unwarranted here and in the context of Ephesians where the point is clearly that the principle of subordination has "structure." It does not teach that this structure is somehow vitiated by our shared relationship in Christ. If that were Paul's understanding, one wonders why he would spend so much time talking about it here.

"So also the man has his birth through the woman" (v. 12) is added to establish a balance. The principle of submission is supported by the order of creation. The principle of mutual dependency is supported by the order of procreation. In Genesis 2 the woman came out of the man. In Genesis 4:1 the man came out of the woman. So have all men since. This is a corollary of the previous declaration that woman was created "for man." It is not simply the case that she was created, as it were, to serve his every whim. Rather, the very continued existence of the man depends on the woman and her voluntary submission to this role. In the final analysis, of course "all things originate from God" (v. 12). With this the writer reminds us that this is precisely the order that God has established. It is not ours to remake or destroy in the interest of modern visions of human ecology.

In verse 13 Paul returns to his principle of headship and asks, "Is it proper?" ("Is it becoming?"). One's natural sense of propriety dictates that a woman pray with her head covered. "Nature itself" (v. 14) speaks of "the recognized constitution of things." "If a man has long hair, it is a dishonor to him" (v. 14) is a difficult passage to understand—especially in a culture where nature does not seem to dictate it. It cannot mean that nature naturally grows short hair on men and long hair on women, since we know this is not the case either—perhaps he should have said *no hair* on some men! Several factors must be considered. First, the context: Paul is talking about differentiating between the sexes. When he uses the verb *komao*, "to wear long hair," he has in mind long hair like that of a woman. It cannot be said that he has in mind a specific kind of haircut. He is simply saying that it is shameful for a man to wear his hair in an effeminate way. As Barrett also comments, the "horror of homosexuality" is no doubt also in the background here.[22] What nature dictates is that men and women naturally differentiate themselves in obvious ways—hairstyles being one of them.

Another factor has to do with culture. In Paul's experience, he knew of no culture, whether Hebrew, Greek, or Roman, that did not consider long hair a disgrace to a man. The only exception to this rule was the Nazirite (Num. 6:5; and Ezek. 44:20). Thus, to Paul it was significant that worldwide cultures naturally emerged with the same sense of propriety regarding long hair on men. The same principle holds true today. The vast majority of cultures regard effeminacy of hair and dress as distasteful and shameful to a man. "But if a woman has long hair, it is a glory to her[.] For her hair is given to her for a covering" (v. 15). The logic is obvious. In the natural order of things, human cultures the world over have universally observed this convention. "Whether or not this corresponds with modern scientific observation, it would certainly correspond with Paul's observation, as study of Hellenistic portraiture will confirm."[23]

This is not to say, incidentally, that the additional covering is unnecessary. That would contradict everything he has already said on the subject. Since (as he has observed) everyone recognizes that it is shameful for women to shave their heads and that it is natural for them to wear their hair as they do, Paul would have had no reason to bring this up if that is all he wanted to say. Rather, the discussion underscores his argument that the covering is appropriate because it is evident from experience that it is universally recognized.

Finally, having appealed to his readers' sense of wisdom and propriety, he ultimately appeals to his own authority as an apostle. But he does so only last and inserts his appeal almost as a footnote. In keeping with his approach to Christian liberty, he hopes there will be a voluntary submission to the principles he has laid out in this chapter.

An important distinction comes clear at this point in Paul's argument. First, there is the *principle* of headship as it relates to the recognition of the structures of authority. These are rooted in creation and the purpose for which the man and the woman were brought into the world. The principle is normative and binding on all believers. Second, there is the concrete *expression* of obedience to the principle. Here Paul develops his argument from custom and experience. For Paul in his context, a "covering" was the appropriate symbol to demonstrate obedience to the principle. That this was the universal custom of his time is evident in his conclusion: "If one is inclined to be contentious, we have no other practice, nor have the churches of God" (v. 16). In other words, there is no other precedent. To violate this principle is to go against a standard that is maintained in every church with which Paul is familiar. So the specific *way* this principle is observed—be it a covering or some other commonly accepted symbol—seems not to be as important as the principle itself. The only thing that is not allowed is that nothing be done to acknowledge it.

The history of the interpretation of this text shows that Christians throughout most of our history have followed this practice in one way or another. Only in recent decades have women decided to follow cultural fashion (hats are not "in") or, worse—emboldened by feminist philosophy—to discard the covering along with all other supposedly antiquated ideas respecting the divine structure of authority. This is something each of us must prayerfully consider. If we do not practice the "covering," then by what means do we show our respect for the principle? Is it possible that we are missing something that might bring great blessing to our churches? Would it not be a refreshing change in our Christian worship if we were to leave the culture of Corinth at the door and begin to "practice the presence of God"? What if the wives of the church would honor their husbands openly in some way? Is it possible that we might once again see a revival of male interest in the church?[24]

Reverence for the Table of the Lord (11:17–34)

The Corinthian believers were to be commended for keeping the "traditions" (v. 2), but they deserved sharp criticism for the manner in which they did so. In the observance of the Lord's Supper, they have been guilty of carnality (vv. 17–22). They are desperately in need of correction (vv. 23–26), and they are in danger of chastisement from the Lord (vv. 27–34).

Verse 17 begins with "But" (*Touto de*, "Now this"). The reference is to what follows. "In giving this instruction, I do not praise you." In an obvious contrast to his earlier complement, he goes on, "You come together not for the better but for the worse" (v. 17). Your congregational gatherings are more debilitating than edifying.

"For, in the first place, when you come together as a church, I hear that divisions exist among you" (v. 18; cf. 1:10). The expression is intended as irony—"come together" is linked with "divisions." What is described is a party spirit in the assembly. It is evident in what follows that the factions were largely divided between the rich and the poor. "And in part, I believe it" (v. 18). What Paul knew of the Corinthian assembly compelled him to accept at least part of what he had heard.

The expression "For there must also be factions among you" (v. 19) sounds strange. The term "factions" is apparently used in a nonecclesiastical sense. Note Acts 5:17 and 15:5, translated "the sect." Paul was certain that some divisions would occur in the assembly, if only to bring to light those who defend the truth. It is significant that God in His sovereign purpose uses dissension and disorder in the assembly to put His people to the test. "Therefore when you meet together, it is not to eat the Lord's Supper" (v. 20). It is a supper but not the Lord's. It is a disorderly gathering of people going through the motions.

"For in your eating each one takes his own supper first; and one is hungry and another is drunk" (v. 21). In the early church, the Lord's Supper was commonly preceded by a fellowship meal, later known as the agape feast. Eventually, so many problems accompanied these feasts that, at the Council of Carthage (A.D. 397), they were strictly forbidden. And such was the case at Corinth. In their coming together, they were not eating together, hence it would not be called *communion*, and their behavior was so dishonoring to the Lord that it could hardly be called the *Lord's* Supper. Some were actually getting drunk.

Verse 22 continues, "Or do you despise the church of God, and shame those who have nothing?" Paul's indictment is twofold: They disgraced the Lord's house, and they embarrassed the poor in their midst who were not invited to participate in the fellowship dinner. This being the case, they could just as well do this at home.

Having given ample expression of his sentiments about how not to come to the Lord's Supper, Paul now goes on to give instruction as to how it ought to be done. By declaring, "For I received from the Lord" (v. 23), Paul traces his authority to the Lord Himself. He does not indicate how Christ gave him the instruction. It is likely that he received it through the apostles. Without modification it was "that which I also delivered to you" (v. 23). Evidently, this was not the first time Paul had been through this with the Corinthians. He takes his readers back to the upper room and traces the events of the Last Supper. This does three things. First, it bases what he has to say in history, not dogmatism. Second, it forces his readers to think back with him to Calvary, which, of course, is what the Lord's Supper is all about. Third, it delineates precisely what the Lord instructed so that his readers cannot escape the authority and significance of it.

"This is My body" (v. 24) is not to be taken literally, but figuratively. His actual body was there in the midst participating with the disciples in the element of the bread, which speaks of His incarnation. "Which is for you" signifies the sacrificial and vicarious character of the death of Christ. Christ is memorialized at this table, not as a great example, or teacher, or even prophet, but as the Lamb of God who takes away the sin of the world. "Do this in remembrance of Me" (v. 24) is contrasted with the thoughtless and reckless gathering of Corinthian believers at their so-called love feast.

Reverence in Worship

The magi fell down before the child Jesus and worshipped (Matt. 2:2, 8, 11).

Lepers worshipped Jesus (Matt. 8:2).

Rulers worshipped Jesus (Matt. 9:18).

God the Father seeks those who worship Him in spirit and truth (John 4:23).

Present your bodies a living, and holy sacrifice to God, which is your spiritual service of worship (Rom. 12:1).

The Holy Spirit must fill (or control) the believer to worship (Eph. 5:18).

Part of worship may be singing and "giving thanks" for all things to God (Eph. 5:19–20).

God is to be worshipped in the Spirit (Phil. 3:3).

All the angels of God worship the Son of God (Heb. 1:6; cf. Ps. 97:7).

The sacrifices in the Old Testament could not make the worshiper perfect (mature) in conscience (Heb. 9:9)

"This cup is the new covenant in My blood" (v. 25). Christ is the mediator of the new covenant who "through His own blood . . . entered the holy place once for all, having obtained eternal redemption" (Heb. 9:12). The emphasis is on the blood. This signifies our Lord's death, which in turn signifies the ground on which eternal salvation is secured for the believing sinner. "Do this, as often as you drink *it*" (v. 25). Note that the observance is commanded, but the frequency is not. In the apostolic church, communion was generally a weekly practice.

"You proclaim the Lord's death until He comes" (v. 26). The service at the Lord's Table looks both back and ahead. It recalls the accomplishments of Calvary and anticipates our Lord's glorious return. Incidentally, the fact that this is observed "until He comes," indicates that our Lord intended this ordinance to be observed throughout the Church age.

Paul concludes his discussion of the Lord's Supper with a warning to his readers that they were facing the sure chastisement of the Lord unless they corrected their abuse of the Lord's Supper. "Therefore whoever eats the bread or drinks the cup of the Lord in an unworthy manner, shall be guilty of the body and the blood of the Lord" (v. 27). This is defined in verse 29 as "not judg[ing] the body rightly." In other words, an irreverent and careless attitude is displayed at the Lord's Table. This expression is not to be taken to prove the doctrine of consubstantiation.[25] Rather, the intent is to show that when one violates this sacred institution, he or she is, in effect, despising the body and blood of our Lord. In the same sense as it is expressed in Hebrews 9:26, they profane the institution and crucify the Savior all over again. Instead of being cleansed by His blood, they are guilty of His blood. For this reason, it is imperative that "a man examine himself" (v. 28). Before one partakes of the Lord's Supper, it is essential that we take stock of ourselves as we take stock of our Lord. There is no room here for callousness of heart or carelessness of mind.

Coming to the Lord's Table with the wrong attitude and the wrong approach may cause a man to eat and drink "judgment to himself, if he does not judge the body rightly" (v. 29). Sacerdotalism directs too much attention to the vertical dimensions of this rite and not enough to its horizontal implications. William Baird notes:

> To eat and drink without discerning the body, then, must mean to ignore the true character of the body, to fail to distinguish it from what it is not . . . the body metaphor has been used earlier with little ambiguity. "Because there is one loaf," Paul has written, "we who are many are one body" (10:17). In that statement bread stands for the body, and the body means church. This is precisely the meaning Paul presents at length and with clarity in chapter 12; the body of Christ is the church. Is it possible to conclude that discerning the body means recognizing the reality of the church in the service of the Supper?[26]

But there is also more. The kinds of judgments the apostle has in mind are enumerated in verse 30: "For this reason many among you are weak and sick, and a number sleep." Paul knows that the judgments of God many times take the form of physical illness and even death (cf. Acts 5:1–10). It is his conviction that such judgment has already occurred. The verb *koimao,* "sleep," when referring to death, always refers to the death of believers (cf. John 11:11–12; Acts 7:60; 1 Cor. 15:6, 18, 20, 51; 1 Thess. 4:13–15; 2 Pet. 3:4). Judgment here is physical and temporal, not eternal. The exhortation of verse 31 goes back to verse 28. "If we judged ourselves rightly" corresponds to self-examination. The benefit of such examination is that "we would not be judge." Paul gives his readers a choice. They may either exercise their own judgment upon themselves, or they may await God's judgment.

Lest his readers misunderstand what he means by judgment, Paul adds, "But when we are judged, we are disciplined by the Lord" (v. 32). Discipline or *chastening* is evidence of sonship (cf. Heb. 12:6). The purpose is "in order that we may not be condemned along with the world" (v. 32). The sin of which the Corinthians were guilty was worthy of the certain judgment of God, but it was not unpardonable. And true to his previous exhortation to the church, Paul's primary interest is not reprobation, but restoration.

"Wait for one another" (v. 33). In the last two verses of this chapter, Paul concludes his discussion of the Lord's Supper with a practical exhortation that the Corinthian believers show proper concern for one another. He implies his disapprobation of the common love feast in the words "eat at home" (v. 34). And he again demonstrates pastoral concern when he expresses the thought "that you may not come together for judgment." Paul takes no delight in the chastening hand of the Lord. "The remaining matters I shall arrange when I come" (Greek, *diataxomi*, refers to outward practical arrangement; cf. 9:14; 16:1; Matt. 11:1; Gal. 3:19). Any other details pertaining to the Lord's Supper, Paul will clarify upon his promised visit to the city.

Study Questions

1. How does Paul see spiritual order and authority in the church and spiritual order between men and women?

2. Does Paul's argument mean that women are less than men before God?

3. What is the ultimate point the apostle is trying to make?

4. For a woman, is the head covering to be a veil or her hair? Or both? Explain.

5. Concerning a head covering, is Paul giving a cultural or a doctrinal argument?

6. How could a woman's hair be her glory? Explain.

7. Do you think that what Paul says here is applicable for our generation?

8. Does Paul say in verses 17–34 how often a church should commemorate the Lord's Supper?

9. Does the Lord's Supper impart "grace" to the recipient, or is it simply a remembrance?

10. What does the apostle mean when he says of the Corinthian church that some are "weak and sick, and a number sleep" (v. 30)?

11. For what reason were many in this church coming to partake in the Lord's Supper?

CHAPTER 15

Concerning Spiritual Gifts
1 Corinthians 12:1-31

Preview:

Paul addresses three dominant issues in this epistle: division, godly separation, and the understanding and exercising of spiritual gifts. In this chapter, Paul turns his attention to the final matter. What are spiritual gifts? Who has them? How are they to be exercised? For what purpose have they been given? Are some more significant than others? The first two of these questions will be answered in this chapter.

In chapter 11, Paul transitions from his concerns about maintaining Christian standards in contact with the *outside* culture to matters pertaining to life on the *inside* of the church family. If chapters 8—10 relate mostly to separation issues, chapters 12—14 deal with ministry issues. Paul turns his discussion in this new direction by looking at the general subject of Christian worship and using it as a hinge to respond directly to a question the Corinthian believers have addressed to him. It also gives him an occasion to touch on some things they had not necessarily asked about. So in the previous chapter he moves the discussion forward by offering a much-needed corrective regarding authority and practice in public worship. This effectively reframes the subject under review and—anticipating what he will say in the next chapter—he provides a contextual foundation for how he will respond to their question regarding spiritual gifts.[1]

The section before us encompasses three chapters—all of which are to be taken as a unit. Here Paul strives to achieve three objectives: (1) to show that spiritual gifts are for the benefit of the body—the church (chap. 12). This constitutes the *theological* argument. (2) To show that spiritual gifts are instruments for loving (chap. 13). This is the *teleological* argument. (3) To show that spiritual gifts are primarily for ministry (chap. 14). In the final argument, Paul draws from *experience*, also addressing the importance of tradition and authority. In each of these sections, Paul shows that the gifts are primarily directed away from the individual who exercises the gift and toward others for whom the gift is primarily intended—to edify them, love them, and minister to them in meaningful ways. In keeping with the previous sections of this letter, Paul is working throughout to correct their misunderstandings of the issue and to redirect both their thinking and their actions.

Gifts Are for the Benefit of the Body

Much like the first century, the twentieth century was a time of great change, a time of social and technological upheaval. It was also a time that required believers to "test the spirits to see whether they [were] from God" (1 John 4:1). Many in our churches are struggling with a wave of *charismata*[2] that has overtaken contemporary Christianity. Most evangelicals who dismissed the phenomenon in the 1950s and 1960s as cultic and transient now accept it as mainstream. Many churches struggle with their identity as charismatic styles of worship usurp more traditional and staid hymns of praise and worship. To make matters worse, there is a new kind of (New Age) spirituality afoot that has nothing to do with the *Holy* Spirit. This new secular spirituality is popularized to suggest ways for people to "resonate with the universe" or to get in touch with their inner "spiritual" selves. Such forms of spirituality are man-centered rather than God-centered and represent a whole new challenge to those who wish to be faithful to Scripture and authentically related to the person and work of the Holy Spirit.

The character and importance of what Paul has to say on this vital issue could not be timelier. Leon Morris calls it "epoch-making."[3] What appears to us as "new" on the horizon is not really new at all. Such alternate forms of spirituality were current in Paul's day, and it was against them that much of what is contained in these chapters is directed. In what follows, the writer shows that the ministry of the Holy Spirit is not identified with a tingle down the spine, sensuous enthusiasm, ecstasy, or human ingenuity. It will be known by the place given to the lordship of Jesus Christ (v. 3). This is the "touchstone"[4] to which all proper teaching on this subject is to be brought. And it is central to Paul's theological argument, which follows.

On Not Being Ignorant (12:1-3)

Paul opens with a word of introduction in which he shows the relevance and importance of the ministry of the Holy Spirit in the life of the individual believer and in the wider circle of the believing community.

This is a pertinent issue (v. 1). He turns the spotlight on the subject "concerning which" (*peri de*, v. 1) the Corinthians had solicited his advice. This is without doubt the most difficult section of 1 Corinthians to interpret. The comment made by Archibald Robertson and Alfred Plummer more than sixty years ago is still pertinent today: "The difficulty of the passage lies in our ignorance of the condition of things to which it refers."[5] This will be noted as we progress through the text. The subject to which Paul turns in verse 1 is introduced with the expression "spiritual *gifts*" (Greek, *pneumatikon*, "spirituals"). This is not the ordinary term used for the gifts, *charisma*, the term from which *charismatic* is derived. It is in the plural and conveys the idea of "the things of the Spirit." In using this term, the writer links this teaching with a subject introduced in 2:13, where he contrasts the "spiritual person" with the "natural" and the "carnal." Using the plural, he also opens up his discussion to the wider venue of matters having to do with the presence and ministry of the Holy Spirit in, with, and through the individual members of the body of Christ. In the masculine, *pneumatikon* would refer to "gifted individuals" (cf. 2:13-14). When it occurs in the neuter, the emphasis is on the "gift itself."[6] It is with respect to a range of issues pertaining to these gifts that Paul goes on, "I do not want you to be unaware" (v. 1). This is a common Pauline expression to specify a subject of importance (cf. 10:1; 2 Cor. 1:8; 2:11; Rom. 1:13; 11:25; 1 Thess. 4:13). While we have noted the soft irony of the expression in this epistle, it is probably best to see this here as simply a characteristic way Paul calls attention to a range of concerns relating to the nature and exercise of the gifts.

This is a problem issue (v. 2). "You know that when you were pagans, you were led astray to the dumb idols" (v. 2). Paul seems to be reflecting on Habakkuk 2:19:

> "Woe to him who says to a piece of wood, 'Awake!'
> To a dumb stone, 'Arise!'
> And that is your teacher?
> Behold, it is overlaid with gold and silver,
> And there is no breath at all inside it."

This is both a statement of fact and an insinuation. Paul's readers need to face the fact that before they were saved they were led about into all forms of superstition and blind impulse. The pagan worship at Corinth not only involved immorality and the worship of mute idols, but it also involved a pagan exercise of tongues. The practice of "ecstatic utterances" was common in the mystery cults and in the worship of various Greek gods and goddesses.[7] The insinuation is that they are still being "lead." This expression has the force of being controlled by an influence they could not resist (cf. Gal. 2:13; 2 Pet. 3:17).[8] Such would reflect on the addictive power of sensuous religion.

The heathen are pictured, not as men freely following the gods their intellects have fully approved, but as under constraint, as helpless, as men who know better. There is something pathetic about idol worship. "Dumb idols" characterizes their deities as totally unable to answer those who call upon them. They could give no revelation. They could make nothing known to their worshipers. Far from reaching the dignity of the sons of God, they were continually led about. And no matter how they were led, they were brought only to dumb deities.[9]

This is a paraclete issue (v. 3). The other Paraclete (cf. John 15:26, "the Helper") was Jesus' reference to the coming of the Holy Spirit, of whom it was said that He would bear witness of Christ. His work would be identified by two criteria. Paul begins with the negative one: "Therefore . . . no one speaking by the Spirit of God says, 'Jesus is accursed'" (v. 3). "Therefore," ties with verse 2 and indicates that Paul's readers are in need of instruction. While Paul is about to deal with the entire range of gifts the Holy Spirit will bring, it is clear from the start that the emphasis is on speaking in tongues. Robert Gromacki points out: "Notice this closeness of sounds in this verse: 'if any man love not the Lord Jesus Christ, let him be Anathema Maran-atha' (16:22). Thus, it could have been that a person tried to simulate a real tongues utterance with faulty pronunciation, resulting in a heretical declaration."[10] Doubtless, this comment echoes something that must have happened in a Corinthian service. Since it is such an egregious misuse of a speech gift and because it strikes at the heart of Paul's central affirmation on these matters, he mentions it. When spiritual gifts are legitimately exercised, Christ will not be blasphemed or dishonored by them.[11]

This alerts us to the possibility that Paul is approaching his subject in much the same way he did the matter of meats sacrificed to idols (chaps. 8—10)—he shows them how their free expression of previous pagan ideas and actions were corrupting the *koinonia* that was unique to the new community. By calling attention to this in his opening statement, Paul had to have caused chagrin with his readers. If and when this occurred in their worship, they had to know that something was wrong. It is not unlikely that this, in fact, is what occasioned their question to him in the first place. Reference here to abuse also alerts us to the need in this section to discern between passages that are merely *descriptive* in nature and passages that are *prescriptive*. For example, when Paul says in 14:2, "For one who speaks in a tongue does not speak to men, but to God; for no one understands," we must ask whether this is instruction concerning the proper exercise or merely descriptive of something they are doing that requires correction.[12] This verse has occasioned no small controversy and has often been used to draw a distinction between tongues in Corinth and tongues in Acts. I believe, since there is nothing to indicate otherwise, that Paul's references to *glossa* ("tongues") complement but do not contradict Luke's references in Acts to the same gift.

The second criterion by which the authentic ministry of the Holy Spirit is identified is a positive one. "No one can say, 'Jesus is Lord,' except by the Holy Spirit" (v. 3, cf. John 20:28; 1 John 4:2–3). To speak of Jesus as *kurios* ("Lord") was to identify him with *Yahweh* of the Old Testament. This was the title the Greek translation of the Old Testament (the LXX) used to translate the most sacred name for God. How a person speaks determines the nature of the spirit within. There is a character to the authentic ministry of the Holy Spirit that corresponds to Jesus' instruction in the upper room when He said of the Holy Spirit, "He shall glorify Me; for He shall take of Mine, and shall disclose it to you" (John 16:15, cf. 14:26; 15:26–27). When a "gift" brings attention to itself, or when it brings inordinate attention to the "Spirit," it is not what the Holy Spirit ordinarily enables believers to do.

In many of our churches, as in Corinth, there are times when the Spirit witnesses with our spirit (Rom. 8:16) that Christ is not being honored by what we see or hear. It may be in the speaking or the music or the incongruity between the message and lifestyle of the messenger. It may be the absence of love (cf. chap. 13). It may be due to distractions caused by a lack of orderliness. These and many other types of concern unique to the Corinthian situation addressed here are also common today. The mere fact that someone claims to be speaking through the unction of the Spirit is not enough—what he or she is saying must honor Christ. The mere fact that someone in the audience is offended because the style of music or speaking is not in keeping with their culture-savvy tastes or their felt needs misses the point. Worship is to God, and it honors His Son if and when the Holy Spirit is involved. This is not to say that the only legitimate music has to be at least a century old or that there is no place for anecdote, humor, church suppers, or recreational activities. But when the body is gathered and Christ is in the midst, it is He who must be magnified and none other.

Everyone Has a Gift (12:4–7)

In the first three verses, Paul shows that the Spirit is in control. This says something of the *quality* of what is done in the legitimate exercise of gifts. In verses 4–7 he argues that the Spirit is central, and this says something about the *consistency* of what is done in the exercise of gifts. In speaking as he does of "varieties of gifts . . . varieties of ministries . . . varieties of effects," Paul is not classifying the gifts into three categories. Rather, he is using the Trinitarian formula as a rhetorical device to show how all the "manifestations" of the Spirit come together in relation to "Spirit . . . Lord . . . God." They are the gifts given by the Spirit, used in ministry by the Son, and energized (Greek, *energeo*, "to work") by the Father. As there is no disunity among the persons of the Godhead in the distribution of the gifts, there should be no disunity in their display. Paul anticipates his rebuke of the Corinthian's tendency to use even the gifts of the Spirit as an occasion for jealousy. He adds, "But the same God . . . works all things in all *persons*" (v. 6). Since there are *varieties* of gifts, it is evident that no one has all of them. By saying they are given to *all*, Paul is declaring that every believer has at least one. "Gifts" are supernatural endowments for service. They refer to *what* the Holy Spirit contributes to the body of Christ through each one. "Ministries" are supernatural appointments for service. They speak of *where* the Holy Spirit does this work. "Activities" are supernatural enablements for service. They suggest *how* the Holy Spirit does this work. Taken together they suggest that for each there is a specific *gift* that correlates with a specific *place* and a specific *work*. As he proceeds, Paul weaves these three ideas in and out of his teaching on the subject.

"But to each one is given the manifestation of the Spirit for the common good" (v. 7). This does not exactly equate with "diversities of gifts" in verse 4. Rather, he wants the reader to understand that when the Spirit gives gifts, they will be demonstrated. The emphasis here is not on the particular gifts being considered but on how they are used. They are for "the common good" (Greek, *sumphero*, "to bring together," "to be profitable"). One of the common misconceptions of the biblical teaching on spiritual gifts is that they are for the personal benefit of the one to whom they are given. Another misconception, in our analysis, is that they can be cultivated. In fact, and quite to the contrary, Paul seems to view them as having been given exclusively for the profit and mutual benefit of the body of Christ. Furthermore, they are "gifts," not products of human effort and training. They are neither privately owned nor can they, like skills, be developed. Their function is to offer to the body something that it would not have if the individual through whom they are intended to be exercised cannot or will not use them for the mutual benefit of the body (see below, vv. 15–27ff.). Implicit in this exercise is that the gift honors the One who gave it (cf. v. 3).

I realize that this suggests a slightly different perspective than the commonly held view. Thus, a few observations are in order. (1) Spiritual gifts in this text are not talents or skills; they have reference to distinctive ways the Holy Spirit enables believers to contribute in positive, Christ-honoring ways to the spiritual edifying of the entire body. (2) Spiritual gifts are coordinated in Paul's discussion with one's placement in that body. Accordingly, for those who wonder what their gift might be, where a person is placed in the body may be the best indicator of the spiritual gifts they should be sharing. (3) The primary reference to the body in this context is the "local" body—not a "universal" body. That is, they are given *in situ*. If someone says he has the gift of "pastor-teacher" (cf. Eph. 4:11), for example, we may assume that he is already situated as a pastor-teacher in a local church. The gift is not given proleptically (for example, at salvation) as something to be developed or enhanced by training. What Paul is teaching here is that we are to bloom where we are planted. And the fragrance of our lives under the control and empowerment of the Holy Spirit is our gift—our *spiritual* gift—to the body into which God has placed us. (4) On this account, it is also evident in this passage that gifts are given as the body has need (cf. 12:15–27). To suggest that someone has only a specified gift and may only contribute that one (or few) "gift(s)" to the body seems to limit the sovereign action of the Holy Spirit (cf. 12:11). If believers should find themselves in situations requiring expressions of mercy to others, Paul invites them to ask for that gift. If they desire a gift of healing for their brothers or sisters, they may ask for that gift (James 5:14–15). (5) Before he finishes, Paul will show that any one of these gifts may potentially be sought in the interest of loving one another. They are not ends in themselves; they are instruments of God's love shed abroad in our hearts through the Holy Spirit who has been given to us (Rom. 5:5).

Not Lacking in Any Gift (12:8–10)

In the list that follows, we have an unusual glimpse into the affairs of the early church of Corinth. Paul had said that they were "not lacking in any gift" (1:7)—that is, in relation to spiritual gifts, they had all they needed. From the list, it is evident that the gifts they had experienced in this church were an impressive display of God's power. Paul is careful throughout to communicate the divine source of each of these manifestations. Spiritual gifts are "given . . . through the Spirit" (v. 8). The Holy Spirit is indicated, not just an impersonal *spirit* of unity (cf. vv. 3, 11, 13). "The word of wisdom" (v. 8) has to do with the exposition of wisdom. It is speech that has wisdom as its content.[13] Wisdom is knowledge skillfully applied to life. Gordon Fee notes that Paul brilliantly does two things here against the "worldly wise" of this church "(a) He uses one of their own terms to begin his list of 'manifestations' in the assembly that demonstrate the great diversity inherent in the one Spirit's activities; and (b) he reshapes that term in light of the work of the Spirit so as to give it a significantly different content from their own."[14] They, as many in our own time, had equated *their* experience with *true* experience.

Paul's Teaching on the Gifts

Gifts Given by the Holy Spirit (1 Corinthians 12:7–11)

Wisdom

Word of knowledge

Faith

Gifts of healing

Miracles

Prophecy

Distinguishing of spirits

Various kinds of tongues (languages)

Interpretation of tongues

Possessing special knowledge (13:8)

Gifted Workers Appointed in the Church by God (1 Corinthians 12:28–31)

Apostles

Prophets

Teachers

Workers of miracles

Workers of healing

Workers of helps

Workers of administrations

Workers of various kinds of tongues

Gifted People Given for the Equipping of the Saints (Ephesians 4:7–12)

Apostles

Prophets

Evangelists

Pastors and teachers

> ### General Gifts Given to the Church "in a Measure of Faith" (Romans 12:3–8)
>
> *Prophecy*
>
> *Service*
>
> *Teaching*
>
> *Exhortation*
>
> *Giving*
>
> *Showing mercy*

"The word of knowledge" (v. 8) is associated in context with mysteries and prophetic utterances (see 13:2; 14:6). It seems to be identified here as a revelatory gift.[15] In fact, it was with this gift that Agabus had prophesied the famine under Claudius (Acts 11:28) and would later speak a similar word of knowledge concerning Paul's imprisonment (Acts 21:10–11). Likewise, "Faith" (v. 9) is not saving faith but the wonder-working faith to "move mountains." "Gifts of healing" (v. 9) is a double plural, "gifts of cures." The expression has in mind gifts whereby the healing of the sick was effected (cf. Acts 4:30). Two important facts should be noted here. First, the use of the plural suggests that a special gift is necessary each time a healing occurs. Second, the expression emphasizes the results, not the process. The gift does not provide for divine *healers* but divine "healings" (cf. James 5:14–15). "Effecting of miracles" (v. 10) is more comprehensive than the gifts of healings. It has in mind such manifestations as are recorded in Acts 5:1–12; 9:32–43, and 13:8–12. "Prophecy" (v. 10) is the communication of special revelation from God.[16] It could have been a "foretelling," as in Acts 11:28, or simply "forthtelling." Most of the New Testament epistles fall into this category. When it results in Scripture, it associates with inspiration. After the canon of the New Testament was completed, the special needs for this gift were substantially diminished. It is generally considered that these gifts became subsequently identified with the *preaching* and *teaching* ministries of elders and pastors (cf. Eph. 4:11–12; 1 Tim. 3:2; 6:2; 2 Tim. 2:2). Such ministries are prophetic insofar as they communicate the faith once for all delivered (Jude 1:3). When pastors "preach the word" (2 Tim. 4:2) they are in effect *forthtelling* the revealed Word of God. We do well not to neglect the awesome power of such preaching in favor of soft therapeutic drivel too often served up in modern pulpits.

"Distinguishing of spirits" (v. 10) was also vital during this period when Scripture was still being formulated and the foundation of the church was being laid. A class of individuals gifted with discerning true prophets from false prophets was necessary. This seems to be what John has in mind in 1 John 4:1 (cf. also 14:29; 1 Thess. 5:20–21). However, discerning of spirits may be required in any age.

"Tongues . . . the interpretation of tongues" (v. 10) requires some explanation. The gift of speaking in tongues in the book of Acts appears to have been limited to speaking in "known languages" (cf. Acts 2:4; 10:46; 19:6). In the Acts 2 passage it does not appear that the gift of interpretation was necessary, since "every man heard in his own dialect" (Acts 10 and 19 are not as clear). At Corinth, however, it seems that the exercise of tongues involved more than just speaking with "known" languages. Here there is a question of whether Paul is talking about a different kind of gift from that recorded by Luke in Acts 2 or whether Paul is simply saying that when the gift is properly exercised someone will be present for whom it is intended and who, in turn, can interpret. This poses a special problem for the interpreter of the New Testament. We know that this gift was a problem for the Paul, for he devotes almost an entire chapter to it (chap. 14). In the book of Acts it is associated only with the first instance of the gospel in Jerusalem (chap. 2), the home of Cornelius (chap. 10), and Ephesus (chap. 19). Thereafter, the New Testament is silent about it.[17] Its appearance in Corinth is the only time tongues are mentioned outside Acts in reference to the spiritual gift. And it is the only time the gift is mentioned anywhere in connection with the regular worship of a local assembly of believers. In every instance in Acts, it is referenced with respect to the manifestations of the Holy Spirit when the gospel was first delivered and an initial cohort of people responded. And even in those instances there seem to be unusual circumstances requiring a special "sign" to those present. For a fuller discussion of the nature and exercise of these gifts, see my exposition of 13:1 and 14:1–40.

All Are Baptized into One Body (12:11–13)

The doctrine of spiritual gifts is rooted in our relation to Jesus Christ. The risen Lord taught Paul this truth in Acts 9:4. The body equals Christ. Paul comes back to this in 15:22, "As in Adam all die, so also in Christ all shall be made alive." In Colossians 1:18 Paul says that Christ is the "head of the body, the church." The point is simply this—one cannot be "in Christ" and not be "in His church." The reverse is also true—and this is the point that is being made here. If one is truly in the church, that one is also *in Christ*—that is, in His body. And just as the life of Christ includes all who are part of that body, so also the presence and the gifts of the Spirit are given to all. The phrase "all these things" (v. 11) has in mind all the above-mentioned gifts.

In relation to each, "one and the same Spirit works." While the gifts are diverse, the source is a common one. "Distributing to each one individually just as He wills" (v. 11) shows that the Holy Spirit not only produces these gifts but also distributes them—and He does so according to His own will, not according to the wishes or merits of the individual. Notice here that the apostle Paul attributes to the Third Person of the Trinity one of the qualities of personality (viz., "will"). This underscores that the Holy Spirit is not a force but a person.

"The body is one and *yet* has many members" (v. 12). The church is viewed as an organism. Like the human body, it reflects both unity and diversity. It is "one body" (v. 12). While there are many members, the body is one. This truth is further emphasized in Rom. 12:4–5; Eph. 1:23; 4:4, 16. "So also is Christ" (v. 12). That is, the body of Christ, which is the church. This expression is appropriate because Christ is the Head of that body. Gromacki rightly notes: "The equation of Christ with His . . . body, the church, can be seen here. Christ said to Saul who had devastated the church: 'Why persecutest thou me?' (Acts 9:4; cf. Eph. 5:23; Col. 1:18)."[18] "For by [*en*, "in/with"] one Spirit we were all baptized into one body" (v. 13). The preposition *en* is to be taken as a "means" or "instrument"—not "agency."[19] This has the same force as the expression "and we were all made to drink of one Spirit" (v. 13). The event fulfills Matthew 3:11; John 1:33; and Acts 1:5, where it was promised that (as John baptized "in/with" water), the One coming after him would "baptize you with the Holy Spirit and fire." In contrast to water baptism, this refers to the work of Christ by which each believer is identified with Him. This act is equated with being baptized "into one body" (v. 13). The body is the church, which, through its immersion *(baptizo)* in the Spirit, is caused to become one organism with many members. That this baptism is common to all believers at Corinth is implied by the fact that Paul does not exhort them to *be* baptized by the Spirit. Rather, he declares that they *have been* baptized. The imagery speaks eloquently of the events recorded later by Paul's companion Luke in Acts 2.[20] It was then that the believers who had been joined to Christ first shared in this new ministry of the Holy Spirit who was promised to come and indwell them in a way that they had never experienced before (John 7:37–39). However, it would not happen until after Christ returned to the Father; as He said, "For if I do not go away, the Helper shall not come to you; but if I go, I will send Him to you" (John 16:7). That this was the fulfillment of Jesus' promise was recalled by Peter in Acts 11:15–16 as he reflected on the significance of what happened at the house of Cornelius (Acts 10). He reported: "And as I began to speak, the Holy Spirit fell upon them, just as *He did* upon us at the beginning [in Acts 2]. And I remembered the word of the Lord, how He used to say, 'John baptized with water, but you shall be baptized with the Holy Spirit.'"

Just as the Old Testament saints were "baptized into Moses in the cloud and in the sea" (1 Cor. 10:2), so now these saints have been "baptized" into Christ and "whether Jews or Greeks, whether slaves or free . . . were all made to drink of one Spirit" (v. 13). Paul is still chipping away at the ethnic and socioeconomic barriers to unity in this church. Here the powerful incentive to put these aside is the truth of the baptism of the Holy Spirit that has joined us together in one body—*e pluribus unum.* Those who suggest that Paul is teaching that this refers to a higher tier of Christian experience for the spiritual elite not only miss the point entirely, they do serious injustice to the unity of the body that is hereby made possible.

To summarize Paul's teaching on the baptism of the Holy Spirit, the following may be said. First, it is the fulfillment of the promise that Christ would do a *new* thing. He would baptize with the Holy Spirit—it is not a continuation of a ministry that was part of the Old Testament dispensation. Second, the baptism has already happened—it is not enjoined upon them to pray for it. Third, it has happened to all of them—not just the most spiritual. Fourth, it constitutes the dynamic and incentive for unity—not a reason to separate from one another.

One is left with only the question as to *when* this happened for the Corinthians. The only rational answer to this question is that it happened in the same way it happened for the believers in Acts 19. It happened *when they believed* (cf. Acts 19:1–7). After leaving Corinth (Acts 18), Paul's next extended ministry was in Ephesus. It was here that he encountered the disciples of John who, after Paul explained the gospel and they believed, experienced the coming of the Spirit. While the events recorded in Acts 2, 8, and 10 are unusual because they are "transitional" from the old dispensation to the new,[21] Acts 19 is given to establish the normative way this is to happen throughout the remainder of the church age.[22] It is, in the progress of revelation, the "last word" on this important topic.

God Has Placed Us (12:14–19)

Here the illustration of the body is further developed with emphasis on the diversity and placement of each member. One cannot escape the force of Paul's argument: For a body to be a body it must have diverse members. It is absurd to expect everyone to have the same gift. But by the same token, it is utterly wrong to imagine that there are some members that are unnecessary. "God has placed the members, each one of them, in the body, just as He desired" (v. 18). Paul stresses the sovereignty of God in this process. It is not only foolish but disobedient to covet another person's gift. The place and gifts of each member are determined by the Lord. In an age when self-image and positive feelings about oneself are emphasized ad nauseum, the reflexive character of this argument is important. Each member is vitally important to the body, without which a crucial contribution simply will not be made. When people get their feelings hurt, they have a tendency just to leave. This is tantamount to a body part cutting itself off from the body because of an offense. In such an analogy, it is the body part that will ultimately die if this happens. And the body, of course, will be permanently disfigured. The appropriateness of this analogy for the situation in Corinth is transparent.

No Freelance Christians (12:20–26)

Not only may I not say that the body can do without me, but I may not say that I can do without the body. "But now there are many members, but one body" (v. 20) speaks of a mutual dependency. Based on the theological fact of organic unity, Paul is now going to show that each member is interdependent on all the others. None is permitted to say, "I have no need of you" (v. 21). There is no such thing as a freelance Christian. No part of the body can take leave of the other members as though they were unnecessary. He adds, "The members of the body which seem to be weaker are necessary" (v. 22). As in the human body, some members are weaker than others. Likewise, there are some "we deem less honorable" (v. 23). Some parts of the body seemingly receive more attention and exposure than others, while other parts of the body that are "less presentable"[23] are never noticed. As God views the body, He does not see it in parts but as a whole. "Composed" (v. 24) was used to speak of mingling elements[24] to form a compound or of mixing two colors to create a third.[25] The union thus formed is indissoluble: "that there should be no division in the body" (v. 25). What is discerned from this imagery is that the whole is greater than the sum of the parts. When yellow and blue are combined, the result is not another shade of yellow or blue—it is green—an altogether new color. When each one contributes its "color," the result is something that could not even exist without the constituent parts contributing to the final product.

Divisions and alienation of feelings should find no place in the body of Christ. Rather, "the members . . . have the same care for one another" (v. 25). The body is one, and it has a common life and consciousness; therefore, "if one member suffers, all the members suffer with it" (v. 26). Likewise, "if *one* member is honored, all the members rejoice with it" (v. 26). The application to Paul's readers is abundantly clear: There were people in the church who had little more than disdain for the "weak" and were guilty of offending these "little ones." Of these Paul underscores that they are all vital to the health of the body. We cannot dishonor one member without violating the whole. Likewise, when the least of its members is celebrated, the whole shares in the joy.

Every Member Is Important (12:27–31)

There is a design to this body (v. 27). "Now you are Christ's body, and individually members of it" (v. 27). In one succinct statement, the apostle expresses both the unity and the diversity of the body of Christ. In the original, the definite article does not appear before "body." The thought is not that this particular local assembly constituted the body of Christ—although in one sense it does. But here the stress is on quality. Since they are of the body of Christ, their actions and their attitudes toward one another should reflect His character.

Paul gives a further listing of the gifts with some additions to those included in verses 4–11. Here the stress is twofold. First, he stresses the source: "God has appointed" (v. 28). And second, he stresses priority. The list is so arranged as to put the most important first and the least important last. In this arrangement, "apostles" are first while "tongues" are last. It is doubtful that the apostle ever intended that this list be exhaustive.

There are differences in this body (vv. 28–30). "All are not apostles, are they?" (v. 29). Just as a body possesses many different members, even so the members of the church possess a variety of gifts (vv. 29–30). It is both absurd and sinful to expect otherwise.

There is development in this body (v. 31). "But earnestly desire the greater gifts" (v. 31). The original is more explicit than the English translation allows. It is a second person plural—"you people"—and it may be understood as present indicative or imperative. If it is indicative, it should be translated "you people desire." Our text (as most translations) prefers the imperative. In context, either can easily be seen. They were indeed "coveting" gifts, so it might not surprise the reader to see reference to it. However, the imperative would tend to telegraph ahead to chapter 14, where Paul makes it clear that the desire for spiritual gifts is a good thing, but only if it is driven by love (chap. 13) and if it is exercised for the purpose of building up the body of Christ. This then would explain why the apostle has arranged the list in verse 28 in order of priority. He wants his readers to be clear in their own minds as to which gifts are the best. Obviously, his intent is to steer them away from the more spectacular gifts such as tongues. "Earnestly desire" then is not to be construed negatively but is to be understood in relation to the prioritized listing above. This also shows why it is a mistake to imagine that each believer is given a discrete allotment of gifts at the time of conversion. Paul makes it clear in this text that there is a wide array of gifts that God has given to the church for its mutual edification—and He will give these sovereignly according to His will—to those who ask. But there is something even more important than seeking gifts. And so Paul adds, "And I show you a still more excellent way" (v. 31). The import of this statement is to be seen in chapter 13. Paul will show them a better "direction" altogether—not *striving* but *loving*.

S. Lewis Johnson notes correctly:

> The last clause of chapter 12 has been misunderstood. Many feel that Paul is here showing *how* the gifts are to be administered, i.e. in love. However, the use of "way" (*hodos*) in the sense of "a road" instead of the "way" (*tropos*) in the sense of "manner," and the statement of 14:1 indicate that Paul was, rather, pointing out a path of life superior to a life spent seeking and displaying of spiritual gifts."[26]

Study Questions

1. Why is verse 3 so important in the testimony of individual Christians? Compare Galatians 4:6.

2. From verses 4–6, show how the Godhead, the Trinity, is involved in the giving of spiritual gifts.

3. List at least five reasons from this chapter why spiritual gifts are given to the body of Christ.

4. From verses 7, 11, 18, and 28, explain how the giving of gifts is the sovereign "gifting" from God.

5. What is the baptism of the Spirit?

6. Is the baptism of the Spirit a spiritual work, or does it refer to water baptism?

7. In the body of Christ, are some members more important than others? How does Paul prove his point on this issue?

8. As Paul describes it here in this chapter, is the body of Christ the local church or the fellowship of all believers scattered everywhere?

9. Is every individual Christian given all the spiritual gifts? In other words, is the gift of tongues given to every child of God? Explain.

CHAPTER 16

Gifts Are for Loving the Body
1 Corinthians 13:1-13

Preview:

Paul closed the previous chapter with a teaser: "I show you a more excellent way." Throughout his letter it is evident that the Corinthians had a problem with love. They had placed knowledge, rights, and gifts over love. Paul places this chapter concerning the "greatest thing in the world" in the center of his corrective to remind them that love is more important than everything else they had placed before it.

Paul's interest here is not to instruct his readers how they may best use their gifts. Rather, he is redirecting their priorities. It is love for which they should be striving, not spiritual gifts. Love is the *end*, not the *instrument*. This is Paul's teleological argument. To desire a spiritual gift is a good thing (12:31) but only as an instrument through which one may love his or her brothers and sisters in the Lord. In other words, love is not the means by which the *gift* is exercised; rather, the gift is the means by which *love* is exercised.[1] The chapter breaks quite naturally into three sections: the contrast of love (vv. 1–3), the character of love (vv. 4–7), and the constancy of love (vv. 8–13).

The Contrast of Love (13:1–3)

Henry Drummond, the Continental scholar whose life was profoundly changed through his association with D. L. Moody, began his classic, *The Greatest Thing in the World*, with this observation: "Love was not Paul's strong point. The observing student can detect a beautiful tenderness growing and ripening all through his character as Paul gets old, but the hand that wrote "The greatest of these is love," when we meet it first, is stained with blood."[2]

Paul, himself, would be the first to concur (Gal. 1:13; 1 Tim. 1:15). The Word of God is a two-edged sword. The writer knows how it cuts into his own life. So now with the skill of a surgeon, he appropriates its truth to lay bare the real disease of the heart that has caused division, compromise, and distorted priorities in the church—the absence of love.

The expression "tongues of men and of angels" (v. 1) is important in two ways. First, it shows that the content of chapter 13 is directed foremost against the abuse of the gift of tongues[3] (contrast 12:28 where speaking in tongues is listed last). Second, it shows that at least in this situation, tongues involved both known and unknown languages. The Corinthians apparently considered these tongues to be languages of the angels.[4] Such was the association of tongues-speaking in pagan worship at Corinth. When a priest or devotee spoke in tongues, it was considered that he spoke in the language of the gods.[5] The first hint that the writer is concerned about syncretism is in 12:2, where he reminds his readers that they were "led astray to the dumb idols." Ironically, it was to these mute gods that many of the people were formerly drawn and with whom they communicated in various forms of ecstatic speech.

The apostle does not explicitly accuse his readers of incorporating this pagan activity into their worship. Rather, his approach in the next two chapters is to circumscribe the exercise of the gift in such a way that the inordinate exercise of it will be eliminated. Whether my gifting be natural or supernatural, it is worthless if it does "not have love" *(agape)*. The King James translation, "charity," derives from the Latin and unfortunately has lost much of its force in contemporary usage. "Charity" has been used to distinguish the dynamic of Christian giving from all such parallel expressions in the ancient world.

Love is shown to be superior to the very best of the spiritual gifts. It is also superior to philanthropy—"if I give all my possessions to feed *the poor,*" (v. 3)—and personal dedication—"if I deliver my body to be burned" (v. 3).[6] Without love these things "profit me nothing" (v. 3). In the Greek and Roman world, people gave, but their giving always had the character of *eros*, not *agape*. Giving was a sort of investment in the community and was a response to the beauty or value of the object of the gift. One did not give because of a need, but because the object of the gift was deserving of the gift. Or one might be interested in a quid pro quo—having his or her name attached to the gift in some way. "Erotic" love always expects a "return" for the attentions given. One may describe this as *contract* giving. In the New Testament the term *agape*, which is rare in secular Greek literature, is adopted from its use in the

Septuagint to describe the character of God's love.[7] The love of God is unique because it is rooted in His grace and responds selflessly to the needs of the object loved. It is for this reason that the term *charity* (from the New Testament term for "grace") was used to designate this form of giving. It is that which acts in conformity to the character and nature of God. It is not benevolence, yet it produces it. It is not motivated or moved by external circumstances yet always acts appropriately in response to them. It is no wonder that the apostle considered that though a person possessed any or all of the gifts but was destitute of love she or he was nothing.

The Character of Love (13:4–7)

What Paul does here is what Jesus did with His audience in respect to the keeping of the Law. Jesus said that if his followers "love God" they will fulfill the Law. Rather than striving to keep the Commandments, if they will just love God with all their hearts, their behavior will follow (Matt. 22:37). Here too, rather than going all out to do the works of righteousness or to have a prominent place in the assembly, Jesus' followers are to love. Paul undertakes now to show us what this looks like.

Love "is patient" (v. 4). It is not easily roused to resentment (cf. James 5:7). It "is kind" (v. 4). This term appears only here in the New Testament. From the root *chrestos*, it has the idea of "useful," that is, inclined to be of good service to others. Love "does not brag" (v. 4). It does not sound its own praises. And it is "not arrogant." It is not swelled with pride (cf. 4:6; 8:1). Love is "not provoked" (v. 5). It is not exasperated (cf. Acts 17:16). It "does not take into account a wrong *suffered*" (v. 5). The sense here is that it "does not reckon evil." This expression of love does not keep track of the offenses committed against it. Love "does not rejoice in unrighteousness" (v. 6). It does not take delight in that which is offensive to God. Rather, it "rejoices with the truth" (v. 6). This may be taken in an instrumental sense "rejoices together *with* truth,"[8] or it may be taken in the locative sense as reflected in the KJV—"rejoices *in* truth." The latter is probably more consistent with Paul's thought in the context (cf. also John 3:21; Rom. 1:8; 1 John 1:26). Love "bears all things" (v. 7; "covers all things"; cf. 1 Pet. 4:8). When Paul says that love "believes all things" (v. 7), he does not suggest that it is gullible, but that it will believe well of others unless convinced otherwise. In any case, it always "hopes all things" (v. 7). Rather than having a negative and critical spirit, it is always positive and hopeful. And love "endures all things" (v. 7). This is a military term; it means to sustain the assaults of an enemy (cf. also 2 Tim. 2:10; Heb. 10:32; 12:1–2).

The Constancy of Love (13:8–13)

All spiritual gifts are temporary. Unlike them, love will never be outmoded, unnecessary, or eliminated. Everything, as Sam Johnson used to say "has an end on't." The average mammal, in a lifetime, has less than a billion heartbeats. The average human has 3 billion heartbeats. There is an end to youth. Here we are told there is an end to gifts. There is even an end to faith and hope. But love abides.

"Love never fails" (v. 8; *ekpiptei*, "falls off"; cf. Luke 16:17). Unlike the leaf or the flower, love never fades or falls off (cf. James 1:11; 1 Pet. 1:24). "Gifts of prophecy, they will be done away" ("be abolished"). "Tongues, they will cease" (v. 8). No special significance need be attached to the Greek term *pauo*[9] ("stop") in its use with tongues, except to say that it was the most appropriate term in the Greek language that the apostle could use for an activity involving speaking (cf. Luke 11:1; Acts 5:42; 6:13; 20:31; Eph. 1:16). Perhaps what is most significant is that they *will* stop. Some have argued that tongues are the language of heaven. If that were true, Paul could hardly have said that they will stop. "Knowledge, it will be done away" (v. 8) signifies "be abolished." This is the same word used in reference to prophecy above. It is not knowledge in general but the "gift" of knowledge (cf. 12:8; 13:2).

"For" (v. 9) suggests reason. "We know in part, and we prophesy in part" (v. 9). Knowledge and prophecy as we now know them are suited only to an imperfect state of existence. "When the perfect comes" (v. 10) is best understood in light of 1 Corinthians 2:6, in the sense of "mature" (cf. also Col. 3:14; Heb. 6:1). It cannot be a reference to the completion of the canon of Scripture, since this would imply perfect knowledge in this age. Furthermore, not even the Word of God, which is a mirror, wherein we now behold the glory of the Lord (2 Cor. 3:18), can compare to seeing Him face to face (cf. v. 12). Paul employs the neuter because he does not contemplate an individual, but the corporate body of Christ. "The partial will be done away" (v. 10). The body growing up as a perfect, or mature adult (cf. Eph. 4:12–13) will eventually outgrow the need for certain things associated with immaturity, as verse 11 shows. This becomes a metaphor for the "Church triumphant," where the physically challenged will stand once again on their own because the Great Physician will see to it; and where there will be no more need for a "pastor-teacher" because the Great Shepherd will be there. We will no longer need prophets and elders, for a Prophet greater than Moses will be there. And we will no longer need discerners and exhorters, for "we shall be like Him, because we shall see Him just as He is" (1 John 3:2).[10]

The apostle illustrates his point by likening it to the maturation of a person from infancy to manhood. A child speaks, reasons, and assimilates knowledge at the level of his or her maturity. Paul's use of "speak . . . think . . . reason" (v. 11) seems to correspond respectively to "tongues," "prophecy," and "knowledge" above. The apostle goes on to say, "When I became a man, I did away with childish things" (v. 11). A child's speech is undeveloped, his or her understanding crude, and knowledge incomplete. Thus, attention is focused on developing the skills of speech, coming to terms with truth, and assimilating knowledge. But when the child becomes an adult, his or her speech becomes subject to the mind, understanding is tempered, and knowledge is complete. Paul is not implying that his readers had attained such a level of maturity, but as Philippians 3:7–15 teaches, that is the end toward which they should be striving.

Paul is exceedingly practical here. As there is an end to childhood, there is an end to those special ministries associated with the spiritual infancy of the church. Living things change. This is true of individuals as well as of families and societies. And it is true of the church. In Ephesians 2:20 Paul speaks of the "foundation" ministries of the apostles and New Testament prophets with Christ as the cornerstone. In 1 Corinthians 3 he spoke of the responsibility of each to build on that foundation—not to try to lay it again. There is a pattern in such texts that suggests the larger context of Paul's thinking here. Is it possible, in fact, that many of these more unusual gifts are being associated with apostolic/foundational ministries (cf. 2 Cor. 12:12)? I think so.

"Now we see in a mirror dimly" (v. 12; literally, "for yet we see through a mirror in a riddle"). Paul seems to be alluding to the incident in Numbers 12:8 that describes how God spoke, as it were, "mouth to mouth, even openly, and not in dark sayings." On another occasion Paul says the writings were an enigma compared to the revelations contained in the gospel (cf. 2 Cor. 3:12–13). The apostle understands that complete maturity will not be achieved until we see the Lord "face to face" (v. 12). At that time, we will not only achieve complete maturity but perfect knowledge. As Paul puts it, "but then I shall know fully just as I also have been fully known" (v. 12). The gifts are fragmentary and serve only as means to an end. Paul's advice is to keep your eyes on the goal and not on the means toward achieving it.

"But now abide faith, hope, love, these three" (v. 13). "Now" is best understood in a temporal sense (cf. Rom. 8:24–25; 2 Cor. 5:7; Heb. 11:1). If the present Christian experience were to be reduced to three essential qualities, they would be faith, hope, and love. "The greatest of these is love." Faith will one day vanish into sight (cf. Jer. 16:14–15), and hope will give way to reality (Job 19:20). "For I consider that the sufferings of this present time are not worthy to be compared with the glory that is to be revealed to us. For the anxious longing of the creation waits eagerly for the revealing of the sons of God" (Rom. 8:18ff.). Love alone abides. Its clearest expression is seen on Golgotha's hill. Thus Paul's approach is not to decry the possible abuses at Corinth but to challenge them to something much better. As Augustine says:

> And now as to love, which the apostle declares to be greater than the other two graces, that is than faith and hope, the greater the measure in which it dwells in a man, the better is the man in whom it dwells. For when there is a question as to whether a man is good, one does not ask what he believes, or what he hopes, but what he loves. For the man who loves aright no doubt believes and hopes aright; whereas the man who has not love believes in vain, even though his beliefs are true; and hopes in vain, even though the objects of his hope are a real part of true happiness; unless, indeed, he believes and hopes for this, that he may obtain by prayer the blessing of love.[11]

Study Questions

1. Is Paul saying he actually spoke in the tongues of angels? What does he mean?

2. Is Paul saying he could literally do all the things that he lists in verses 1–3?

3. What is the apostle's most important thought in these verses? What message is he trying to get across to the Corinthian church?

4. Make a list of all the qualities that are found in love. Elaborate on them. Do most people understand love as Paul here explains it? Why or why not?

5. What is unique about the three gifts Paul cites in verse 8? Why does he specifically say that they will someday no longer be in operation?

6. Put into a paragraph what you think Paul's central thought is in verses 11–12.

CHAPTER 17

Gifts Are for Ministering to the Body
1 Corinthians 14:1–40

Preview:

God gives gifts to build up the body of Christ. When people place the exercise of their gifts ahead of the purpose for which they are given, both the use of the gift and the purpose are perverted. If gifts are used in the service of love, the individuals exercising them will want to have only those that are most beneficial to the body toward which they are directed. Comparing prophecy (the better gift) with tongues (the lesser gift), Paul hopes to divert his readers' attention away from the sensational gifts toward those that edify. He concludes with a challenge to do all things decently and in order.

While the acquisition and exercise of spiritual gifts in general constituted a problem at Corinth, it appears that the most serious difficulty was centered on the gift of tongues. Earlier (12:10) Paul listed tongues among the last of the spiritual gifts. Later in 12:28 he listed tongues among the least of the gifts. In this chapter he is going to compare it with the greatest of the gifts (i.e., prophecy). Much as he did in chapters 8—10, Paul has taken on a problem relating to the admixture of truth and error. He established a foundation for his teaching on this issue in the previous chapters by detailing the nature of the authentic ministries of the Holy Spirit and by showing how they relate to Christian worship and character. But he still has a problem. What this church seems to be practicing in reference to tongues is being practiced with sincerity but not with understanding (14:2, 11, 14). And the result is a demonstration without edification. There is a display of what is said to be the gift of the Holy Spirit, but since there is no one to interpret, no one can say for sure if it is even genuine—in one case, at least, it clearly was not (12:3). To make matters worse, for these reasons, it is not in conformity with the Pentecostal experience. Paul has already raised the specter of syncretism (12:2). He associates their experience with immaturity (13:11), and since they have construed that their experience is to be coveted, and the writer has said that the desire for the gifts is a good thing (12:31; cf. 14:1), he now needs to spell out what a "better gift" might look like in contrast to the lesser gift.

Paul's approach is very similar to that with which he addressed the idol meat issue. First, he states the issue (12:1). He then identifies a matter for serious concern with which most of them would have to agree (12:3). In the remainder of chapter 12, he presents his theological argument for the nature and practice of spiritual gifts. In chapter 13 he shows that in reality the matter of spiritual gifts is subordinate to the superior expressions of love. This is Paul's teleological argument. Now, in chapter 14, Paul presents his argument from experience. He calls upon the church to consider what they have observed in their own exercise of the gifts. What have they seen in Paul's example? How have their various ministries been received—contrasting tongues with prophecy? Finally, Paul challenges them to mature reflection on the problem(s) they have brought before him, rebuking them for the chaotic character of their services and challenging them to peace and orderliness.

Tongues: Pentecost Versus Corinth

"Pursue love, yet desire earnestly spiritual gifts" (14:1) forms the connecting link with Paul's final comment in chapter 12 while, at the same time, embracing the principle of chapter 13 that love is prior and gifts are subordinate to it. He then addresses the central purpose for the gifts and compares this to their experience of tongues versus their experience of prophecy (vv. 2–25). In the concluding section (vv. 26–40), Paul offers practical advice on ways to follow up on his instruction by taking steps to bring the participants under control. Here the footprint widens slightly as he introduces additional matters only tangentially related to tongues but very much related to order and harmony in their services.

A word needs to be said here about the specific nature of the gift of tongues as used in this chapter. Earlier in the comments on 12:10 I suggested that there is an apparent difference between the exercise of tongues in Acts and their use in 1 Corinthians. This is asserted for several reasons. First, in 1 Corinthians 14 tongues are under the control of the speaker, apparently to initiate or to cease as he wishes (cf. 14:6, 27–28). This is not the case in Acts 2, 10, or 19. Second, the tongues-speaking in Acts seems to have a special significance as a dispensational sign (cf. Acts 2:15–21). However, in 1 Corinthians 14 the primary purpose seems to be to edify the speaker (14:4). Third, the exercise of the tongues in Acts was not regulated according to the rules listed in 1 Corinthians 14. For example, more than three spoke in each case. Also, no interpretation is mentioned.

One may very well ask, at this point, Since Paul and Luke were companions in the gospel, why is it that they would both use the term *glossa* to express two different ideas without providing explanation? One would expect that if a distinction is made between the ways each uses it, such a distinction would be spelled out. Furthermore, since Paul wrote 1 Corinthians before Luke wrote Acts, it is in Acts that one would expect to find the clarification. This is only logical since it would be incumbent on the later writer to show the distinction. This, in fact, is the case. As Luke describes the events at Pentecost, he is careful to point out that as the apostle spoke in "tongues" *(glossa)*, every man heard in his own "dialect" *(dialektos)*. Note the interchange between those two terms in Acts 2:6, 8, and 11.

It is my contention that the differences are not to be explained in terms of two legitimate (albeit different) gifts. Rather, the accounts recorded in both of these texts are *experiential* and *historical*—not *theological*. Luke records what happened on Pentecost. Paul records what was happening in Corinth. The question as to which of these experiences is to be considered normative—Acts 2 or 1 Corinthians 14—may be answered in several possible ways. One could say that the Pentecostal experience is normative and that the legitimate exercise of gifts must conform to that initial one. Or one could say that both are normative for two different kinds of experience—one for the inauguration of the church and one for the institution of the church. A third option might be that the Corinthian experience is normative and that Acts 2 must be made to conform to it. Finally, we could say that neither is necessarily normative—they are merely descriptions of two different experiences manifested in the early church. I believe the Pentecostal experience of Acts 2 (the first option above) should be considered normative for understanding the purpose and exercise of the gift of tongues, and my discussion will show that a careful exposition of the text supports this thesis.

The phenomenon in Acts clearly involved speaking in a "known" language. (1) In Acts 2:6 and 8 the term "language" is used synonymously with "tongues." (2) The adjective *heteros*, in Acts 2:4 does not denote ecstatic utterance but simply a language that was different. (3) In each case (Acts 2, 10, 19) there is evidence that foreign Jews were present. (4) Since the gift of interpretation does not appear in the book of Acts, it is only reasonable to assume that either it was not necessary or it was included in the tongues experience itself. If the Pentecostal experience is normative, then it is to be explained in the sense that every person heard in his or her own language.

That the experience in Corinth, however, is not to be taken in the sense of known language is asserted for two reasons. (1) It was understood not so much for communication as for the edification of the one speaking (14:4). (2) In the exercise of the gift, Paul calls for an interpreter to be present (1 Cor. 14:28). This refers to a spiritual gift of interpretation (cf. 1 Cor. 12:10). Tongues in Corinth, then, involved languages unknown to *anyone* in the assembly and profitable to them only if an interpreter was present. There are also several applications of this gift unique to the Corinthian situation. (1) It was used for prayer (2 Cor. 14:23ff.). (2) It was used in speaking to the assembly (1 Cor. 14:26). Additionally, it is evident that the practice of the gift in 1 Corinthians 14 does not entirely match the instruction regarding its proper use in 1 Corinthians 12.

My position is that the interpreter must do two things. First, he or she must overlay the *historical* data with the *theological*. That is, where there are apparent "contradictions," it is necessary to evaluate the experience by the doctrine. This is what Paul does. He lays out the theological and teleological foundation in chapters 12 and 13 and then evaluates the Corinthians' experience in light of it. Readers are forced to consider whether their experience matches the theological grid. Second, one must read Acts 2 as further clarification of the initial experience of Pentecost as Luke's way of making it abundantly clear what the experience entailed. There is no doubt that the Corinthians sincerely thought their experience was the same as that at Pentecost, but it was not. Paul's challenge throughout this text is to gently prod them back to orthopraxy with a careful application of orthodoxy.[1]

Pursue Love (14:1)

"Pursue love" (v. 1) ties the preceding thought to what follows (cf. 12:31; 13:13)—"desire earnestly spiritual gifts" (v. 1). Paul is concerned that his readers do not misunderstand him. He does not mean by what he says in chapter 13 that spiritual gifts have no value at all; he simply wants his readers to keep the gifts in perspective. Thus, he especially desires that they may prophesy (v. 1). As for desiring spiritual gifts, it is only proper to seek after those gifts that will best fulfill the mandate of love. Since prophecy issues in the greatest benefit to the greatest number of people, it is only appropriate that one seek that gift above all others.

Tongues Are for a Sign (14:2–25)

In light of the fact that all the gifts are for the edification of the church, Paul carefully shows that what the Corinthians are experiencing fails this litmus test and should be laid aside in preference to those gifts that will be beneficial. In this section he seems to role play from the perspective of the Corinthian position. This is reflected in the subtle shift from the plural of verse 1 ("desire" and "you may prophesy") to the singular: "For one who speaks in a tongue does not speak to men, but to God; for no one understands" (v. 2). This is a statement of historical fact—not necessarily a statement of what happens when this gift is properly exercised. The Corinthian believers understood that this person "in his spirit . . . speaks mysteries" (v. 2). Even though someone may be speaking spiritual mysteries, the benefit to the hearers is nil because they cannot understand. This of course is in contrast to the gift of prophecy.

"But one who prophesies speaks to men" (v. 3). Continuing his contrast, Paul returns to prophecy—where genuine communication is taking place. The results are "edification and exhortation and consolation." On the other hand, "one who speaks in a tongue edifies himself" (v. 4). When the Corinthians spoke in their tongues, only one person was benefited, but in contrast, "one who prophesies edifies the church" (v. 4). Then Paul adds, "I wish that you all spoke in tongues, but even more that you would prophesy" (v. 5). Admitting the value of tongues, it would still be better if they prophesied. The reason, of course, is "that the church may receive edifying" (v. 5). Since Paul recognizes that there is a legitimate exercise of tongues, he does not deny that here. In fact, he need not do so, as we shall see.

"But now, brethren" (v. 6) means "Well, now, let's look at the facts and take a concrete example."[2] "If I come to you speaking in tongues, what shall I profit you?" The question is, What benefit is it to you if I come speaking in tongues? Paul really doesn't answer the question except by way of contrast. By "Unless I speak to you" (v. 6), Paul is saying that if you are benefited, I must speak "either by way of revelation" (apostolic gift), "knowledge" (the gift of knowledge), "prophecy" (the gift of prophecy), "teaching" (the gift of teaching). Any of the above gifts is far superior to *the* gift of tongues because it communicates and edifies.

"Even lifeless things" (v. 7) demonstrate Paul's point. He goes on to add more examples. An instrument "producing a sound," must also be distinctive to be understood as "either the flute or the harp." This is clearly understood by the soldier who follows the sound of a trumpet. How could he "prepare himself for battle" (v. 8) if the signal were an indistinct "sound?"

Now Paul pulls his readers further into the web of his argument. His example now deftly moves them away from the legitimacy of unintelligible "languages" to compare their experience to "a great many kinds of languages in the world" (v. 10). There are many kinds of languages, "and no kind is without meaning" (v. 10). They are all intelligible to those who use and receive them. On the other hand, if I do not know a specific language "I shall be to the one who speaks a barbarian" (v. 11) Paul's use of "barbarian" here simply has the general sense of "foreigner" (cf. Acts 28:24; Rom. 1:14; Col. 3:11). It is much better then if the one who wants to communicate uses a language that conveys meaning to the hearer. So he adds, "Seek to abound for the edification of the church" (v. 12), that is, seek after gifts that will benefit the church. Note that where Paul gives direction to his argument, it moves toward Acts 2 as the normative experience.

Realizing that many in this assembly feel God is directing them to get up in the assembly and speak in tongues, Paul suggests that one way to test whether this is from God is to pray that they may interpret (v. 13). Paul is not saying that speaking in a tongue and praying are coterminous, but that if one is wishing to speak in a tongue, he or she should ask God for the gift of interpretation also. In the Pentecostal experience, the tongue and the interpretation of the tongue were never a problem, since both the speaker and the hearer understood.

"For" (v. 14) indicates the reason for Paul's advice in verse 13. In the language of indirect discourse, Paul continues. If I put myself in your shoes, he says, "my spirit prays." This is a difficult expression but probably means "the Holy Spirit in me" in the sense that his spiritual gift is being exercised. "But my mind is unfruitful" suggests "I do not understand what I am saying." What is the conclusion to all this discussion? "I shall pray with the spirit and I shall pray with the mind also; I shall sing with the spirit and I shall sing with the mind also" (v. 15). If I should pray or sing in tongues, intelligible praying and singing (that is, with the tongues interpreted) will accompany the tongues. Again Paul presses the theological grid onto their experience by showing that their experience must match the purpose of edification implicit in all spiritual gifts. "Otherwise . . . how will the one . . . say the "Amen" at your giving of thanks . . . ?" (v. 16). Even if a person should bless the Lord in tongues, it would be impossible for anyone else to join in because no one would know it. "For you are giving thanks well enough, but the other man is not edified" (v. 17). What has been said may be good, but no one has been spiritually benefited by it.

"I speak in tongues more than you all" (v. 18) is a curious claim. This is the only place Paul (or any other New Testament writer) makes mention of his speaking in tongues. Is it possible that he is using irony again? If he had the gift but they never heard him use it, this would raise the obvious question, why not? He goes on to answer this implied question. "However, in the church I desire to speak five words with my mind, that I may instruct others also, rather than ten thousand words in a tongue" (v. 19). Words have meaning only as they are understood, and it is Paul's intent that he might instruct others. There was never a legitimate occasion for Paul to use this gift, and so he explains that his ministry was evangelism and discipleship—not the display of unusual gifts.

Continuing his contrast with prophecy, Paul goes on to show that in the essential purpose of spiritual gifts, prophecy was to be preferred. "Do not be children" (v. 20). This is the second time the apostle has measured the Corinthians' spiritual maturity by this term (cf. 13:11). "In your thinking³ be mature." Paul associates the gift of tongues with spiritual immaturity. He anticipates that as the church matures, her concerns will be less in the arena of the spectacular and more in the stimulation of understanding.

"In the Law it is written" (v. 21) has in mind the entire Old Testament Scriptures. In this case, Paul has in mind Isaiah 28:11–12 (cf. John 10:34; Rom. 3:20). "So then tongues are for a sign, not to those who believe, but to unbelievers" (v. 22). Paul's use of this text to show the legitimate exercise of the gift of tongues is one of the strongest indicators thus far that his understanding of the gift is fully consistent with Luke's account of the Pentecostal experience. When Israel was in the situation where the language of the Assyrians was the dominant language, it was a sure sign that they were under the judgment of God for their unbelief. It was in this context that the sign was given repeatedly in Acts (see Acts 2:4–12, 22–23; 10:45; 11:2, 15–18; 19:1–7). That is, God had judged Israel and was speaking to them in the language of their captivity to announce to them that His mantle of blessing was now on the Church. Paul applies this principle to the situation in Corinth. This gift, he asserts, is not for the assembly of believers. It is for unbelievers. Why would they want to use it in their church?

"But prophecy is for a sign, not to unbelievers, but to those who believe" (v. 22). Insofar as the church is for the gathering of saints and not unbelievers, prophecy is by far the more appropriate gift. Yet, even in this case, since the circumstances are so different from the inaugural experiences relating to God's judgment on Israel, tongues is not the appropriate gift even for the unbelievers who might come into their gathering. Paul asks, "Will they not say that you are mad?" (v. 23). In other words, the very purpose of the gift is mitigated by the improper exercise of it.

On the other hand, it is almost impossible to misuse the gift of prophecy. Should an unbeliever wander into the assembly and be exposed to the

truth of God being taught through prophecy, "he is convicted by all, he is
called to account by all" (v. 24). Thus, instead of being repelled by the service,
"he will fall on his face and worship God" (v. 25). He will be convinced of his
sin and of God's righteousness and will repentant and believe.

Chaos Is Not of God (14:26–40)

Having established the theological argument for the proper use of spiritual
gifts and having concluded that there are some gifts that are more generally
edifying than others, there is one more thing left to do. Paul now turns his
attention to the practical matters having to do with the order—and disorder—
of their services. The matter of tongues is still to be considered, and his
approach continues to establish biblical parameters that are designed to eliminate abuse. If their experience is not legitimate, it will be through the application of these standards that it will become evident and the problem will die
a natural death (vv. 26–29). He then goes on to suggest how the prophets are
to be ordered (vv. 30–35). And finally he has a concluding challenge with
respect to the women of the church who were causing confusion during the
service—to which he appends a similar charge to everyone that everything is
to be done "decently and in order" (vv. 36–40).

The contrast is between harmony and confusion. The key verse here is "For
God is not a God of confusion, but of peace, as in all the churches of the
saints" (v. 33). As Paul comes to a close in this section, he draws upon the
example of other churches with which he has been privileged to work.
Harmony signifies order. Confusion signifies disorder. God is interested in
how we worship Him. Some forms of worship are not permitted. While this
was and is difficult to accept, Paul wishes to make it clear that their worship
should follow an acceptable standard of conduct.

Peace and worship (vv. 26–33). Paul argues first for *balance* (vv. 26–28).
The central principle in the exercise of any gift is, "Let all things be done for
edification" (v. 26). Throughout this chapter this has been the overriding
directive that continues to dominate the apostle's thinking as he regulates the
proper exercise of these gifts. This paragraph is also significant because it gives
"us the most intimate glimpse we have of the early church at worship. Here
we are able to see something of what the early Christians actually did when
they assembled to worship God."[4]

"If anyone speaks" (v. 27) is evidence that worship services of the early
church were not dominated by one individual; rather, there seems to have
been an open and free participation in the worship service by all who were led
to participate. Thus, in this situation, if a person should speak in a tongue,

Paul says, "it should be by two or at the most three" (v. 27). It is permissible for as many as three to speak in tongues and "each in turn" (v. 27)—that is, one at a time, not all together. "And one must interpret" (v. 27). "But if there is no interpreter, let him keep silent" (v. 28). To speak in tongues without an interpreter is forbidden in the church (see above).

Second, Paul argues for *order* in relation to the prophets (vv. 29–31). "Let two or three prophets speak, and let the others pass judgment" (v. 29). Those who would share a special truth revealed to them by God were to do so in order and no more than two or three. The only exception to this would be in the event that a person felt unusually constrained, while someone was speaking, to interject a thought—and in this situation the first one must keep silent (v. 30). In other words, the new communicator was entitled to be heard at once. It is not difficult to imagine that some were trying to out-shout one another in the interest of being heard. So Paul adds, "You can all prophesy one by one" (v. 31). Again this is to be understood in the light of verse 29. Paul is not saying that any number of people may prophesy, but that the two or three may prophesy one at a time. And in the case of possible interruption, the two are not to prophesy simultaneously but one at a time.

Finally, Paul argues for *control* (vv. 32–33). "And the spirits of prophets are subject to the prophets" (v. 32). In contrast to tongues as being exercised in Corinth, where it appears that the spirit of an individual is out of control, Paul emphasizes that in the exercise of the prophetic gift, all is done decently and in order. "God is not a God of confusion" (v. 33). The service that is disorderly, confusing, and disruptive is not of God, for God is the author of "peace" (v. 33).

Peace and the women (vv. 34–35). The women are to keep silent in the churches.[5] This must be interpreted in light of 11:5, where it is clear that Paul permitted women to prophesy and to pray in the service so long as they did so in ways that honored their husbands and the elders of the church. Several general interpretive possibilities are suggested for this directive. One suggestion is that Paul is forbidding the women to speak in tongues.[6] But that would seem odd, since he does not forbid the exercise of any other gift in this way. Beyond that, such a prohibition would entail a contradiction with what follows—in verse 39 he comes back and tells them "do not forbid to speak in tongues." Another is that it is not a reference to Paul's teaching at all; rather, it refers to something the Jewish faction in the church is teaching,[7] or it is a copyist's interpolation.[8] While we have noted that Paul sometimes inserts the arguments of his detractors, that does not seem to be the case here. We would expect a clear refutation to follow, but only a circular argument can discern this in verses 36–40.

Most prefer to understand this as a prohibition against "disruptive speech."[9] While dogmatism is difficult, this option seems best. It would connect naturally to the preceding context and to verse 35: "If they desire to learn anything, let them ask their own husbands at home." They were not allowed to disrupt the service by asking questions and talking while the service was going on. If the seating arrangement corresponded to that of the synagogue, it is likely that the women sat to the back (or in a gallery) with their children, while the men sat to the front.[10] The very fact that they would be "asking their husbands" something during the service suggests that they would have to be disruptive when they did so. If the reference is to "judging" the prophets (v. 29), this injunction should be understood as a universal principle. If it is understood more in the context of idle chatter, we should imagine that Paul is addressing a situation peculiar to the Corinthian assembly and related to the cultural situation shared generally in the Graeco-Roman world. In this latter sense, it is likely the first readers in Corinth would have understood exactly what he was talking about—including the names of those who were causing the trouble! The principle would be normative. The specific situation to which it applies here would not. The directive to come to worship with a spirit of reverence, quietness, and readiness to hear the Word of God is applicable to all churches in every age. The customary seating arrangement that may have caused this problem is unique to the ancient church, but problems associated with seating arrangements, congregational participation, and the care of small children continue to present similar problems in our churches to this day.

Peace and the Word (vv. 36–38). Paul offers a bit of sarcasm with, "Was it from you that the word of God first went forth? Or has it come to you only?" (v. 36). Are you the only repository of God's truth? If there is anyone in the assembly who considers himself a prophet or spiritual, he must acknowledge that "the things which I write to you are the Lord's commandment. But if anyone does not recognize this, he is not recognized" (vv. 37–38). Paul's challenge here is similar to what he does in 2:14–17. If they are "spiritual" and have the "mind of Christ," they will agree. If there was anyone who would refuse to acknowledge his authority, he was not going to waste his time trying to convince them. Gordon Fee observes:

> This is the third instance in this letter where Paul attacks their own position head-on with the formula "If anyone thinks he is . . ." (see 3:18 and 8:2). Each occurs in one of the three major sections of the letter (chaps. 1—4; 8—10; 12—14); and the argument in each case indicates that by this formula Paul is zeroing in on the Corinthians' perspective as to their own spirituality. They do indeed think of themselves as "the wise" (3:18) and as "having knowledge" (8:2), probably in both cases because they also think of themselves as being *pneumatikoi* (see on 2:15 and 3:1).[11]

As Paul did on the idol meat issue, he also asserts his authority as the Corinthians' spiritual father and an apostle responsible to deliver God's commandments to them.

Summary and conclusion (vv. 39–40). "Desire earnestly to prophesy, and do not forbid to speak in tongues" (v. 39). Again, Paul compares the two gifts and in so doing asserts the legitimacy of the gift of tongues and the primacy of the gift of prophecy. They are not to forbid one another the legitimate exercise of their gifts—whether prophecy or tongues or any other gift for that matter—but in every case, the gifts should be exercised according to the standards given. "But all things must be done properly and in an orderly manner" (v. 40). Public worship was to be reflective of the One to whom it was directed, thus it was to be beautiful and harmonious. Priority one: Seek gifts that edify. Priority two: Don't quench the Spirit. Priority three: Be orderly.

Study Questions

1. In this chapter, which gift—tongues or prophecy—does Paul say is the most important? Why?

2. What is another way of defining the English word *tongue?* What specifically is Paul writing about?

3. What must accompany tongues-speaking? Why?

4. In writing about tongues, what is most important to Paul—the fact that the gift of speaking in tongues has been exercised or that a clear message has been given forth?

5. Is Paul writing here about an ecstatic experience or the giving forth of an understandable spiritual message?

6. What will cause the unbeliever great conviction, whereby he declares that "God is certainly among you"?

7. Why is it important that order be established in the congregation when messages are going forth?

8. What controls the giving forth of prophecy? As Paul describes it here, is prophecy "forthtelling" into the future, or a special gift of teaching in unusual circumstances?

9. From what Paul says about women in verses 34–35, is he against women, as some say? What possibly was the problem in the church of Corinth that caused him to write these words?

10. While verse 40 particularly relates to the context of this chapter, could it also express a broader principle that may be applicable in many situations? Explain.

Section IV: Teaching

Behold, I Tell You a Mystery

1 Corinthians 15:1 — 6:24

CHAPTER 18

The Resurrection
1 Corinthians 15:1-58

Preview:

Of all the problems addressed in the Corinthian letters, this is probably the most serious, because it involved a matter central to the faith. Some of Paul's readers apparently were willing to concede that Christ was resurrected but in the same breath denied the bodily resurrection. This is a problem unique to the context of Greek believers for whom the idea was entirely counterintuitive. Paul shows that it is crucial to the faith, crucial to Christian living, and crucial to the blessed hope.

The only doctrinal "error" to which the apostle addresses himself in this epistle is contained in this chapter. What were the historical factors behind this problem? One possibility is that he is challenging the faulty thinking of one of the parties mentioned in 1:12. By process of elimination, the party of Apollos is usually suggested. However, this does not agree with what we know of Apollos and of his ministry (cf. also 16:12; Acts 18:24-28). Another suggestion is that they were the moral libertines mentioned in chapter 6 and against whom the apostle urges the resurrection in 6:14. The problem with this is that if they doubted the resurrection, Paul could hardly have used it as an argument for moral purity. Another view is that the problem came from converted Sadducees (cf. also Acts 24:6-9; 26:6-8). However, there is no evidence of any such maverick breed at Corinth. Others suggest that the opponents of the doctrine were Epicureans (note the reference to material indulgence in 15:32).[1] It is evident from Acts 17:32 that many of the philosophical breezes of the day could be felt in the crosscurrents of this cosmopolitan seaport. There is also significant evidence that many of Paul's readers would have fallen under the influence of the general worldview of the Epicureans that would have lead them either toward libertinism or asceticism.

Recent archaeological evidence suggests a significant preoccupation with death in first-century Corinth.[2] The popularity of Epicureanism seems to be associated with this preoccupation. The fear of death was removed in their philosophy by arguing that at death the individual simply ceases to exist. Accordingly, there is nothing to fear. Here the reference in 15:32 argues that the careless lifestyle is a consequence and not a cause of the denial of the resurrection. Acts 17:18 observes certain Epicurean and Stoic philosophers in Athens who were willing to hear Paul out. It should be remembered that Corinth was a Roman colony when Paul came there. The aristocracy of the city was typically Roman, and it was they who were especially enamored with Epicureanism.[3]

Nevertheless, the tenets of Greek platonic philosophy had generally pervaded the Hellenistic world. Dualistic systems considered that the material universe was unsuited to a spiritual existence. The Gnostics even went so far as to suggest that the body was intrinsically evil. It is likely that all of these currents of thought formed the background for both 1 Corinthians 15 and Colossians 2:8–23. (See also 2 Timothy 2:17–18.) How this influenced the thinking of the Corinthian believers is still unclear. Perhaps some of them, like the Thessalonians were uncertain about those of their number who had already died (1 Thess. 4:13ff.; cf. 1 Cor. 11:30). Perhaps they were speculating that only those who were alive at the coming of Christ would be able to participate in His kingdom. Influenced as they were by conventional thought as to the impossibility of corpses coming to life, they failed to realize that the resurrection of Christ also included a "blessed hope" for all who trust in Him— not just to share with Him in His kingdom, but to share with Him in a glorified body.[4] In any event, Paul is not intending to answer the supposed philosophical objections. Rather, he is instructing his readers with respect to the fact of the resurrection of Christ and the appropriateness of their confidence that believers will one day share in that glorious reality.[5]

The Gospel Which I Preached (15:1–7)

In rhetorical fashion similar to that used in his previous discussion of idol meat and spiritual gifts, Paul begins his defense of the resurrection with a reference to theological common ground shared by all who had received Christ. By establishing this central teaching, he will then be able to move on to some of their apparent defections. How will believers share in this resurrection?

What exactly is this resurrection "body" like? Is it different only in degree to what I experience or is it different in kind? So, his argument is not (as it were) a set of proofs to serve as an apologetic for the resurrection—although its apologetic value cannot be discounted.[6] Rather, it is a discussion of the significance of the resurrection for our own sharing in this hope and for understanding exactly what it means to be raised from the dead. It is evident that some were willing to concede that Christ is raised, but they were not clear on the nature or implications of this. Much as liberal theology of the last century redefined the resurrection, "life in the Spirit meant a final ridding oneself of the body, not because it was evil but because it was inferior and beneath them."[7] The idea that the body would be raised was repugnant.[8]

Introduction (1–2). "Now" (v. 1) tells us that Paul has finished his answers to the Corinthians' questions, and he goes on to a new subject. "I make known to you" (v. 1) primarily looks ahead to verses 3–5. "The gospel which I preached to you" is the good news the Corinthians have "received, in which also [they] stand, by which also [they] are saved unless [they] believed in vain" (vv. 1–2). "In vain" may mean "without cause," that is, blind faith[9] (cf. Gal. 2:18). Or it may mean "without effect," that is, to no purpose (cf. Gal. 3:4; 4:11). The latter idea seems to fit the context best—looking ahead to the discussion that follows. If, as some are saying in Corinth, there is no resurrection, then their faith is vain and worthless (cf. v. 14). Paul is now at the very heart of the gospel message.

A common creed (3–5). Paul says, "For I delivered to you as of first importance" (v. 3), that is, in order of priority, "what I also received" (v. 3). In both the Jewish and Greek world, the term for "received" (*paralambano*) has the technical meaning of "traditions" of teachers, rabbis, or philosophers.[10] The teachings to which Paul refers in this passage relate to the facts of the gospel he received and preached. Barrett paraphrases this with "I ask you to note with what form of words I preached the gospel to you."[11] The tradition thus does not originate with Paul; it predates his ministry.[12] It also conforms to the earliest preaching recorded in Acts. (See Luke 24:45–47; Acts 13:16–41.) There is strong evidence that verses 3–5 constitute an early confessional formula originating in Palestine.[13] In any event, this passage gives testimony to the essential facts of the gospel, including the death, burial, resurrection, and attestation of the risen Lord.[14] It is likely that Paul received this from the apostles or from his association with the believers of Antioch at the time of his first visit there (c. A.D. 42).[15] Paul asserts elsewhere that "his gospel" was given to him directly by the Lord (Gal. 1:12). It is entirely possible that the Lord confirmed these truths to Paul by revelation. Each line is introduced with *kai hoti*, "and that," emphasizing the content of each statement.[16]

- *"that Christ died for our sins according to the Scriptures"*
- *"and that He was buried"*
- *"and that He was raised on the third day according to the Scriptures"*
- *"and that He appeared to Cephas, then to the twelve"*[17]

The four "independent propositions, not subordinated to one another, reflect the nature of proclamation."[18] The propositions each are laid down without explanation. Two probable factors account for this. One is that the formula seems to be in a fixed form. The second factor is that this calls to the minds of the hearers the message they had already heard from Paul and on which there would be no reason to elaborate—it is a statement of faith most surely affirmed by them all.

Having said that, it is difficult for a modern reader to not ask the obvious question: What would the "unabridged edition" look like? When he gives the first truth of the gospel with "Christ died for our sins according to the Scriptures" (v. 3), had he fleshed this out with them? The sublime theology of substitution and satisfaction (Rom. 3:23–26) must surely have already been preached in Corinth. It would only be a few years later that Paul would pen those words to Rome while on a subsequent three-month visit to this very city (Acts 20:1–4).[19] And one wonders what Scriptures he has in mind according to which Christ would die for our sins. We are tempted to think of Isaiah 52—53 or of Passover (cf. 1 Cor. 5:7).[20] Certainly these messianic texts made their way into the common faith of the early believers. But a more likely source is reflected in the early preaching of Acts—as recorded by Paul's companion, Luke. Concerning these great salvific events, Peter drew from Joel 2:28–32; Psalms 16:8–11; 89:3–4; and 110:1. It would be from these texts that he would discern God's predetermined plan that Christ would be slain, that he would be buried, that he would nonetheless not see corruption (that is, would be raised), and that he would ascend to the right hand of God (cf. Acts 2:14–36). Later Peter again would make use of Psalm 118:22 and Daniel 9:24–27 (see Acts 4:23–31).

Such proclamations laid the bedrock of scriptural truth according to which Christ's work would be understood and defined by the early Church. That these were decisive texts for Paul is clearly reflected in his sermon in Acts 13:16–41, where the essential content is identical to that outlined here and where he makes explicit use of Psalms 2 and 16 in addition to Isaiah 55 and Habakkuk 1. While he does not cite these texts on Mars Hill, he makes copious use of the Old Testament in his message (Acts 17:16–31). It is said of Apollos that he was "mighty in the Scriptures" (Acts 18:24) and that he "refuted the Jews in public, demonstrating *by the Scriptures* that Jesus was the Christ" (18:28, emphasis mine). One further thought concerning this first truth of the gospel is that such language shows how the death of Christ presupposes a condition that exists between God and sinful humanity. There is an alienation requiring a substitutionary atonement imbedded in this earliest of Christian confessions.[21]

The second truth of the gospel is "that he was buried" (v. 4). This evidences the reality and totality of Christ's death. Emphasis on his burial is important to Paul's argument because it relates to Christ's body. Many even today follow the same reasoning that influenced the Corinthian church to affirm a *spiritual* resurrection but not a *bodily* one. It was in the body that the Son of God died. It was His body that went into the grave. And it was in a glorified body that He arose. He does not repeat the supportive, "according to the Scriptures," but Peter's use of Psalm 16:10 shows us the commonly held interpretation that presupposes the idea that Christ's body would go down into "Sheol" (a reference to "grave"), from which it would be rescued before it would see corruption. As noted above, Paul is also known to have used this text to make the same point.

The third truth of the gospel is "He was raised" (v. 4). Paul uses the aorist tense to speak of Christ's death and burial as singular events. Now He uses the perfect passive tense to stress abiding results. Elsewhere Paul uses similar language to speak of God's miraculous power in the performance of the resurrection (Acts 13:22, 30-37; Rom. 4:24-25; and especially as this impacts the believer, Rom. 8:11, cf. 1 Cor. 15:20 below). The expression "On the third day" (v. 4) was important because it shows that the resurrection was not a special feeling experienced by Jesus' followers. It happened before they knew or expected it. This is not an existential event; it is a historical event[22] occurring once for all (as the perfect tense emphasizes) as evidenced by the empty tomb. The added phrase "according to the Scriptures" (v. 4) is not as easily interpreted. As seen from our review of early apostolic preaching, it is clear that "an early tradition saw the combined evidence of Psalms 16:8-11 and 110:1 as bearing witness to the Messiah's resurrection (cf. Acts 2:25-36); and that it happened "on the third day" was probably seen in terms of the variety of Old Testament texts in which salvation or vindication took place on the third day"[23] (cf. Matt. 12:39-40; 16:4; Luke 11:29-30 on the sign of Jonah), or it may be an allusion to Hosea 6:2.[24] The facts of the gospel are not only important historically, but prophetically as well. They occurred as had been predicted (cf. Ps. 16:10; John 20:9; Acts 26:23).

The fourth vital truth of the gospel is "that He appeared to Cephas" (v. 5; cf. Luke 24; 34). Christ appeared after the resurrection, not to a few but to "Cephas, then to the twelve" (v. 5). Interestingly, the confession skips over the first appearance to the women (Luke 24:1-12), whose testimony did not have the weight Peter's had. This is reminiscent of John 4:39-42, where the woman at the well brought the men from her town to the Lord with her testimony. But after hearing Christ for themselves, the men found it necessary to discount

her word as being decisive ("no longer because of what [she] said," John
4:42). Rather, it is "because of what [Jesus] said that we believe" (v. 43). The
reader has to smile, because we all know that it was really both/and; not
either/or. For, had she not testified, they would not have been brought to Jesus
in the first place.

Likewise, had it not been for the testimony of the women, we wonder
how Peter might have made the discovery. Jesus and Paul (Gal. 3:26–29) both
challenge the status quo of the Jewish and Graeco-Roman world with regard
to the place and importance of women. Nevertheless, it is Peter who later
becomes the champion—to whom is given the "keys to the kingdom" and is
decisive in opening the doors to the New Testament church to the Jews (Acts
2), the Samaritans (Acts 8), and the Gentiles (Acts 10). And it was his testimony that was decisive. So in the confession, it is the reference to "Cephas"
that carries the day.

Paul's Doctrine of the Resurrection of Christ

For the resurrection of Christ, Paul was put on trial (Acts 24:21).

By His resurrection, Christ now proclaims light to the Jews and Gentiles (Acts 26:23).

By His resurrection, Christ was proclaimed the Son of God with power (Rom. 1:4).

Believers will be united in the "likeness" of Christ's resurrection (Rom. 6:5).

Christ was raised up through the power of God (1 Cor. 6:14).

Christ was raised on the third day (1 Cor. 15:4).

Christ appeared to Cephas (Peter) (1 Cor. 15:5).

Christ appeared to the twelve disciples (1 Cor. 15:5).

Christ appeared to five hundred brothers (1 Cor. 15:6).

Christ appeared to James and all the apostles (1 Cor. 15:7).

Christ appeared to Paul (1 Cor. 15:8).

God raised Christ from the dead (1 Cor. 15:15).

The last Adam (Christ) by resurrection became a life-giving spirit (1 Cor. 15:45).

Because God raised up Jesus, He will also raise up the believers (2 Cor. 4:14).

The Father raised the Son from the dead (Gal. 1:1; Eph. 1:20; 1 Thess. 1:10).

Paul desired to know the power of Christ's resurrection (Phil. 3:10).

What is most important here is that the risen Christ was seen. The function of this entire discussion is still directed toward those who will affirm the resurrection of Christ and yet reject the idea that His resurrection included the body (cf. 15:35–57). This is so important that Paul expands the list. The additional claim "then to the twelve" (v. 5) may or may not have been part of the original formula. However, to us, it has the *ring* of belonging to the confession because "the twelve" would be a code for the original inner circle of Jesus' followers, and it is not a term that occurs naturally in any of Paul's other writings (cf. Luke 9:1, 12; John 6:67–71, passim).[25]

Whereas the essential truths of the gospel were demonstrated by the Scriptures, Paul now turns to extrabiblical evidence: "After that He appeared to more than five hundred brethren at one time" (v. 6). It is not certain when this last event occurred. The most likely possibility is the event recorded in Matthew 28:16–20. Since Jesus had previously announced this meeting (cf. Matt. 26:32; 28:10, 16), it is unlikely that anyone would have intentionally missed it. What is important is the adverb *ephapax*, "at one time." One commentator has rightly observed:

> There appears to be a conspiracy of silence with regard to this adverb; it is ignored by all the commentaries and studies that I have been able to check. If Paul had merely written "he appeared to five hundred brethren," the most natural interpretation would have been to understand it as a reference to a mass vision. Why, then did he need to emphasize this point? The most obvious explanation is that he intended to underline the objectivity of the experience.[26]

"Then He appeared to James, then to all the apostles" (v. 7). James here is probably the Lord's brother (Matt. 13:55) since the *apostle* James is included in "the twelve" above. James was earlier mentioned as an unbeliever (cf. John 7:5) and later with the assembly of believers (cf. Acts 1:14). It is "at least possible that Jesus converted His brother by appearing to him, as He did later to Paul. Hence it is not correct to say with some opponents of the gospel that Jesus is not reported to have appeared to any unbelievers, and that, therefore, the accounts are suspect because they all come from persons who expected the resurrection."[27] Subsequently, James was a leader in the Jerusalem church (cf. Acts 12:17; 15:13; 21:18). One wonders if this was not the turning point of James's life. By referencing James (not of the twelve) with "all the apostles" (v. 7), Paul seems to be paving the way for inclusion of himself (below) in that exclusive list. This also underscores that when he is using this expression, he is not suggesting "apostle" in the widest possible sense, but in a special limited sense as related to Peter, James, and the apostles called directly by Christ (cf. also Gal. 1—2).[28]

Not I, but the Grace of God (15:8–11)

Finally, "Last of all, as it were to one untimely born [an "abortion"], He appeared to me also" (v. 8). In Paul's characteristically self-effacing way, he cites the fact that he too had the honor of seeing the risen Lord (cf. Acts 9:1–6). The use of the term *ektroma* is interesting.[29] One cannot help but speculate that such language was used of him by his enemies in Corinth. What the Corinthians "see as weakness and therefore as evidence of a lesser standing, he sees as the true evidence that his apostleship is from the Lord. Thus in 2 Corinthians 10–13 where all this comes to a head, he defends himself once again by glorying in his weaknesses (cf. 1 Cor. 2:1–5 and 9:1–27)."[30] He adds, "For I am the least of the apostles" (v. 9)—not because he was simply the last to see the risen Lord, but because he was "not fit" ("unworthy"). Paul has not yet recovered from the "wonder of it all" that he should be elevated to the honor and office of apostleship, "because I persecuted the church of God" (v. 9).[31]

"But by the grace of God I am what I am" (v. 10). Paul does not magnify his personal credentials; he exalts the sovereign grace of God. Yet this least of the apostles "labored even more than all of them" (v. 10). Whether this is taken to mean any of the apostles individually or all of them collectively, the intent of the apostle is not to boast "but the grace of God with me . . . . So we preach" (vv. 10–11). Paul's message and that of the other apostles is the same. Furthermore, both included the message of the resurrection. "And so you believed" (v. 11). If some of the Corinthian believers are now questioning the resurrection, they are departing from their initial starting point. If they believed the message of the gospel, they believed in the resurrection. Paul knows that these believers agree on this point, so he will now proceed to show that this is not merely incidental to their faith; rather, it constitutes the central core without which their faith in Christ is "in vain" (v. 2).

This passage is interesting *historically*. It reflects Paul's association with the Church—from Saul the persecutor to Paul the preacher; from arrogant Pharisee to apostle to the Gentiles; from the feet of Gamaliel to the feet of the risen Christ. Often the people who have been saved from the greatest sin are those who respond the most decisively when the purity of the gospel is challenged.

This text is also interesting *psychologically*. It reflects on Paul's "self-image." Paul was anything but in denial. He does not deny his past and so does not fall into self-righteousness. He does not delight in his past, and so we see a constant awareness of the seriousness of his prior sin. Yet he does not dwell on his past either. He was not morbidly introspective and preoccupied with his interior. Rather, Paul knows what he was yet finds no reason to despair. He knows what he is yet finds no room for pride. And he knows what he has accomplished in Christ yet finds no cause to glory in himself.

Finally, the text is of interest *theologically*. In many ways, Paul's experiences with this church reflect on our own experiences today. Like Paul and the Corinthian believers, we too struggle with the past. We are gifted to serve. And we see God miraculously change lives through our efforts. The immediate crisis in this church was a doctrinal heresy. But the response to it is an unusually candid confession of the apostle. He shows that the dynamic that empowered him was none other than the risen Lord. Nothing less would do for the crisis at hand. Nothing more could be added to improve his chances.

We Are False Witnesses of God (15:12–19)

Perhaps it was because Paul had already been a false witness of God that he has such a sustained allergic reaction to the possibility that it could be happening again. A false witness of God is one who testifies to lies about God through self-deception, rebellion, or blind traditionalism. Paul knew what it was like to "kick against the pricks" (Acts 9) and to persecute even the Church of God in the name of God. The two questions are the same: What if Christ is not raised? And what if we were all false witnesses? If the answer to the first is affirmative, the answer to the second is likewise the same.

At least since Luther it has been recognized that the argument that follows is not one that would be very convincing to pagans. Rather, it is given to believers to show the vital connection between the resurrection of Christ and their own.[32] It explains with a *reductio ad absurdum* in two parts to show (1) that if we question the reality of "resurrection" in general, we cannot at the same time affirm that of Christ (vv. 13, 16); and (2) that if that be the case, our faith is also vacuous, since it is established upon this truth (vv. 14, 17).[33]

Verse 12 stands as a focal point around which the first nineteen verses revolve. "Now if Christ is preached, that He has been raised from the dead" recalls the first eleven verses. "How do some among you say that there is no resurrection?" In keeping with the rhetorical style evident throughout this epistle, Paul establishes their common ground and then launches his challenge in the form of a question: "How do some among you say . . . ?" This question looks ahead to verses 13 through 19. Paul has established first of all that the bodily resurrection is an essential article of faith—one concerning which they all agree. He now tabulates the logical consequences of denying that we will share in it.

Truth and Faith (15:13–15)

Salvation depends on the factual and finished work of Christ—not on how we feel about it. For Paul, there were those in the assembly who were in denial about the resurrection because, in their point of view, it just didn't make any sense. This form of skepticism is deadly, as Paul will show. If one denies the possibility of the bodily resurrection, it will require an overhaul of the gospel, for "not even Christ has been raised" (v. 13). The first consequence is that Christ is still in the grave. The nature of Paul's argument here does not suggest that his objectors denied the resurrection of Christ—only that their approach toward the resurrection, in principle, led to an unthinkable conclusion for any genuine believer. The logic is inescapable. But beyond this, "If Christ has not been raised, then our preaching is vain" (v. 14). The proclamation of the gospel as outlined in verses 1–11 is hollow. Not only that, but "your faith also is vain" (v. 14)—that is, "groundless." Faith in a dead Savior is both preposterous and pathetic. And not only so, but "we are even found *to be* false witnesses of ['against'] God" (v. 15).

Truth and Significance (15:16–17)

If Paul's preaching affirms something that God did not really accomplish, his message and ministry are opposed to God. They perpetrate a lie about Him. Paul summarizes his logic here and goes on to suggest yet another consequence: "You are still in your sins" (v. 17; cf. v. 3). Since the resurrection of Christ is essential to our justification (Rom. 4:25), the denial of it vitiates the forgiveness of our sins. Victims of modernity who have been subjected to preaching that denies the core value of the resurrection for the gospel are told that it doesn't matter what one believes as long as he or she believes in something! The result is an obsession with religious *activity* instead of the *truth*. And there is a disconnect between their real spiritual problem and the only cure for it.

Truth and Hope (15:18–19)

If we deny the resurrection, "those also who have fallen asleep in Christ have perished" (v. 18). The expression "fall asleep in Christ" is used to speak of those who die in Christ (cf. 1 Thess. 4:14 and Rev. 14:13). Only when a person is in Christ can his or her death be said to be as simple as "falling asleep." But if Christ is not raised, then death is a fearful thing—tantamount to "perdition." "Only" (v. 19) is to be taken with the entire opening clause. If our hope in Christ does not take us beyond this present life, then "we are of all men most to be pitied" (v. 19). Indeed, we are both deceived and unwitting deceivers. What a sad lot the Christian becomes.

Paul now goes on to show the vital link to biblical eschatology. Some people believe that faith is useful if only to make life more bearable—a kind of Epicurean Christianity. Against such a vacuous faith, they become obsessed with the fleeting joys of a dying planet. The real answer to this malaise is to reconnect truth to faith, significance, and hope. When people understand the real pain, loneliness, and disappointments that come with the reality of sin, with Paul they realize that the Savior they need cannot be a fantasy—He must be true!

Christ: The Firstfruits (15:20–28)

Christ is risen. This is a *fact*. He is risen from the dead. This is also a *first*. In the preceding section, Paul showed the absurdity of the position of those who challenge the viability of the resurrection by pointing out the consequences for them and for their faith. There it was noted that a vital connection exists between faith and facts. And this is all the more important since Christ did not come to change our feelings or point of view. He came to release us from sin and death. "But since all of that was hypothetical, Paul now turns to demonstrate that Christ's resurrection, which both he and they believe (vv. 1–11), has made the resurrection of the dead both necessary and inevitable."[34]

In what follows, Paul shows that the resurrection comes in stages. Clark summarizes the argument, "First, Christ's resurrection negates the death we inherited from Adam. It also looks forward to the resurrection of believers at Christ's return. With death abolished, and all things in subjection to Christ, Christ will deliver up His kingdom to His Father that God may be all in all."[35]

The New Man (15:20–22)

The first important truth is that Christ is risen. He has become "the first fruits of those who are asleep" (v. 20; cf. Lev. 23:9–14). The "firstfruits" in Israel always anticipated a harvest. "For since by a man *came* death" (v. 21) is to be understood in the light of the parallel idea in verse 22, "by a man also *came* the resurrection of the dead" (v. 21). If the death Adam brought is physical death, then the life Christ brings also includes physical life.

The plight of all the descendents of the first man is that they must pay the consequences of Adam's sin. "As in Adam all die, so also in Christ all shall be made alive" (v. 22). The two occurrences of "all" are to be understood in a restricted sense. In the first instance, it is qualified "in Adam." All who are born of Adam are included—but not all will necessarily die. In the second instance, it is qualified "in Christ." All who are born again in Christ are included—not the entire human family. This may seem trivial, but it is critical in determining how inclusive the resurrection to life is understood to be. Paul does not subscribe to universalism (i.e., that all are saved) as some have taught. It is only *in Christ* that the sinner receives life. And note that in referring to the first Adam, "all die" is present tense. The second "all" is changed to the future. We "shall be" made alive—referring to the resurrection.[36] There is much more to this truth that Paul extracts elsewhere, as Gordon Fee observes: "This is the first use of the Adam-Christ analogy in Paul's extant letters" (see also vv. 45–49 and Rom. 5:12–21).[37] It will become one of the writer's favorite ways to articulate the implications of the work of Christ on behalf of sinful humanity. For Paul, Adam's race is natural, sinful, condemned, and dying. The new race of the "second Adam" is spiritual, righteous, justified, and living (cf. also Heb. 2:9–10, 14–17).

The New Order (15:23a)

The second truth is that Christ will reign. Each is in his or her own "order" (literally, "rank"). "Christ the first fruits" means that He is the first to experience the resurrection of the body from the dead. "After that those who are Christ's at His coming" (*parousia*) will be made alive. When Christ comes for the church at the Rapture, believers will also experience the resurrection (15:50–58; 1 Thess. 2:19; 3:13; 4:14–17). "Then" suggests an interval in the same way "afterwards" (cf. v. 23) suggests an interval of an indeterminate length of time. "The end" (v. 24) refers to when Christ "delivers up the kingdom to the God and Father" (v. 24). At that time He will have "abolished all rule and all authority and all power." Such language shows both precision and flexibility. The events relating to Christ's coming, the resurrection, His kingdom, and the final denouement before God the Father offer a clear outline of future events. However, the exact chronology is not given. The promise of Christ's coming is presented as a blessed hope for the believer of the New Testament. It is not given in such a way as to simply satisfy our curiosity about the future.

The New Age (15:23b–26)

The messianic kingdom is imagined in three stages. The first relates to the man in heaven (Dan. 7:13; Col. 4:1; 1 Thess 1:10; 1 Pet. 3:22; Rev. 4:2). The risen Christ is the first fruits. He is the first man to enter heaven, and it is from there that He will come and receive His own (2 Thess. 1:7). The second stage is at "His coming" (v. 23) to establish His reign on the earth (cf. Rev. 20:1–10). Only then will he sit on David's throne (2 Sam. 7:12–17). At that time the believers of this age will rule and reign with Him (cf. 6:3; 15:51–52; 1 Thess. 4:13–17).

After the Tribulation (not mentioned here) the Old Testament saints will also be raised (Dan. 12:1–2; Rev. 20:4). It is then that "all shall be made alive" (v. 22). The third stage is the "end" (v. 24), when He will deliver up the kingdom to God. In the end, the earthly kingdom will be delivered up to the Father, the "rest of the dead" will be brought to judgment (Rev. 20:5, 12–15), and a new heaven and a new earth will appear, including a new Jerusalem where the "bride" shall dwell in the eternal state (Rev. 21—22). "The last enemy that will be abolished is death" (v. 26). Of the enemies to be vanquished by the Lord during His reign, this is the last. The writer of Hebrews would add, "Since then the children share in flesh and blood, He Himself likewise also partook of the same, that through death He might render powerless him who had the power of death, that is, the devil; and might deliver those who through fear of death were subject to slavery all their lives" (Heb. 2:14–15).

The Consummation (15:27–28)

The final truth is that even the Son is subject to the Father. "Then the Son Himself also will be subjected to . . . Him" (v. 28). This is a difficult expression and has often been misunderstood to suggest that the apostle subordinated the Son to the Father. However, two facts must be accounted for here. First, when Paul says that the Son is subject to the Father, he is not speaking of the Son in terms of His essence, but in terms of His function, or ministry, as the incarnate Son. Second, the force of Paul's statement is best understood dispensationally. At this present time the administration of the messianic kingdom is given to the Son (cf. Matt. 28:18). However, at the conclusion of the messianic kingdom, this function will be returned to the Triune God, "that God may be all in all" (v. 28).

Most commentaries see this expression as denoting God's ultimate sovereignty. While this cannot be entirely discounted (especially with reference to the subjugation of His enemies), the expression "all in all" was fairly common in the ancient world to designate special relationships. When someone was said to be "all things," it was to denote love, friendship, or commitment. We employ a similar expression in our own language in much the same way. If we understand the expression in this way, it fits well with 9:22, where Paul says that he is "all things to all" that he might "save some." If we stress "sovereignty" here, we run the risk of trivializing the Son's deity and nullifying the special relation of creation to the Creator.[38] David Fredrickson offers some practical implications of this.

> When all things have been subordinated to Christ—that is, when all things receive their identity from their participation in the Son—then there will be no barriers for God to be in direct and personal relation with all of creation

as the Father is directly related to the Son. In other words, God becoming all things to all is made possible by the participation of all things in Christ, whose identity is generated in his filial relation to the Father.[39]

Such an intimate vision of the eternal state is reflective of Psalm 119:89–91:

> Forever, O Lord,
> Thy word is settled in heaven.
> Thy faithfulness *continues* throughout all generations;
> Thou didst establish the earth, and it stands.
> They stand this day according to Thine ordinances,
> for all things are Thy servants.

Psalm 73:25–26 adds,

> Whom have I in heaven *but Thee?*
> And besides Thee, I desire nothing on earth.
> My flesh and my heart may fail,
> but God is the strength of my heart and my portion forever.

As the hymn writer has said of that day, "things that are not now, nor could be, soon shall be our own." This will be so, not because we have the "things" we so often desire, but because we have Christ!

Baptism for the Dead (15:29–34)

The misunderstanding of verse 29 has made it much easier for genealogists today to trace their roots. I am certain that my pilgrim ancestors (paedobaptists that they were!) would be disheartened to know that their descendants in Utah are being baptized for them. Modern-day Mormons perpetuate the practice of "baptism for the dead"—a practice inaugurated more than a century after Paul penned these words. They, as did their ancient counterparts, continue a practice that has never enjoyed the sanction of orthodoxy.[40] Since Peter (2 Pet. 3:16), it has been readily acknowledged that some of Paul's writings are "hard to understand, which the untaught and unstable distort, as they do also the rest of the Scriptures, to their own destruction."

The expression "those . . . who are baptized for the dead" (v. 29) is obscure. The practice of vicarious baptism, such as that practiced by Mormons today, appeared as early as the second century[41] as an observance of this text. Some suppose that the custom had already been introduced into Corinth.[42] However, I think Charles Hodge and the majority of modern commentators on this text are wrong. As Joel White has observed, "One searches in vain for any independent historical or biblical parallel to the practice of baptism for the dead."[43] This observation is all the more noteworthy since the extensive archaeological evidence amassed in recent years on ancient Graeco-Roman funerary practices has provided "absolutely no evidence anywhere in the ancient world for anything like baptism for the dead."[44] It is also extremely doubtful that the apostle would have made reference to this heretical practice without condemning it in the same breath.

In attempting to understand a text such as this one, we must submit to the principle of the *analogia fidei*, that is, we must allow Scripture to interpret itself. Three views that are much more aligned with Pauline doctrine are suggested. The first is that the expression refers to young converts who took the place of the older saints in the church who had died so that it would be properly rendered "baptized in the place of." The Greek preposition *huper* allows this sense (cf. 2 Cor. 5:15; Philem. 1:13). With such a young congregation, however, it would seem odd that they would even have reason to think this way.

A second alternative is that the expression is to be taken synonymously with verse 30. It would thus be rendered "baptized with reference to the dead." This would be a nonsacerdotal use of the term *baptism*. That is, the people of whom Paul was speaking were being immersed in such severe persecution that they were dying for their faith. And behind them were those who took their place in the front lines of the "Church Militant."[45] However, while we know that Paul, himself, underwent life-threatening persecution, there is no evidence that the Corinthians were suffering in this way.

A third alternative is to relate the "dead" to those, like Paul, who give their lives ("die daily) to bring people to Christ. One way to acquire this sense is to change the punctuation of the verse. The verse might read: "Otherwise what will those do who are being baptized on account of the dead (that is, the dead, figuratively speaking; that is, the apostles)? For if the truly dead persons are not raised, why at all are people being baptized on account of them (that is, the apostles)?"[46] White appeals to 1 Corinthians 4:9; 2 Corinthians 2:14; 4:7–12; and 6:1–10 to show that this is a commonplace in Paul's teaching.[47] A variation of this view, perhaps requiring no change in punctuation, is that of John Reaume, who suggests that the "dead" refers to people (now dead) whose witness brought others to faith—and thus to baptism. The latter would then take their place.[48] The logic of the passage would thus connect to the import of resurrection. People (now dead) have proclaimed the message and have led others to faith in the same gospel promising life and participation with Christ at His coming. What will we do if we now say that there is no resurrection and that the dead are simply gone?

Suffice it to say that there are several interpretive options fully consistent with Paul's theology and Christian orthodoxy. It is not likely, however, that we will ever reach a consensus on this difficult text. In each of the above options, nevertheless, the function of the passage would be to show the absurdity of submitting to baptism upon the word of those who are dead or dying for their faith when in fact there is no resurrection. Indeed, why would they or Paul or anyone suffer hardship when in the end it is for naught? This is certainly consistent with what follows.

"Why are we also in danger every hour?" (v. 30). If there is no resurrection, there is no sense in suffering persecution for Christ. On the contrary, it is only logical that one would do whatever is necessary to prolong life on earth. "I die daily" (v. 31). This does not teach that Paul mortified the flesh every day. The context tells us that he, in effect, faced the "wild beasts" (v. 32) every day. Paul's life was in such constant jeopardy that he never knew when he might be called upon to give his life for the gospel. On the occasion of his subsequent visit to Corinth (Acts 20:1–4), Luke records that there were people plotting for his life. Paul is not talking about specific incidents here. Rather, he is speaking of the general danger he found himself in on any given day. It is also evident that in Corinth there were "gladiatorial combats not known elsewhere in Greece. Lenschau cites the so-called thirty-fifth letter of the emperor Julian (409A), which criticizes the Corinthians' purchase of bears and panthers for "hunts" in theaters."[49] Thus, while the reference to such hypothetical situations might not have carried much weight elsewhere, it is evident in this "Roman" colony that there was much "non-Greek flavor"[50] in the city with which Paul was acquainted.

We may as well "eat and drink, for tomorrow we die" is a quotation from Isaiah 22:13. The language is also used in Plutarch to caricature the dissolute life believed to be taught in Epicurean philosophy.[51] In the same breath, Paul borrows a proverb from the Greek poet, Menanders: *Thais*, "Bad company corrupts good morals." Evil is contagious. By this the apostle implies that those who are denying the resurrection are in fact false teachers. Perhaps with this he is suggesting that they separate from them.

"Become sober-minded as you ought, and stop sinning" (v. 34). Wake up to righteousness, open your eyes to the delusion of your spiritual superiority. "For some have no knowledge of God" (v. 34). The denial of the resurrection suggests that those who hold to such a view are literally "ignorant of God" (cf. Matt. 28:22). "I speak *this* to your shame." It is both incredible and shameful that a church so gifted of God could have allowed persons in their assembly to call such a cardinal truth into question.

In the first half of this chapter, Paul argues on the basis of known truth and thereby commends the preaching of the resurrection. In the remaining part of the chapter, he develops the doctrine, based on new revelation, to provide his readers with insights into the blessed hope of the believer. How do we understand the nature of the resurrection and how does it relate to the coming of Christ when we read that the believer, too, will be changed?

What Is the Resurrection Body? (15:35–49)

First, the Doctrine Is Reasonable (15:35–38)

The first questions (vv. 35–36) Paul answers are "How are the dead raised? And with what kind of body do they come?" While both questions are distinct, they must be taken together. The first deals with how life can come from death, and the second deals with the nature of the resurrection body. Paul answers the first question with an analogy from common life. "That which you sow does not come to life unless it dies" (v. 36). Whenever a seed is sown in the ground, it must first die before it can germinate (cf. John 12:24). The second question requires more explanation, so Paul uses examples from nature, experience, and Scripture.

Examples from nature. "That which you sow, you do not sow the body which is to be, but a bare grain" (v. 37). That which is produced is very different from that which is planted. A grain is sown, a plant is the result. "God gives it a body" (v. 38). All of nature illustrates the providential control of God. The precise nature of the body of every living thing is determined by the good pleasure of God. In the ancient world, even among the philosophers, the precise way life came to be from the seed, or for that matter, from the sperm of a man, was a great mystery. Paul understood that it was God who gives life, whether in nature or in the resurrection.

Second, the Doctrine is Unique (15:39–50)

Paul again draws upon nature to show that even in the natural realm a distinction must be made between the seed and the plant issuing from it. They are connected, but they are not the same.

It is like sowing and reaping. "All flesh is not the same flesh" (v. 39). It is clear in nature that diversity exists among all living things. Such diversity is not only reflected in the earthly sphere but also in the heavenly. The expression "So also is the resurrection of the dead" (v. 42) is to be understood in the context of reaping and sowing. It thus reflects the same principle of unity and diversity. The resurrection body is related to the earthly body in the same sense that the plant is related to the seed. Yet it will be different. "It is sown a perishable *body*, it is raised an imperishable *body*" (v. 42). Paul continues by enlarging upon the contrast between the two. The one is sown in "dishonor," "weakness," "a natural body" and it is raised in "glory," "power," "a spiritual body" (vv. 43–44).

Adam-Christ analogy. Paul returns with a new emphasis to his Adam-Christ analogy. "So also it is written" (v. 45) is tantamount to saying, "and this agrees with Scripture." "Adam became a living soul" seems to have in mind the earthly animal nature given to Adam in the original creation. This seems to suit the parallel ideas in verses 46–49. "The last Adam became a life-giving spirit" (v. 45). The expression "last Adam" was coined by the apostle Paul as a reference to Christ (cf. also Rom. 5:14). The contrast here is not so much between the soul and the spirit as it is between *zosan*, "living," and *zoopoioun*, "life giving." The principle of life is common with all men. The second Adam brings infinitely more than that (John 5:26). The one partakes of temporality, the other of eternality.

Examples from experience. However, it was the "natural" (v. 46) that came first; it was the "spiritual" that came afterward. Adam is "from the earth" (v. 47); Christ is "the second man . . . from heaven." The former is thus "earthy" (v. 48); the latter is "heavenly." The certainty of the resurrection is verified by the reality of human, earthly existence. "As we have borne the image of the earthy, we shall also bear the image of the heavenly" (v. 49). Thus, the human body, instead of becoming an argument against the resurrection, becomes an argument in its favor.

Resurrection and Rapture (15:50–58)

But what of those who are alive at the coming of Christ? How shall they be distinguished from those who have died? Paul's final statement in the chapter is to turn his attention to the nature of the resurrection for those who are still living at the time of the second coming of Christ (vv. 50–58).

It is a mystery. First he states a principle: "Flesh and blood cannot inherit the kingdom of God" (v. 50). This is not to suggest a denial of a "bodily" resurrection; rather, a change is necessary if the believer is ever to realize his promised blessings. "I tell you a mystery" (v. 51; cf. 2:7). Not all believers will "sleep" ("die"), but we can all be assured of one thing: "We will all be changed." The new truth that was given to Paul by revelation from God in a "mystery" is that at the coming of Christ we shall all—living *and* dead—be "changed"[52] like unto His glorious body (cf. 1 John 3:2). Thus, the teaching of the apostle here coincides with 1 Thessalonians 4:13–17.

It is at the last trump. How will that occur? "In a moment, in the twinkling of an eye" (v. 52) expresses the suddenness with which it will occur. The time is indicated "at the last trumpet" (v. 52) This is not the last trump of

Revelation 11:15 but the last trump of 1 Thessalonians 4:16. It is so designated because it signals the end of the present age. Then we who are "alive and remain" will be gathered together with the saints to meet the Lord in the air.

It includes the living and the dead. Two groups are distinguished. "The dead will be raised imperishable, and we shall be changed" (v. 52). The term "dead" refers to those who have died in Christ. The term "we" refers to those who are still living at the time of the Rapture. Both groups are alike in that they are "perishable" (v. 53) and "mortal" (v. 54). That to which both groups are changed is likewise the same, designated as "imperishable" and "immortality."

It destroys the fear of death. "Death is swallowed up in victory" (v. 54b) is taken from Isaiah 25:8. Such hope and assurance issue in a great song of triumph (v. 55). The context of Isaiah 25 is especially appropriate. It speaks of a time when Israel laid in ruin yet looks with hope to when God will "remove the reproach" and bring them to life again as a nation. It was from this text that the rabbis had long discerned the hope of the resurrection, using it during funeral lamentations as reference to the final elimination of death.[53] It is not surprising that Paul appropriates it here. He follows this with Hosea 13:14. "'O death, where is your victory? O death, where is your sting?' The sting of death is sin," and Paul would answer, "And yet I am forgiven." And "the power of sin is the law" (v. 56), and Paul would exclaim, "And yet I am pardoned." "Now we can *invite* Death to do its worst, knowing that the final victory will be ours in Christ. Then we shall be able to mock that immemorial Enemy because his worst will be—nothing! After all, death got his hold on us through the Law, but we can thank God that we are delivered from all this through Jesus Christ."[54]

It gives assurance in the present trial. No man can take credit for this victory. It comes "through our Lord Jesus Christ" (v. 57). And this blessed hope, this blessed assurance issues forth in a challenge in verse 58: "Be steadfast, immovable, always abounding." How does this relate to the doctrine of resurrection? Paul answers, "knowing that your toil is not in vain." For Paul it was more than faith. It was knowledge. It was the sure conviction that one day he would share in the glory of the resurrection. Of course, Paul has a small hidden agenda here too. Abounding in the work of the Lord will include participation in the collection for the saints in Jerusalem. But that's a matter for the next chapter.

Study Questions

1. From verses 3–8, list the elements that Paul considers so important in describing the gospel.

2. In verses 8–9, why does the apostle feel so unworthy as a minister of the gospel?

3. Did Paul labor more than or less than the apostles for the sake of Christ? What do you think he means by this statement?

4. What is the central historic issue about the gospel? And why is this so important?

5. In Paul's argument, could Christianity exist without the resurrection of Christ from the dead? Explain.

6. Is Paul making some kind of universal statement when he writes that "in Christ all shall be made alive"? What does he mean by this?

7. Verse 29 has sometimes been a problem passage. Explain it from the context and in your own words.

8. What is the difference between the first Adam and the last Adam? Compare what Paul teaches on this in Romans 5:14.

9. Paul makes a comparison between the natural body and the spiritual body. Is he saying that the resurrected spiritual body will not be real and that it will be somewhat "ghost-like"? What is the apostle saying?

10. From verse 50, is Paul saying that there will be no one in the kingdom in a "natural" body?

11. Describe and list the various elements Paul gives about the Rapture in verses 51–52. Compare this with 1 Thessalonians 4:13–18.

12. How is the final triumph over death to be accomplished? What is the role of Christ in this victory?

13. What positive message is Paul giving in verse 58? How does this fit with his lengthy discussion of the blessedness of the resurrection? How should this verse sustain Christians as they live out the problems and disappointments of life?

CHAPTER 19

A Great Door Is Opened
1 Corinthians 16:1-24

Preview:

Paul concludes his letter by suggesting a practical way the Corinthian believers can abound in the work of the Lord through participation in the benevolence offering for the suffering saints in Jerusalem. He closes with special greetings from their mutual friends and his coworkers.

The purpose of the giftedness of the church was that they should be able to minister and speak the truth in love (Eph. 4:15). This theme permeates this first letter of Paul to the Corinthians. Throughout he has mixed doctrine (truth) and exhortation (loving instruction). Sometimes, as when a mother warns of a hot stove, it has been shown to be a *painful* truth. Throughout, Paul has shown that the truth of God's Word should issue in a distinctive behavior for the child of God. For Paul, it has been shown that two basic truths are axiomatic for his life and ministry. He based his *life* on the truth of the finished work of Christ on Calvary. He based his *hope* on the resurrection of Christ and the promise of His coming. These have influenced his lifestyle, his priorities, his work, and his strategy. In his closing challenge, Paul also demonstrates his strategy for ministry. In effect, he sees himself positioned between the cross and the kingdom. He was driven by the cross, but he had his eye on the crown (cf. Phil. 3:14). As he draws to a close, lest they become so heavenly minded they are no earthly good, he uses the promise of the coming of Christ and the resurrection as a segue to talk about mundane matters. His final word was that in light of the blessed hope, they should be "always abounding in the work of the Lord" (v. 58). The truth of the resurrection should loosen our grip on material things and open our hearts to the spirit of loving service.

The Strategy for Giving (16:1–4)

Love will pay a price. Any parent knows this. Solomon understood it when he said, "Faithful are the wounds of a friend, but deceitful are the kisses of an enemy" (Prov. 27:6). When God challenged Israel concerning their commitment to Him, He said, "'Bring the whole tithe into the storehouse, so that there may be food in My house, and *test Me now* in this,' says the LORD of hosts, 'if I will not open for you the windows of heaven, and pour out for you a blessing until it overflows'" (Mal. 3:10, emphasis mine). "If you love Me," God challenges, "show me!" Here too Paul is asking the Corinthians for the same kind of confirmation to demonstrate both the integrity of their commitment to Christ and their love for him.

It is a benevolence offering. As noted, "Now concerning" (Greek, *peri de*)[1] (v. 1) is the common formula used in the epistle to introduce matters about which the Corinthians had queried the apostle. In this case, it had to do with "the collection for the saints" (v. 1). The believers at Corinth were aware that the apostle was gathering funds for the Jerusalem church, and apparently they had written to inquire to what extent they could participate in this collection. "As I directed" suggests that this was not an optional matter for the Corinthian believers any more than it was for the "churches of Galatia."

There is a pattern for giving. Notice that giving was commanded (v. 1). It was regular (v. 2). It was comprehensive (v. 2). It was proportional (v. 2). It was planned (v. 2). And it was protected (vv. 3–4). The church was to gather these funds "on the first day of every week" (v. 2). Their giving was to be systematic and planned. "Each one of you [is to] put aside and save." This obligation extended to everyone "as he may prosper." The amount of each gift was proportionate to the giver's income. When Paul says, "that no collections be made when I come" (v. 2), he makes it clear that the obligation is theirs. The apostle was also desirous that the collection be taken before he came, probably for two reasons. First, through systematic and planned giving, he knew that the amount would be more. Second, he did not want to apply pressure when he came.

"When I arrive" (v. 3) suggests that Paul's arrival in Corinth was yet indefinite. He is stressing that the church be prepared with the collection at any time. "Whomever you may approve, I shall send them with letters" (v. 3). Placing himself above suspicion, the apostle shows that he is not so much interested in handling their money as in assuring that it got to Jerusalem. He suggests that they appoint stewards to carry their money "if it is fitting" (v. 4). If it be substantial enough "for me to go also," then they would all go together. Paul was willing, if their contribution was especially large, to rearrange his schedule and go with the group to Jerusalem. It is important to note that although the priesthood of the Old Testament and the temple are gone, the principle of giving remains. While it is here only applied to a special need in the Jerusalem church, Paul will later draw on Deuteronomy 25:4 and the teaching of the Lord (Matt. 10:10) to expand his understanding of this principle (1 Tim. 5:17–18).

The Strategy for Outreach (16:5–9)

"But I shall come to you after I go through Macedonia" (v. 5). Paul changes his original itinerary. This would subsequently provoke his enemies to charge him with being fickle (cf. 2 Cor. 1:15–17). Paul's plans at this time are to spend the winter at Corinth. "If the Lord permits" (v. 7) reflects how the apostle was always subject to the will of God above his own. But his plan is to "remain in Ephesus until Pentecost" (v. 8). The time is near the close of his three-year stay at Ephesus, and the season is early spring (cf. introduction).

"A wide door" (v. 9) is used here metaphorically for opportunity. "Many adversaries" is best taken with the previous expression. The apostle seems to have in mind his pending trip through Macedonia and is accounting for why he is staying a little longer in Ephesus (cf. 15:32; Acts 19:1–4). When one considers Paul's imprisonment in Philippi and the uproar that ensued in Thessalonica, his being driven from Berea and scoffed at on Mars Hill, and the threats that would be made on his life before he would get to Jerusalem, one is amazed at Paul's attitude. He only hints about the opposition: "there are many adversaries." One might add, "But that's hardly worth mentioning!" Paul was an optimist when it came to his ministry. We would do well to adopt his strategy. Instead of focusing on the problems, let's consider the possibilities.

The Strategy for Success (16:10–14)

Paul appreciates a willingness to work. "Now if Timothy comes" (v. 10; cf. Acts 19:22). At this time Timothy was traveling through Macedonia, and the apostle anticipated that he would be reaching Corinth eventually (cf. 4:17). "See that he is with you without cause to be afraid" (v. 10; "he is fearless toward you").[2] Barrett raises the question as to the particular circumstances that might have caused Timothy to be fearful. If it relates to the church per se, we have no knowledge of the details. If it relates to fear "within Timothy himself, [we would be hard pressed] to answer the question why Paul had chosen a coward as his confidential agent."[3] More recent rhetorical studies suggest that the mirror reading of these texts has entirely misrepresented Timothy, who is shown throughout the book of Acts and the New Testament to be a worthy envoy of Paul. He appears as a man of character, courage, and resourcefulness under whose leadership many crisis situations in the fledgling New Testament churches were confronted (cf. Acts 16–20; Phil. 2:19–24; 1 Thess 3:1–6). Indeed, as Christopher Hutson has noted, commenting on 1 Corinthians 4:16–17, "Following Timothy is the functional equivalent of imitating Paul."[4] Thus, Paul is not being patronizing when he commends Timothy's ministry to them, saying, "he is doing the Lord's work, as I also am."

Paul encourages a positive attitude. "Let no one therefore despise him" (v. 11) is reminiscent of the advice given to Timothy in 1 Timothy 4:12. If the Corinthians are inclined to disdain Paul, he requests that their dislike of him not be extended to Timothy. "Get over it!" he is saying; and let's not allow these issues to get in the way of the Lord's work.

Paul models an openness to change. "But concerning Apollos our brother" (v. 12)—Paul had asked Apollos if he would be willing to go to Corinth to adjudicate some of their problems. Apparently, at that time he was not able, but "he will come when he has opportunity" (v. 12). Now Paul begins a series of closing remarks, exhortations, challenges, and greetings.

Paul commends godly character. Like a military leader, he exhorts the brethren to "be on the alert" (v. 13), that is, be wakeful and alert to your spiritual enemies. "Stand firm in the faith." Don't be unsettled in your mind. Don't be afraid to be firm in your convictions. Don't be as the Sophists who called everything into question. "Act like men." Be courageous. Be strong. Characteristic of Paul, he sees the Christian life as though he were in the arena. Faith, conviction, and courage are the essential ingredients for success and victory.

Paul calls the church to unity. In closing he returns to his challenge to unity with the words, "Let all that you do be done in love" (v. 14). This, of course, calls to mind all that he said in chapter 13 and returns to his challenge in 1:10 to be of one mind and to the central theme of the book, "God is faithful, through whom you were called into fellowship with His Son, Jesus Christ our Lord" (1:9). The truth of the gospel offers a new start. The promise of Christ's coming offers a new direction. Exemplified in Paul's strategy, the text suggests that we act rather than react to the circumstances about us. For each of us as individuals and as a church there is always an "open door," regardless of the "obstacles." But we need a strategy. Paul's challenge is that we move forward intentionally with a plan and a commitment to execute.

A Strategy for Ministry	
1. Ask:	What is God leading me/us to do?
2. Examine:	What am I doing to accomplish this?
3. Plan:	Write it down.
4. Execute:	"Just do it!"
5. Test:	How well did I/we do?
	Go back to Step 1

The Close (16:15–24)

The closing paragraph reads like a list of those for whom special certificates of honor are acknowledged.

First to believe. "The household of Stephanas" (v. 15, cf. 1:16) "devoted themselves," that is, they devoted themselves in a self-imposed duty to the believers. This was the very first family to receive Christ in Paul's ministry in Achaia, and Paul had personally baptized them. The reference to "Achaia" does not conflict with Romans 16:5, which in the better texts do not read "Achaia" but "Asia."

First in service. "Stephanas and Fortunatus and Achaicus" (v. 17) were three members of the Corinthian assembly who ministered to Paul's needs in Ephesus. Note the Latin names. This is not surprising since the new city of Corinth was largely composed of Romans (cf. introduction). It is also generally considered that these are the individuals who brought the report to Paul, which along with the report of Chloe's people, precipitated his writing of this letter.[5] "They have refreshed my spirit and yours" (v. 18). Here Paul has in mind both their ministry to him, in terms of reporting the progress of the Corinthian assembly, and their ministry to the Corinthians, in terms of sharing the ministry Paul had with them in Ephesus. "Therefore acknowledge such men" seems to suggest that these individuals are seen as leaders of the Corinthian assembly and that they will be returning to the city. For this reason, they are generally credited with having brought the letter from the church that contained their questions to the apostle. And they are likely the ones who were the bearers of this letter upon their return.[6]

First in hospitality. "Aquila and Prisca" (v. 19) had been exiled from Rome (Acts 18:2). Paul first met this couple in Corinth. They have since moved on to Ephesus (cf. also Rom. 16:3–5). Apparently, wherever this couple went they made their home a sanctuary where Christ was honored and believers gathered to share the Word together and worship. And so Paul sends greetings from "the church that is in their house."

"Greet one another with a holy kiss" (v. 20; cf. Rom. 16:16; 2 Cor. 13:12; 1 Thess. 5:26; 1 Pet. 5:14). In the custom of the day, this was an expression of friendship. In other words, the Corinthian believers were to put away their divisive spirit and unite in the bonds of love. "In my own hand" (v. 21) has reference to the salutation, not the entire epistle. In Galatians 6:11 Paul remarks about the large letters he wrote with his own hand. This may have been due to his poor sight. Paul ordinarily dictated his letters to a secretary then wrote the salutation with his own hand as a sign of authenticity (Col. 4:18; 2 Thess. 3:7). No doubt it is with the pen still in his hand that he appends the challenge with which the epistle comes to a close.[7] William Baird comments: "How much it is like the man from Tarsus—how abrupt, how terse, how compact! He hurls an anathema at anyone who 'has no love for the Lord' (v. 22). He utters the eschatological hope: 'Our Lord, come!' (v. 22). He offers a simple benediction."[8]

"Accursed" (v. 22; *anathema*, "devoted to destruction"; cf. 12:3; Rom. 9:3) is to be understood in light of Paul's own usage elsewhere. In particular he invokes such language against those who would preach or teach a *heteros* ("different") gospel that deviates from that which he delivered to them. The overtly friendly greetings of the previous verses do not extend to those who stand opposed to the gospel. Patterson cautions: "This does not constitute a command for any sort of action on the part of the church with regard to those who do not love the Lord. It is merely an observation of the state that exists. Those who do not love the Lord will be set aside for destruction. This is to be noted especially in light of the fact that the Lord is coming."[9] *Maranatha* is, properly, two words in the Aramaic. It expresses one of two possible ideas. It may be taken in the sense of "our Lord is come," signifying Christ's first coming. Or it may mean "our Lord comes," signifying His second coming. The latter seems to be in view here. It is much like John's concluding remarks in Revelation: "Come, Lord Jesus." (Rev. 22:20). In using this term, Paul also offers indirect testimony to the antiquity of the claim that Jesus is Lord. That it came to be a "slogan" in the Aramaic suggests that the very earliest of New Testament believers affirmed that it was so.[10] Taken together with *anathema* the general sense is that of an invocation: "May the Lord soon come in judgment to redress wrong and establish right."[11]

"The grace of the Lord Jesus be with you. My love be with you all in Christ Jesus" (v. 24) is a tender expression of affection by the Corinthians' spiritual father. His love is extended not only to those who agree with him, but to all in the assembly—even his enemies. The greatest example these Christians have is the incomparable apostle himself. The epistle ends as it began, with a reference to their place "in Christ"[12] and its implicit reinforcement of the theme that runs throughout this epistle—their incomparable place and unity in Christ's body, the Church.

The epistle ends, but the story does not. It continues on and occasions further communication, including the subsequent letter known to us as Second Corinthians. This will be examined in a companion volume of this series.

Study Questions

1. Describe the way Paul urges the Corinthians to prepare for their collections for the Jerusalem church. List and discuss the steps he lays out for that collection.

2. In going to Corinth, why do you think Paul wished to remain there with the believers for a while? What do you imagine his purpose would be for such an extended visit?

3. Why would Timothy be fearful if he went to Corinth?

4. From verses 10–24, list the many positive and encouraging things the apostle has to say about individual believers with whom he is associating. What lessons do we learn from this about relating to others in the body of Christ?

5. Why did Paul mention that he wrote this lengthy letter in his own handwriting (v. 21)?

6. Write out your overall impression of Paul's first epistle to the Corinthians. What did it mean to you personally? What does it say to churches today?

Bibliography

Barrett, C. K. *The First Epistle to the Corinthians*. New York: Harper and Row, 1968.

Barclay, William. *The Letters to the Corinthians*. Philadelphia: 1956.

Blomberg, Craig L. *1 Corinthians*. Grand Rapids: Zondervan, 1994.

Calvin, John. *The First Epistle of Paul to the Corinthians*. English translation by John Fraser. Grand Rapids: Eerdmans, 1960.

Dods, Marcus. "The First Epistle to the Corinthians." *The Expositor's Bible*. Edited by W. Robertson Nicoll. Grand Rapids: Eerdmans, 1940.

Erdman, Charles R. *The First Epistle of Paul to the Corinthians*. Philadelphia: Westminster, 1928.

Fee, Gordon D. *The First Epistle to the Corinthians*. TNICNT. Grand Rapids: Eerdmans, 1987.

Godet, Frederick L. *Commentary on the First Epistle of St. Paul to the Corinthians*. English translation Edinburgh, 1886. Reprint Grand Rapids: Zondervan, 1957.

Gromacki, Robert G. *Called to Be Saints*. Grand Rapids: Baker, 1977.

Grosheide, F. W. *Commentary on the First Epistle to the Corinthians*. NIC. Grand Rapids: Eerdmans, 1953.

Hodge, Charles. *An Exposition of the First Epistle to the Corinthians*. Grand Rapids: Eerdmans, 1974.

Johnson, S. Lewis. "The First Epistle to the Corinthians." *The Wycliffe Bible Commentary*. Edited by Charles F. Pfeiffer and Everett F. Harrison. Chicago: Moody Press, 1963.

Lenski, R. C. H. *The Interpretation of St. Paul's First and Second Epistle to the Corinthians*. Columbus, OH: Wartburg Press, 1946.

MacArthur, John. "1 Corinthians." *The MacArthur New Testament Commentary*. Chicago: Moody Press, 1984.

Morgan, G. Campbell. *The Corinthian Letters of Paul*. Old Tappan, NJ: Revell, 1946.

Morris, Leon. *The First Epistle of Paul to the Corinthians*. Grand Rapids: Eerdmans, 1976.

Robertson, Archibald, and Alfred Plummer. *A Critical and Exegetical Commentary on the First Epistle of St. Paul to the Corinthians*. ICC. Edinburgh: T. & T. Clark, 1955.

Thistleton, Anthony C. *The First Epistle to the Corinthians*. NIGTC. Grand Rapids: Eerdmans, 2000.

Vaughan, Curtis, and Thomas Lea. *1 Corinthians*. Grand Rapids: Zondervan, 1983.

Notes

Chapter 1—Background of First Corinthians

1. V. P. Furnish, "Paul and the Corinthians," *Interpretation* 52, no. 3 (July 1998): 231.

2. Ibid., 233.

3. E. F. Harrison, *Introduction to the New Testament*, (Grand Rapids: Eerdmans, 1971), 267. Brian S. Rosner, "Temple Prostitution in 1 Corinthians 6:12–20," *NovT* 40, no. 4, 336–51, has argued convincingly that it is impossible to support the idea that these women served in the interest of the cultus in the temple, but rather were more likely included in the festivities following the cult rituals. The "unholy trinity" of eating, drinking, and sexual immorality was the primary target of Paul's admonition in chapter 6. See also Bruce W. Winter, "Gluttony and Immorality at Elitist Banquets," *Jian Dao: A Journal of Bible and Theology* 7 (1997): 77–90.

4. F. W. Grosheide, *Commentary on the First Epistle to the Corinthians*, NIC (Grand Rapids: Eerdmans, 1953), 13, notes: "An inscription found by scholars at Delphi, though badly mutilated, clearly records a letter of the emperor Claudius granting a series of privileges to the city of Delphi. The name of Gallio . . . is found in this inscription and a date is also mentioned. Chronologists, by means of complicated computations which need not be reproduced here, have come to the result that Gallio was governor of Achaia in the first part of 52 A.D."

5. John E. Stambaugh and David L. Balch, *The New Testament in Its Social Environment* (Philadelphia: Westminster, 1986), 157–58.

6. Ibid., 158.

7. Ibid., 159.

8. Winter observes, "The plays of Philetaerus and Poliochus [fourth century B.C. Greek playwrights] carrying the title 'The Whoremonger' *(ho Korinthiastes)* also fuel the perception of proverbial sexual promiscuity paid for by Corinthians. What tends not to be noticed is that this evidence belongs to Greek Corinth and not to Roman Corinth" ("Gluttony and Immorality," 78).

9. J. S. Exell, *The Biblical Illustrator,* vol. 1, 379.

10. The description is found in the *Acts of Paul and Thecla,* discussed in Abraham J. Mahlerbe, "A Physical Description of Paul," *Christians among Jews and Gentiles* (Philadelphia: Fortress Press, 1986), 170. The passage is much discussed as to whether it accurately describes the historical figure or whether it is an idealized representation. While it does not seem to describe "physical attractiveness" as it is ordinarily observed today, Mahlerbe shows that most features mentioned by Onesiphorus of Paul are also found in ancient physiognomy to describe persons of great leadership, courage, wisdom, magnanimity, and even royalty and were not necessarily "unflattering features in the context in which the *Acts* was written" (see pp. 170–75).

11. For a recent discussion of the theological orientation of the Corinthian letters, see Furnish, "Paul and the Corinthians," 237–45. See also Anthony C. Thistleton, NIGTC, *The First Epistle to the Corinthians* (Grand Rapids: Eerdmans, 2000), 41–52, 455–60.

12. For example, see Moffatt, *Introduction to the Literature of the New Testament,* 109. See also Furnish, "Paul and the Corinthians," 229–45.

13. Contra Margaret Mitchell, "Concerning *Peri de* in 1 Corinthians," *NovT* 31 (1989): 229–56. Taken alone, the expression may not mean anything more than that a new topic is being introduced, but the additional reference to their letter and his attention to their questions contained in it argue for the view of most interpreters since Lake that Paul is writing in response to their inquiries of him. See Kirsopp Lake, *The Earlier Epistles of St. Paul: Their Motive and Origin,* 2d ed. (London: Rivingtons, 1914), 136. I agree nonetheless with Mitchell that the epistle is not "organized" by their letter to him. Rather, the epistle is organized around Paul's appeal for unity. See also Saw Insaw, *Paul's Rhetoric in 1 Corinthians 15* (Lewiston: Mellen Biblical Press, 1995), 180ff.

14. It is important to observe that we are not saying these are "canonical letters" that have been lost to the church. Rather, we are saying that Paul wrote, possibly, two letters that were never inspired and were never intended by the Holy Spirit to be part of Scripture. One of the evidences of this is that they were lost. See Matthew 5:18–19. Indeed, even Paul himself wonders out loud if he had been too harsh.

15. Furnish breaks 2 Corinthians into two letters: chapters 1—9 were written in response to the good report of Titus, while chapters 10—13 constitute another letter written only after he became alarmed at the subversive efforts of rival preachers (Furnish, "Paul and the Corinthians," 230–32). I acknowledge the internal evidence for this suggestion but see no reason to disrupt the canonical structure of the text as it has been received. Specifically, reference to the collection in chapters 8 and 9 along with his impending "third visit" (2 Cor. 13:1) squares better with the reconstruction adopted here.

16. D. Stanley, *Epistles of St. Paul to the Corinthians* 8.

17. See also the helpful discussion in Stambaugh and Balch, *The New Testament*, 157–60.

18. Much has been made of the analysis of power relations in Pauline thought in the interest of contemporary gender issues. See, e.g. V. K. Robbins, *The Tapestry of Early Christian Discourse* (London and New York: Routledge, 1996), 220–29. In such ideological analysis, the interpreter attempts to critique Paul's *real* motives as a first-century companion might. What is of primary interest in such an analysis is what Paul is "up to" rather than what he writes. One then attempts to exegete the *subtext* rather than the *text* of Paul's letter. In so doing the interpreter stands over and above the text as a modern-day psychotherapist might a client. And the authority is shifted away from the text to the exegete. This interpreter accepts the authoritative voice of Paul as given in the text and—to use Robbins' categories—understands the text as *representational* rather than *generative* of the situation in Corinth. That is to say that the text correctly *reports* on the historical and social issues rather than *creates* a historical and social reality in service to an ideological objective. Having said that, much attention has been given in the last decade to the sociological and rhetorical analysis of 1 and 2 Corinthians. While I appreciate this work and agree that it has brought new insights into our understanding of these letters, I agree with Graham Tomlin, who

says, "In fairness to earlier scholarship, these more recent approaches do not answer all the questions either. Specifically, there is a danger that a purely sociological or rhetorical approach can tend to ignore what earlier studies saw, namely the existence of a real *ideological* divergence from Paul in Corinth" (Graham Tomlin, "Christians and Epicureans in 1 Corinthians," *JSNT* 68 [1997]: 51-72). As seen here, there is a real danger in reducing Paul's writings to an exercise in pragmatics and losing sight of the apostolic authority implicit in his letters—to say nothing of their authority as inspired Scripture.

19. Anthony C. Thiselton, "Luther and Barth on 1 Corinthians 15," *The Bible, the Reformation and the Church* (Sheffield Eng.: Sheffield Academic Press, 1995), 258-89, argues with Barth that the "of God" (see e.g., 1 Cor. 4:5) forms the "secret nerve" of the entire epistle. And it is the resurrection chapter in which this all comes together and the various threads of issues and ideas throughout the epistle are tied together.

20. See Furnish, "Paul and the Corinthians," 234-35; B. K. Peterson, "Conquest, Control, and the Cross," *Interpretation* 52, no. 3 (July 1998): 258-70.

21. Furnish, "Paul and the Corinthians," 236-37.

22. Ibid., 241.

Chapter 2—To the Church of God at Corinth

1. See F. W. Grosheide, *Commentary on the First Epistle to the Corinthians*, NIC (Grand Rapids: Eerdmans, 1953), 21.

2. See V. K. Robbins, *The Tapestry of Early Christian Discourse* (London and New York: Routledge, 1996), 223.

3. Grosheide, *First Epistle to the Corinthians*, 22. In a footnote Grosheide also observes that the Greek, *ho adelphos*, without the pronoun but with the article, implies that Sosthenes is well known to the readers (cf. 2 Cor. 1:1).

4. V. P. Furnish, "Paul and the Corinthians," *Interpretation* 52, no. 3 (July 1998): 233.

5. Leon Morris, *The First Epistle of Paul to the Corinthians* (Grand Rapids: Eerdmans, 1976), 35.

6. A. A. Trites, "Witness," *NIDNTT*, ed. Colin Brown, vol. 3, (Grand Rapids: Zondervan, 1978), 1038-51.

7. Spiros Zodhiates, *A Richer Life for You in Christ: An Exposition of 1 Corinthians 1* (Ridgefield, NJ: AMG Publishers, 1972), 126–27.

Chapter 3—Dealing with Division

1. C. K. Barrett, *The First Epistle to the Corinthians* (New York: Harper and Row, 1968), 40, captures the thought with "I beg you, brothers, for the sake of our Lord Jesus Christ . . . ."

2. F. W. Grosheide, *Commentary on the First Epistle to the Corinthians*, NIC (Grand Rapids: Eerdmans, 33, 34.

3. Charles Erdman, the great Princeton scholar of an earlier time, wrote, "The name is that 'by which one is known,' or that which one is known to be. Therefore, the name of Christ indicates all that Christ is known to be, as Saviour and Master and Lord. As all believers belong to him, and are under his power and control, the very mention of his name suggests an existing spiritual unity to which outward expression should be given" (*The First Epistle of Paul to the Corinthians* [Philadelphia: Westminster, 1927], 22).

4. V. P. Furnish, "Paul and the Corinthians," *Interpretation* 52, no. 3 (July 1998): 233.

5. See John E. Stambaugh and David L. Balch, *The New Testament in Its Social Environment*, (Philadelphia: Westminster, 1986), 160. It is evident that Corinth, along with most major urban areas in the Roman Empire of the first century, would consist generally of factious people, with tensions often boiling over between various ethnic, religious, and socioeconomic groups (cf. Acts 18).

6. Barrett, *First Epistle to the Corinthians*, 42.

7. Stambaugh and Balch, *The New Testament*, 54–55.

8. Paul customarily refers to Peter by his Aramaic name, Cephas. See note, ibid., p. 43.

9. One is caused to reflect here on the first and second commandments. The first commandment is against the worship of false gods. The second commandment is against the worship of the true God with idols. It is not inconceivable that the Greeks with their "wisdom" were reducing Christ to a "concept." As such they were as guilty as Aaron who built a golden calf with which to worship God. Idols of the mind are just as much a violation of the second commandment as those of wood and stone. See Barrett's discussion of T. W. Manson's suggestion (*Studies*, p. 207) along similar lines in *First Epistle to the Corinthians*, 45.

10. Duane Litfin, "Living in a Culture That Needs Christ," *Decision*, March 2001, 34. See also G. Goetzmann, "Wisdom," *NIDNTT*, ed., Colin Brown, vol. 3, (Grand Rapids: Zondervan, 1978), 1026–38.

11. Furnish, "Paul and the Corinthians," 238

12. Ibid.

13. Ibid.

14. See the discussion of James C. Hanges regarding such *leges sacrae* in "1 Corinthians 4:6 and the Possibility of Written Bylaws in the Corinthian Church," *JBL* 117, no. 2 (summer 1998): 275–98. More of this will be discussed below.

15. While the Gospels typically use this term in its general literal sense, Paul makes much of it in a theological reflection on man's sinful nature, to Christ's humiliation, and to a range of ethical considerations. See. H. G. Link, "Weakness," *NIDNTT*, 3: 993–96.

16. Craig Blomberg, *The NIV Application Commentary* (Grand Rapids: Zondervan, 1995), 57–58. He adds, "James 2:5 parallels 1 Corinthians 1:26–31 in pointing out the sociological makeup of much of early Christianity. But when God 'chose the poor' they were also 'those who loved him,' who recognized their need for help and their personal inadequacy and hence turned to the true and living God. One of the key Hebrew terms for 'poor,' the *anawim* combines precisely these two elements—material poverty and spiritual piety. Historically, Christians have had to guard against the twin errors of spiritualizing 'the poor' as if they could include the materially wealthy, and of politicizing the term, as if salvation could be claimed apart from explicit faith in Christ."

Chapter 4—Developing True Spirituality

1. David E. Aune, *The New Testament in Its Literary Environment* (Philadelphia: Westminster, 1987), 12–13.

2. Fred G. Zaspel, "The Apostolic Model for Christian Ministry: An Analysis of 1 Corinthians 2:1–5, " *Reformation and Revival* 7 (winter 1998): 21–34.

3. F. W. Grosheide, *Commentary on the First Epistle to the Corinthians*, NIC (Grand Rapids: Eerdmans, 1953), 63.

4. Ibid.

5. Lidie H. Edmunds, "My Faith Has Found a Resting Place," *The Hymn for Worship and Celebration* (Waco: Word Music, 1986), 405.

6. David K. Lowery, "1 Corinthians," *The Bible Knowledge Commentary*, ed. John F. Walvoord and Roy B. Zuck (Wheaton: Victor, 1983), 510.

7. See footnote in the *NET Bible* (The Biblical Studies Press, 1998), 509.

8. Grosheide, *First Epistle to the Corinthians*, 63.

9. Lowery, "1 Corinthians," 510.

10. Marvin R. Vincent, *Word Studies in the New Testament*, vol. 2, (New York: Scribner, 1887–1900), 197.

11. W. Schneider, "Judgment," in *NIDNTT*, ed. Colin Brown, vol. 2 (Grand Rapids: Zondervan, 1978), 362–67.

Chapter 5—Developing Maturity

1. Lewis Sperry Chafer, *He That Is Spiritual* (Chicago: Moody Press, 1918), 3–14.

2. Arthur Custance's otherwise excellent and provocative Doorway Papers series includes *Man in Adam and in Christ* (Grand Rapids: Zondervan, 1975). Here he presents a rather eccentric view that carries the logic of his Reformed theology to an extreme as he applies it to his anthropology. He suggests that the "spiritual" dimension of the human died at the fall and that unsaved humanity is born with only the capacities of mind and body, innate to the beast. Only at salvation is the spirit restored—bringing with it the attendant spiritual capacities lost at the fall. Man is a dichotomy before salvation and a trichotomy only after salvation.

3. Spiros Zodhiates, *Getting the Most Out of Life: An Exposition of 1 Corinthians 3* (Ridgefield, NJ: AMG Publishers, 1976), 15.

4. Anthony C. Thiselton, "Humanness, Relationality and Time: Anthropological Terms in Hebrews, 1 Corinthians, and Western Traditions," *Ex Auditu* 13 (1997): 87.

5. Ibid.

6. R. C. H. Lenski, *The Interpretation of 1 and 2 Corinthians* (Columbus, OH: Wartburg, 1946), 120.

7. A. C. Thiselton, "Flesh," in *NIDNTT*, ed. Colin Brown, vol. 1, (Grand Rapids: Zondervan, 1978), 671–82.

8. In Greek thought, following Hippocates and Aristotle, this was how life in nature was understood. "For Ionic philosophy, nature is the growth of plants and animals, both as phenomenon in itself, and as the power of growth" (G. Harder, "Nature," *NIDNTT*), 2:657.

9. David K. Lowery, "1 Corinthians," *The Bible Knowledge Commentary*, ed. John F. Walvoord and Roy B. Zuck (Wheaton: Victor, 1983), 511.

10. Calvin is less than convincing in his attempt to offer a compromise position. "Paul says that men like that can be saved, but on this condition: if the Lord wipes off their ignorance, and purifies them from all uncleanness; and that is what the phrase 'as if by fire' means. Therefore he wants to suggest that he himself does not deprive them of the hope of salvation, provided that they willingly accept the loss of the work they have done, and are cleansed by God's mercy, as gold is purified in the furnace. Moreover, even God sometimes purifies His people by sufferings. I take 'fire' to mean here the testing by the Spirit. In that way God corrects and destroys the ignorance of His people, by which they were controlled for a time. I know very well that many refer this to the Cross, but I am sure that my interpretation will satisfy all of sound judgement" (*Calvin's New Testament Commentaries: I Corinthians*, ed. David W. Torrance and Thomas F. Torrance, trans. John W. Fraser [Grand Rapids: Eerdmans, 1973] 78). From my perspective, there are at least two problems with this. The first is that it fails to account for the fact that this letter is addressed to the "saints" at Corinth. The second is that the "day" of which Paul writes is eschatological and not a reference to our present experience (see 1 Cor. 1:8; 4:5; 2 Thess. 1:7–10; 2 Tim. 1:12; 4:8).

11. Bertrand Russell, *A History of Western Philosophy* (New York: Simon and Schuster, 1945), chap. 31; *The Age of Analysis*, ed. Morton White (New York: New American Library, 1955), 203–5; Rudolph Carnap, *Philosophy and Logical Syntax* (New York: AMS, 1979), 17.

12. See Millard Erickson's excellent discussion of this in his *Christian Theology*, 2d ed. (Grand Rapids: Baker, 1998), 135ff.

13. James Hastings, *The Great Texts of the Bible: 1 Corinthians* (Edinburgh: T. & T. Clark, 1912), 32

14. Ibid., 136.

Chapter 6–Defending Servant Leadership

1. J. H. Thayer, *Greek-English Lexicon of the New Testament* (Grand Rapids: Baker, 1977), 641.

2. Arthur Custance, *Man in Adam and in Christ* (Grand Rapids: Zondervan, 1975), 17.

3. Nigel Turner, *Grammatical Insights into the New Testament* (Edinburgh: T. & T. Clark, 1965), 131–32.

4. Ibid.

5. James C. Hanges, "1 Corinthians 4:6 and the Possibility of Written Bylaws in the Corinthian Church," *JBL* 117, no. 2 (summer 1998): 290.

6. Hanges uses copious examples from contemporary ancient literature to show that "Paul's phrase [here] bears a certain functional resemblance to the kinds of 'internal self-reference' common to Greek *leges sacrae*." An additional argument used to suggest that there was a rudimentary Christian *lex sacra* to which the writer is referring is the formula in 6:12 and 10:23, "it shall be lawful for" (*exeinai* + dative). It is generally accepted, especially since the work of J. C. Hurd, that Paul is quoting a "slogan" used by the Corinthians, which may actually have had its origin in Paul's own preaching. The least we can say is that the phrase represents something with which Paul presupposes the Corinthians to be familiar. Ibid., 293.

7. David K. Lowery, "1 Corinthians," *The Bible Knowledge Commentary,* ed. John F. Walvoord and Roy B. Zuck (Wheaton: Victor, 1983), 512.

8. The oft-repeated phrase is attributed to Gypsy Smith, the great American evangelist of the early twentieth century. It was his answer to the question as to how, after so many years, he was still so moved by the gospel story.

9. Recent scholarship has attempted to deduce from this text that the Corinthians had developed a kind of "over-realized eschatology." See, e.g. A. C. Thiselton, "Realised Eschatology at Corinth," *NTS* 24 (1978): 510–26. This theory has receded somewhat as more attention has been given to the more evident attack against their arrogance. The allusion to living, as it were, in the "kingdom" is entirely rhetorical. See O. L. Yarbrough, *Not Like the Gentiles: Marriage Rules in the Letters of Paul* (*JBL*, 80; Atlanta: Scholars Press, 1985), 117–18.

10. Marvin R. Vincent, *Word Studies in the New Testament*, vol. 3, (New York: Scribner, 1887–1900), 208.

11. In the Pythagorean letters the following is attributed to Pseudo-Theano, Letter to Eubule (Alfons Stadele, *Die Briefe des Pythagoras und der Pythagoreer,* 166–68). "I hear that you are spoiling your children. A good mother's responsibility is not to provide for her children's pleasure, but to lead them to temperance. Be careful, then, not to act like a mother who does not love her children but flatters them. For when pleasure is children's close companion it makes them undisciplined. For what gratifies young people more than pleasure to which they have become accustomed? Children, my friend, should be properly reared and not perverted" (See Abraham J. Malherbe, *Moral Exhortation: A Greco-Roman Sourcebook* [Philadelphia: Westminster, 1986], 83–84).

Chapter 7—Dealing with Immorality

1. J. Sidlow Baxter, *Explore the Book*, vol. 5 (Grand Rapids, Zondervan, 1966), 109.

2. Bruce N. Fisk, *First Corinthians* (Louisville, KY: Geneva, 2000), 23. Fisk lights upon the reference in Sophocles' play to the "unguessed shame" committed unknowingly by the son of Laius against his father. In Paul's view the sin in the assembly is worse than what would ever be allowed even among the "Gentiles." See also the discussion in Will Durant, *The Life of Greece* (New York: Simon and Schuster, 1939), 391ff.

3. Richard B. Hays, "Ecclesiology and Ethics in 1 Corinthians," *Ex Auditu* 10 (1994): 39

4. *Oratio Pro Cluentes* 6.15.

5. P. E. Hughes, "1 Corinthians," *The Biblical Expositor*, ed. Carl F. H. Henry, vol. 3, 267.

6. Commenting on this important text, see Fisk, *First Corinthians*.

7. John Calvin, *Calvin's New Testament Commentaries: I Corinthians*, ed. David W. Torrance and Thomas F. Torrance, trans. John W. Fraser (Grand Rapids: Eerdmans, 1973), 109

8. This phrase is an oft-repeated expression of my pastor, Dr. Jerry Falwell. It expresses well the relationship of a holy God to the problems associated with the presence of evil and the hostile actions of the "evil one" against God's people and His church.

9. Fisk, *First Corinthians*, 27.

10. F. W. Grosheide, *Commentary on the First Epistle to the Corinthians*, NIC (Grand Rapids: Eerdmans, 1953), 125.

11. Fisk, *First Corinthains*, 28.

12. David Hay, ed., *1 and 2 Corinthians* (Minneapolis: Fortress Press, 1993), 87.

13. Hays, "Ecclesiology and Ethics," 39.

Chapter 8—Taking a Believer to Court

1. C. K. Barrett, *The First Epistle to the Corinthians* (New York: Harper and Row, 1968), 135.

2. Charles Hodge, *An Exposition of the First Epistle to the Corinthians* (Grand Rapids: Eerdmans, 1974), 93.

3. Richard A. Horsley, "I Corinthians: A Case Study of Paul's Assembly

as an Alternative Society," in *Paul and Empire* (Harrisburg, PA: Trinity Press International, 1997), 246. Horsley adds, "Indeed, as paralleled in Judean apocalyptic writings (e.g., 1Qp Hab. 5:4; 1 Enoch 1:9; 95:3; cf. Rev. 20:4), at the judgment the 'saints will judge the world'" (6:2).

4. F. W. Grosheide, *Commentary on the First Epistle to the Corinthians*, NIC (Grand Rapids: Eerdmans, 1953), 133.

5. Barrett discusses the influence of the Qumran sect and contemporary Jewish custom but notes correctly that Paul "goes beyond them." He also reviews a significant body of literature on this subject. See his *First Epistle to the Corinthians*, 135–36.

6. Ibid., 139.

7. Brian Rosner, "The Origin and Meaning of I Corinthians 6:9–11" *BZ* 40, no. 2 (1996): 250–53, observes, "In context, I Corinthians 6:9–11 serves as both a warning and an encouragement not to dispute with one another. Paul argues that an eschatological worldview, which the Corinthians lacked or at least failed to appreciate, properly understood would have led them to seek to settle the dispute internally (6:2, 3) or, even better, to suffer gladly the . . . loss over which the dispute arose (6:9–11). Property and material possessions are of little consequence to those destined to inherit the kingdom.

8. S. L. Johnson, "1 Corinthians," *The Wycliffe Bible Commentary*, ed. Charles F. Pfeiffer and Everett F. Harrison (Chicago: Moody Press, 1962), 1238.

9. Barrett, *First Epistle to the Corinthians*, 143.

10. That Paul would cite these vices in particular is not surprising when one considers the depravity of the Roman culture of the day, symptoms of which could be seen throughout the empire. See Decimus Junius, Juvenal, *The Satires of Juvenal*, trans. Rolfe Humphries (Bloomington: Indiana University Press, 1958), especially his Second Satire, "Against hypocritical queens" (in which he satires the homosexuals who have plagued Rome during his lifetime in the first century).

> But this disease is contagious,
> It will infect more men, as the scab spreads all through the sheepfold
> From one sickly ram, as pig mange is epidemic
> From one boar, or a rotten apple spoils the whole barrel.
>
> (lines 80–83)

Chapter 9—All Things Are Lawful?

1. Richard Horsley's valuable discussion on this subject probably goes a little too far in likening Paul's view to the radical Qumranian

movement when he says: "His concern, however, is not simply a parallel to that of diaspora Jewish communities to conduct their own internal community affairs semiautonomously insofar as possible by permission of the Roman authorities. Paul's insistence that the assembly run its own affairs was more of a complete declaration of independence and autonomy, as in apocalyptic literature, where Judean scribes advocate independence of Judea or their own circles from imperial governments in their local clients. Statements of self-government from Qumran and branches of the Jesus movement appear to parallel Paul's statement to the Corinthians (cf. 1QS 5:25—6:1; CD 9:2-8; Matt 18:15-17; Luke 17:2-3; 12:57-59; Matt 5:25-26)" ("1 Corinthians: A Case Study of Paul's Assembly as an Alternative Society," *Paul and Empire* [Harrisburg, PA: Trinity Press International, 1997], 246-47).

2. David K. Lowery is exemplary of those who simply overlook the issue.

3. See the excellent discussion in Will Deming, "The Unity of 1 Corinthians 5—6," *JBL* 115, no. 2 (summer 1996): 289-312. While this writer considers the case to be well reasoned and supported throughout, too many assumptions are required in order to accept the conclusions. If this was the case brought before the courts and alluded to in chapter 6, why does Paul style it as a most outrageous case of immorality (5:1), and then in chapter 6 as "*biotika*," or a "petty issue" ? But more damaging still is that Paul says of the issue before the courts in chapter 6 that it would be better if they had done *nothing* about it, rather than to have brought it to the civil authorities. Such an attitude hardly fits the language of chapter 5 regarding the egregious case of immorality addressed there. See also Rosner's critique of this position in "Temple Prostitution in I Corinthians 6:12-20," *NovT* 40, no. 4 (October 1998): 338ff.

4. This has been generally challenged in recent scholarship. But see Brent Kinman's analysis and defense of the view in "Appoint the Despised as Judges! (1 Corinthians 6:4)," *TynB* 48 no. 2 (November 1997): 345-54.

5. See support for this in C. K. Barrett, *The First Epistle to the Corinthians* (New York: Harper and Row, 1968), 144.

6. See Bruce W. Winter, "Gluttony and Immorality at Elitist Banquets," *Jian Dao: A Journal of Bible and Theology* 7 (1997): 77-90; and Brian S. Rosner, "The Origin and Meaning of 1 Corinthians 6:9-11," *BZ* 40, no. 2 (1996): 336-51.

7. Rosner, "Origin and Meaning of 1 Corinthians 6:9-11," 346.

8. Ben Witherington, *Conflict and Community in Corinth: A Socio-Rhetorical Commentary on 1 and 2 Corinthians* (Grand Rapids: Eerdmans, 1995), 13.

9. Barrett, *First Epistle to the Corinthians*, 144-45.

10. Deming, Rosner, and Winter have reviewed the salient literature on this in Plato, Aristotle, the Stoics, and later Christian writers. In particular the concerns registered had to do with criteria appropriate to those who stood, as it were, above the law. Plato's concerns, for example, regarding a pure democracy had to do with its tendency toward anarchy—i.e., if the majority demanded it, "all things are lawful." For our purposes it is sufficient to note that the expression had a significant currency in the surrounding culture. Socrates' death, it may well be noted, was an intentional demonstration against this idea.

11. In Aristotle, physics, the *phusis* of a thing—especially a living thing— is its end, that for the sake of which it exists. Thus, as Russell has observed, it has a teleological implication. Things have a nature if they have an internal principle of this kind. B. Russell, *History of Western Philosophy* (New York: Simon and Schuster, 1945), 205. It is likely that what Aristotle saw in living things is what a modern biologist would relate to genetics. What is important here is that Paul, writing as he does to a Greek audience, seems to be in touch with what was likely the conventional thought on natural history. And as is typical for him, he adds his own perspective, enlightened as it is from his biblical/theological orientation.

12. A. T. Pierson, *Knowing the Scriptures*: Rules and Methods of Bible Study (New York: Gospel Publishing House, 1910), 108.

Chapter 10—Concerning Marriage

1. In recent rhetorical studies, this analysis has been challenged. Margaret Mitchell has argued that the expression may only mean that a new subject is introduced. See "Concerning *Peri de* in I Corinthians," *NovT* 31 (1989): 229–56. I agree that, taken alone, this phrase may not necessarily indicate a previous referenced communication. However, in this case there are numerous other indicators to suggest that the writer is working off a list of inquiries. These may have been in the form of a letter from them to him, or they simply may have been part of the list of concerns sent by way of "those of Chloe" (cf. 1:11; introduction). Here the writer cites their letter of inquiry (7:1). The use of *peri de* in 1 Corinthians is unique to the rest of Paul's epistles and the New Testament as well. It is entirely possible to surmise that the specific expression was used in their letter to him and that he is simply quoting their text as he states the issue(s). See the discussion in John Coolidge Hurd Jr., *The Origin of I Corinthians* (Macon, GA: Mercer University Press, 1983), 48, 153ff.

2. John Calvin, *Calvin's New Testament Commentaries: 1 Corinthians*, ed. David W. Torrance and Thomas F. Torrance, trans. John W. Fraser

(Grand Rapids: Eerdmans, 1973), 136.

3. Cf. Marvin R. Vincent, *Word Studies in the New Testament*, vol. 2 (New York: Scribner, 1887–1900), 217.

4. "It is the case that, with verbs of saying, the neuter demonstrative pronoun ('this') often introduces the subordinate clause with an implied 'that' (as in, 'I say this, [that] . . .'). We contend that the same construction in 1 Corinthians 7:6 helps to unlock the pattern of Paul's thought in 1 Corinthians 8:24. First Corinthians 7:6 does not refer to the contents of 7:1–5, but emphatically to 7:7a where *de* assumes an adverbial role of 'rather' in Paul's caveat. With the strong adversative 'but' *(alla)* in 7:7b he acknowledges that either singleness or marriage is a divine gift and then proceeds to discuss aspects of these gifts and callings of God in 7:8–24" (Bruce Winter, "1 Corinthians 7:6–7: A Caveat and a Framework for 'The Sayings' in 7:8–24," *TynB* 48, no. 1 [May 1997]: 57–65).

5. Ibid., 65.

6. Cf. Haggai 2:11–13.

7. James H. Moulton and George Milligan, *The Vocabulary of the Greek New Testament* (Grand Rapids: Eerdmans, 1976), 695–96.

8. For the case to be made for this and its import, see Rollin A Ramsaran, "More Than an Opinion: Paul's Rhetorical Maxim in First Corinthians 7:25–26," *CBQ* 57, no. 3 (July 1995): 531ff.

9. See Bruce Winter, "The Seasons of This Life and Eschatology," *Eschatology in Bible and Theology*, ed. Kent E. Brower and Mark W. Elliott (Downers Grove, IL: InterVarsity Press, 1977), 331, nn. 22, 25.

10. Ibid., 333, brackets mine.

11. Ibid.

12. Ibid., 334.

13. Ibid.

14. Ibid.

15. See, e.g., Paul K. Jewett, *Man as Male and Female* (Grand Rapids: Eerdmans, 1975), 112–14, 119, 134–39, 145–47.

Chapter 11—Concerning Christian Liberty: The Principle

1. See, e.g., Leon Morris, *The First Epistle of Paul to the Corinthians* (Grand Rapids: Eerdmans, 1976), 151ff., and discussion below on 11:2–34.

2. I tend to agree with Anders Eriksson's assessment of S. K. Stowers, "Paul on the Use and Abuse of Reason," in D. L. Balch, E. Ferguson and W. A. Meeks, eds., *Greeks, Romans and Christians: Essays in Honor of Abraham J. Malherbe* (Minneapolis: Fortress Press, 1990), 276–84. See also Anders Eriksson, "Special Topics in 1 Corinthians 8—10," *The Rhetorical Interpretation of Scripture*, ed. Stanley E. Porter and Dennis L. Stamps, *JSNT* Supplement Series 180 (Sheffield, Eng.: Sheffield Academic Press, 1999), 283, n. 46. The contrast is not with the weak and the *strong*. It is between the weak and the *wise*. In saying this, it is also evident that Paul speaks of the so-called wise throughout these passages with tongue in cheek. Before the chapter is finished, he will seriously call their self-description into question.

3. Stowers, "Paul on the Abuse and Use of Reason," 77–90; See also Eriksson, "Special Topics," 283, n. 46.

4. In making this acknowledgment and with it a recognition of Paul's use of conventions well known to the Stoics of his day, I maintain nevertheless that the dominant motif of Paul's thought is biblical— that is to say that his central theme relates to the promises of God to Israel and the questions related to how Christ and the New Testament church fit into those promises. See Troels Engberg-Pedersen, *Paul and the Stoics* (Louisville: Westminster John Knox, 2000), for discussions of the work done to date in seeking Hellenistic antecedents in the rhetorical repertoire of Paul's style. Over the past century focus has been primarily on the theological coherence of the Pauline materials. One of the problems with this latter approach has been the theological "bias" often imported from contemporary liberal and neoorthodox presuppositions (e.g., Wrede, Dibelius, and Bultmann). Of course, evangelicals are not exempt from this danger either. Rhetorical analysis attempts to give attention, not just to the *subjects* being discussed, but to the *function* of those literary units in which they appear. Many scholars have begun to recognize in the New Testament texts rhetorical devices common to contemporary Hellenistic literary conventions. Following the rhetorical theory of Aristotle, Cicero, and Quintilian, the world of which Paul was a part was very familiar with these types of speech. David Aune has well noted: "With few exceptions, early Christian letters were either written with a basically deliberative purpose, or included major deliberative elements. The two basic forms of deliberative rhetoric, persuasion and dissuasion, included not only advice but also most of the features associated with moral and religious exhortation: encourage-

ment, admonition, comfort, warning, and rebuke. Most of Paul's let-ters, apart from the opening and closing epistolary formulas, consist of three elements. The first is conciliatory; he compliments the addressees for their past performance. The middle section contains advice. The final section contains paraenesis" (*The New Testament in Its Literary Environment*, 199).

5. Eriksson, "Special Topics," 281. Since the work of Thomas Olbricht, "An Aristotelian Rhetorical Analysis of 1 Thessalonians," in D. L. Balch, E. Ferguson, and W. A. Meeks, eds., *Greeks, Romans and Christians: Essays in Honor of Abraham J. Malherbe* (Minneapolis: Fortress Press, 1990), 216–26, a great deal of attention has been given to the question of whether the New Testament reflects an entirely dif-ferent genre of ancient rhetoric (e.g., "church rhetoric") or whether it fits the more classical categories established in Greek literature. This, as noted above, has led to a new appreciation for the degree to which the New Testament writers—Paul in particular—*reasoned* with their readers rather than merely pronouncing truth, as it were, from a mag-isterial position of authority. This, in turn, has lead to new under-standing of the way the biblical writers interact with their readers to "bring them along" with respect to the issues being considered. While some of this discussion works from presuppositions regarding the text with which we disagree, this new *inventio* phase in modern rhetorical criticism, which displaces the older *dispositio* phase (to use Eriksson's distinction), has offered a fresh new appreciation for the power of the text to *persuade* as well as to teach. Eriksson, in my view, correctly breaks with Olbricht's suggestion that the New Testament represents a fourth kind of rhetoric. Rather, it seems to work with conventions already available in the culture and its language (cf. pp. 273–76).

6. Ralph Earle, *Word Meanings in the New Testament*, vol. 4 (Kansas City: Beacon Hill), 57.

7. For a discussion of the significance of this expression, see comments on 1 Corinthians 15:3–5 below.

8. Eriksson, "Special Topics," 286.

9. Ibid., 282–83.

10. S. Lewis Johnson, "The First Epistle to the Corinthians," *The Wycliffe Bible Commentary*, ed. Charles F. Pfeiffer and Everett F. Harrison (Chicago: Moody Press, 1963), 1242.

Chapter 12—Concerning Christian Liberty: The Portrait

1. Leon Morris, *The First Epistle of Paul to the Corinthians* (Grand Rapids: Eerdmans, 1978), 131.

2. Ibid.

3. This characterization is owed to Eriksson's comment on this text, "Paul hides the issue of his own *ethos* behind the *ethos* of the tradition" ("Special Topics in 1 Corinthians 8—10," *The Rhetorical Interpretation of Scripture*, ed. Stanley E. Porter and Dennis L. Stamps, *JSNT* Supplement Series 180 [Sheffield, Eng.: Sheffield Academic Press, 1999], 285–86).

4. Since Marshall McLuhan's definitive work, *The Medium Is the Message*, published in 1967 (reprint, Corte Madera, CA: Gingko Press, 2001), it generally has been conceded that both text and delivery combine to communicate with the consumer. In recent years a great deal of attention has been given to these issues especially as they relate to American Christianity. An example of this is the penetrating critique of modern market-driven evangelical churches, movements, and attitudes by David F. Wells. See his *No Place for Truth* (Grand Rapids: Eerdmans, 1993), *God in the Wasteland* (Grand Rapids: Eerdmans, 1994), and *Losing Our Virtue* (Grand Rapids: Eerdmans, 1998). As a Brit, Wells writes as an "outsider" in his analysis of the American evangelical scene and offers a perspective not easily achieved by an "insider." He shows significant indebtedness in these volumes to Alasdair MacIntyre, the former Marxist whose acclaimed critique of modern Western thought is also unparalleled in recent decades. These include *After Virtue* (first published in London: Gerald Duckworth and Co., 1981), *Whose Justice? Which Rationality?* (Notre Dame: Notre Dame University Press, 1988), and *Three Rival Versions of Moral Enquiry*, The Gifford Lectures delivered at the University of Edinburgh in 1988 (Notre Dame: Notre Dame University Press, 1990).

5. Perhaps the metaphor was inspired by his own brush with death in the open waters when his ship came perilously close to being lost on a transatlantic trip. The story is recorded by his son, William Moody, in *D. L. Moody* (New York: Macmillan, 1930), 402ff.

Chapter 13—Concerning Christian Liberty: The Practice

1. For insights related to the shape and function of Paul's argument here, I am indebted to the work of Joop F. M. Smit, "'Do Not Be

Idolaters': Paul's Rhetoric in First Corinthians 10:1–22," *NovT* 39, no. 1 (January 1997): 40–53; and "The Function of First Corinthians 10:23–30: A Rhetorical Anticipation" *Bib* 78, no. 3 (1997): 378–88.

2. For a fairly recent review of salient opinions, see Gordon Fee, *The First Epistle to the Corinthians*, TNICNT (Grand Rapids: Eerdmans, 1987) 475–91.

3. Here I am indebted once again to Smit for his helpful analysis of this very difficult text ("'Do Not Be Idolaters,'" 378–88).

4. Ibid.

5. *Rhetorica and Herennium* 2.10.15 and Quintilian, *Institutio Oratoria* 7.7.7, cited in ibid., show that this was the general rule in contemporary handbooks on rhetoric to resolve the dilemma that arises in such cases.

6. Ibid., 388.

Chapter 14–Concerning Christian Worship

1. A. Andrew Das, in "1 Corinthians 11:17–34 Revisited," *Concordia Theological Quarterly* 62, no. 3 (July 1998), notices "the increasing focus in the scholarly literature on the 'horizontal' dimension of the passage" in contrast to the "sacramental aspects of the text" (p. 187). Others show the same tendency to find solutions on even the most obscure references in this chapter by looking "to Paul's cultural and religious context to flesh out the possibilities of his allusions" Jason D. BeDuhn, "'Because of the Angels': Unveiling Paul's Anthropology in 1 Corinthians 11," *JBL* 118, no. 2 (summer 1999): 295.

2. Leon Morris, *The First Epistle of Paul to the Corinthians*, arranges chapters 11—14 under one heading, "Disorders in Public Worship" (pp. 151ff.). I agree with this arrangement because it gives the natural flow of Paul's argument in these sections. Having addressed issues related to problems coming from *outside* the church, he now turns his attention to problems from the *inside*. Nevertheless, I have chosen to separate these since the first chapter (chap. 11) relates more to matters of order and liturgy (see also Das, above), while the next three chapters (chaps. 12—14) relate more to spiritual formation and individual participation in community. The latter section forms a somewhat larger footprint than the rubric of worship per se allows.

3. B. Siede, "Take," *NIDNTT*, ed. Colin Brown, vol. 3, (Grand Rapids: Zondervan, 1978) 751. See comments on 15:3.

4. Harold R. Holmyard III, "Does 1 Corinthians 11:2–16 Refer to Women Praying and Prophesying in Church?" *BibSac*, 154, no. 616 (October–November 1997): 465.

5. Although Holmyard presents a valiant effort to see 1 Corinthians 11:3–16 as referring to "non-church" gatherings in contrast to the latter portion of the chapter and 14:33ff. as referring to more formal gatherings for worship, I remain unconvinced. See D. A. Carson, "'Silent in the Churches': On the Role of Women in 1 Corinthians 14:33b–36," in *Recovering Biblical Manhood and Womanhood: A Response to Evangelical Feminism* 151–53.

6. On this point, I agree with Jason D. BeDuhn's understanding of the presence of subordinate relations here, but he is wrong in his judgment that the distinction drawn is "ontological." This is precisely what is *not* taught here. His suggestion ignores the first four centuries of Trinitarian and Christological reflection that drew the important distinction between the *persons* of the Godhead—who are coequal and coeternal in all attributes of deity—and the *properties* of each person—which were generally sketched out along "economic" lines to specify the unique functions, activities, and acts associated with each person individually. For example, the Father plans the work, sustains the universe, and sends the Son. The Son, in turn, is seen to execute the plan and intercede for His own, and it is He alone who died. The Spirit applies the finished work of the Son, fills the believer, and was known to have descended on the Day of Pentecost for His special work of indwelling and gifting believers. BeDuhn comes to this conclusion because, in his analysis, Paul held to a proto-gnostic anthropogyny that was subsequently rejected in mainstream Christian theology. I agree only that if one makes the unwarranted assertion that the distinction here is ontological, it will indeed lead to a heterodox view of God. (See BeDuhn, "'Because of the Angels,'": 295–320.

7. Khiok-Khng Yeo's striking admission is reflective of the extremes to which people go to sustain this esoteric use of the term *kephale*. "It is true that in the LXX (Paul's 'Bible'), *kekphale* appears 281 times as the translation for *ros* in the sense of chief or ruler, when used of [an] authoritative figure, an *archon* (ruler/originator) or *archagos* (chief/leader)." Citing Fitzmyer, he notes that this usage of the term has been employed to show that Paul's use of the term intends to convey the idea of someone who has supremacy over another. To this he must respond, "But this is to assume that Paul's use of the word cannot exceed the semantic range of his contemporaries." And from

there with no further evidence he asserts that "contextual analysis indicates that Paul is shifting the metaphorical sense of *kephale* from 'authoritative figure' to 'source'" ("Differentiation and Mutuality of Male-Female Relations in 1 Corinthians 11:2–16," *BibRes* 43 [1998]: 16). Others, such as Robin Dowling, don't even go there. She simply asserts: "Almost certainly, the Corinthians would have understood the Greek word for head to mean 'source,' 'origin' or 'fountainhead.' We are probably being influenced by our own culture when we read the word 'head' as 'ruler' or 'boss' (or as referring to 'authority over')" ("Headcoverings: An Exposition of 1 Corinthians 11:2–26," *Evangel* 12 [summer 1994]: 37–40). In a footnote she acknowledges the debate but offers no justification to support her contention that the notion of "source" is to be offered in contradistinction to "authority." I maintain that both are to be seen in this passage and that it is a mistake to bifurcate the two.

8. C. K. Barrett, *The First Epistle to the Corinthians* (New York: Harper and Row, 1968), 249

9. BeDuhn, "'Because of the Angels,'" 300.

10. Dowling, "Headcoverings," 37.

11. Ibid., 299.

12. BeDuhn, "'Because of the Angels,'" 299, goes on to say that "Paul's basic point is clear: men and women have distinct appearances appropriate to them in the setting of religious practice. To violate these norms is to bring disgrace to the person above one in the hierarchical scale of 'headship.'" See also Barrett, *First Epistle to the Corinthians,* on the "literal" versus "metaphorical" uses of *kephale* (249–50).

13. Much recent attention is given to Oster's discussion in "When Men Wore Veils to Worship: The Historical Context of 1 Corinthians 11:4," *NTS* 34 (1988): 481–505. See Holmyard, "Does 1 Corinthians 11:2–16 Refer to Women Praying . . . ?" 470, n. 27; and BeDuhn, "'Because of the Angels,'" 296, n. 5.

14. Morris, *First Epistle of Paul to the Corinthians,* 172, uses the expression "inspired speech." Since "inspiration" is ordinarily associated with the work of the Holy Spirit in the deliberate action of biblical writers to "write," it is best not to confuse the gift of prophecy with that kind of terminology.

15. See Holmyard, "Does 1 Corinthians 11:2–16 Refer to Women Praying . . . ?" 465, and discussion noted above.

16. See BeDuhn, "'Because of the Angels,'" 300, n. 20.

17. It is unlikely that Paul is thinking here about the practice of a woman shaving her head as a mark of mourning and separation (see Deut. 21:12), since the respective contexts are entirely unrelated.

18. Barrett, *First Epistle to the Corinthians*, 252–53.

19. BeDuhn, "'Because of the Angels,'" 303–4.

20. It is at this point that we must take leave of BeDuhn's otherwise helpful analysis of this text. It is my view that his conclusion has the net impact of discrediting Paul's position by identifying it with proto-gnostic influences in the region and requiring an approach to the text that necessitates the abandonment of its normativity to say nothing of its inspiration and inerrancy.

21. Contra Holmyard. See also Grosheide, *Commentary on the First Epistle to the Corinthians*, NIC (Grand Rapids: Eerdmans, 1953), 251–52.

22. Ibid., 257.

23. Barrett also offers several examples from Epictetus and Lucian to reinforce this commonplace in Paul (*First Epistle to the Corinthians*, 256).

24. Leon Podles, *The Church Impotent: The Feminization of Christianity* (Dallas: Spence, 1999), documents the frightening decline of men in the churches of Western Christianity. In all but the most conservative of churches, women make up the overwhelming majority of active members. Podles calls upon his readers to begin to address the problem by paying attention to both the theological and the social reasons for this trend. Theologically, we need to define our ideas of masculinity and femininity from Scripture, not the culture. Sociologically, we need to back away from the *feminization* of our churches and address the special needs of men and women alike.

25. As, e.g., R. C. H. Lenski, would feel the need to do. See his *The Interpretation of 1 and 2 Corinthians* (Columbus, OH: Wartburg, 1946), 477–79.

26. William Baird, *The Corinthian Church—a Biblical Approach to Urban Culture* (New York: Abingdon, 1964), 135.

Chapter 15—Concerning Spiritual Gifts

1. I noted earlier in my comments on 11:29 that "discerning" the body had to do with a proper understanding of the church. This clearly anticipates what follows in this chapter concerning the work of the Holy Spirit in creating the body and in gifting the body for service. See my comments on 2:13–14 for Paul's first introduction of the wider issue involved with "spiritual" matters.

2. The term is intended here not as a pejorative but as a statement of fact describing the unprecedented growth of charismatic Christianity around the world. Some estimates suggest that it constitutes the largest

religious movement of all time, growing from rag-tag beginnings at the turn of the century to more than a half-billion adherents world-wide within the first hundred years. Harvey Cox, in *Fire from Heaven* (Reading, MA: Addison-Wesley, 1995), documents this growth and the unprecedented impact it has had on Christianity and the world.

3. Leon Morris, *The First Epistle of Paul to the Corinthians* (Grand Rapids: Eerdmans, 1976), 165.

4. Ibid.

5. Archibald Robertson and Alfred Plummer, *A Critical and Exegetical Commentary on the First Epistle of St. Paul to the Corinthians*, ICC (Edinburgh: T. & T. Clark, 1955), 257. The characterization is ironic because it is precisely on these matters that the writer wishes the reader *not* be ignorant.

6. Since the spelling of *pneumatikos* is the same for both masculine and neuter, the context is determinative in securing the meaning. Here, since the subject before us is so clearly related to spiritual *gifts*, it is best understood as neuter (cf. v. 4; 5:31; 14:1).

7. Johannes Behm has shown that the Corinthian experience seems to have significant correlation with pagan cultic practice. While discounting the historicity of the Acts account, he suggests that the definitive text in understanding the practice in the New Testament is 1 Corinthians 14. See "glossa," in *TDNT*, ed. G. Kittel, vol. 1 722–24. In my analysis I recognize differences but see no reason to discount the integrity of either text. I further suggest that the Pentecostal experience as described by Luke is understood to be normative by both writers and it is with respect to an aberrant practice at Corinth that Paul deals a corrective. See my discussion below.

8. Jean Hering, in *The First Epistle of Saint Paul to the Corinthians*, trans. from the 2d French ed. by A. W. Heathcote and P. J. Allcock (London: Epworth, 1962), 124, notes, "'*Apagesthai*' is used to speak of victims dragged to the altar, which is a very apt idea here; for pagan ecstatics are the victim of demons. Thus a play on words is intended: you thought you were being transported to heaven (*'anegesthe'*), but really you were the victims of the forces of evil (*'apagomenoi'*) which were leading you astray."

9. Morris, *First Epistle of Paul to the Corinthians*, 167.

10. Robert G. Gromacki, *Called to Be Saints* (Grand Rapids: Baker, 1977), 151.

11. As a matter of "fact" this becomes his *stasis* (basic issue) upon which to proceed to build his case against their abuse of the gifts in the assembly.

12. Ellis agrees that there is a real possibility that the Corinthians had adopted an erroneous tendency toward the veneration of angels (as seen at Qumran) along with an "indiscriminate acceptance of ecstatic phenomena even of demonic origin (12:3)." See E. Earl Ellis, "Christ and the Spirit in 1 Corinthians," in *Christ and Spirit in the New Testament,* ed. Barnabas Lindars and Stephen S. Smalley in honor of C. F. D. Moule (Cambridge: Cambridge University Press, 1973), 269–77.

13. F. W. Grosheide, *Commentary on the First Epistle to the Corinthians,* NIC (Grand Rapids: Eerdmans, 1953), 285.

14. Gordon D. Fee, *The First Epistle to the Corinthians,* TNICNT (Grand Rapids: Eerdmans, 1987), 591–92; see also n. 45.

15. Ibid. Fee agrees that this is a revelatory gift and not to be equated with the experience often associated with it in modern Pentecostal and charismatic circles as a special word from God to help churches "going through a time of difficulty or decision." See also n. 48.

16. Some like to use the expression "inspired speech or utterance" to describe this, and it is often associated with "ecstatic" experience. See ibid. and Morris, *First Epistle of Paul to the Corinthians,* 172. I prefer to emphasize the revelatory nature of this gift but do not wish to confuse it with "inspiration," which is reserved for reference to the composition of Scripture.

17. The only possible exception to this is the suggestion by some that the *battalogeo* "meaningless repetition" of Matthew 6:7 is a reference to pagan tongues-speech. See J. Dillow, *Speaking in Tongues* (Grand Rapids: Zondervan, 1975), 12–13, 39ff., 118ff. In my view, while this is an interesting suggestion, there is little evidence to commend it— certainly not to the magnitude Dillow uses it. While few question that the term is onomatopoeic, the exact etymology is obscure and may not signify anything more than "constant repetition" as with, e.g., a mantra. See Delling, *"battalogeo,"* in *TDNT,* 1:597.

18. Gromacki, *Called to Be Saints,* 154.

19. Matthew Brook O'Donnell, "Two Opposing Views on Baptism with/by the Holy Spirit and of 1 Corinthians 12:13: Can Grammatical Investigation Bring Clarity?" in *Baptism, the New*

Testament and the Church, ed. Stanley E. Porter and Anthony R. Cross, *JSNT* Supplement Series 171 (Sheffield, Eng.: Sheffield Academic Press, 1999), 311–36, shows that a significant case can be made for the use of the preposition *"en"* here as denoting *agency*, it requires too much interpolation of the immediate context to follow him there.

20. It is helpful to remember that the composition of the book of Acts was undertaken by a companion of Paul and not until after Paul had written his letters. These two factors taken together help us to understand that the "final word" on these controversial issues came in Acts, not in the Corinthian letters. And this being the case, if one is looking for "clarification" on the issues, he or she should expect to find it in Acts, not the Epistles. Furthermore, since they traveled together, it is unlikely that Paul and Luke held contradictory views on this important subject.

21. The important common denominator in these passages is not the common *experience*, but *Peter*. It is he who appears to be required in each instance to "lay hands" on the believers and to convey the Spirit. This seems to be rendered necessary in God's providence to establish "one" church, not many.

22. Luke does not record any special manifestations of the Spirit in Corinth. Perhaps this is because he knew Paul had already spoken of them. Nor does he bother to address any of the other controversies, such as divisions, idol meat, or immorality. So perhaps little should be made of this fact. When the paper alone for a book the size of Acts might cost the equivalent of a year's salary, there were more reasons than one to apply Occam's razor to the minor details of his history.

23. Hering suggests that these are to be identified with the organs of excretion and reproduction (*First Epistle of Saint Paul to the Corinthians*, 131).

24. In ancient Greek thought, following Hippocrates and Aristotle, it was considered that living things were created with the mingling together of fire and water. "Aristotle and indeed all those who shared his qualitative view on the nature of matter, believed that all material things change and develop. He was convinced that all elementary matter, whether animal, vegetable or mineral, developed in a physiological way." This indeed was the prevailing view, in contrast to modern science, until the end of the eighteenth century. See the helpful discussion in Scott Brodeur, *The Holy Spirit's Agency in the*

Resurrection of the Dead (Rome: Gregorian University Press, 1995), 34–42.

25. Morris, *First Epistle of Paul to the Corinthians,* 177.

26. S. Lewis Johnson, "The First Epistle to the Corinthians," *The Wycliffe Bible Commentary,* ed. Charles F. Pfeiffer and Everett F. Harrison (Chicago: Moody Press, 1963), 1251.

Chapter 16—Gifts Are for Loving the Body

1. Hering rushes too quickly to the conclusion that "this chapter obviously interrupts the discussion on spiritual gifts" (Jean Hering, *The First Epistle of Saint Paul to the Corinthians,* trans. from the 2d French ed. by A. W. Heathcote and P. J. Allcock [London: Epworth, 1962], 134.

2. Henry Drummond, *The Greatest Thing in the World* (New York: Grosset & Dunlap, n.d.), 10.

3. Fee concurs. See Gordon D. Fee, *The First Epistle to the Corinthians,* TNICNT (Grand Rapids: Eerdmans, 1987), 573.

4. E. Earle Ellis, "Christ and the Spirit in 1 Corinthians," in *Christ and the Spirit in the New Testament,* ed. Barnabas Lindars and Stephen S. Smalley in honor of C. F. D. Moule (Cambridge: Cambridge University Press, 1973), 276–77. Also see note on 12:3 above.

5. J. Dillow, *Speaking in Tongues* (Grand Rapids: Zondervan, 1975), 12–13.

6. This probably is not a reference to martyrdom, although that is not impossible (cf. Dan. 3). However, death by burning was not really known in the Graeco-Roman world. It is probably a reference to the practice of branding the bodies of slaves with a hot iron. Christians might have thus sold themselves, as the text suggests, for some noble cause. But without love, it would have been for naught. See Hering, *The First Epistle of Saint Paul to the Corinthians,* 137.

7. Ibid., 135, n.4.

8. Cf. Marvin Vincent, *Word Studies in the New Testament,* vol. 2 (New York: Scribner, 1887–1990), 265.

9. See Myron Houghton's excellent review of the use of this term and its significance in this context (Myron J. Houghton, "A Reexamination of 1 Corinthians 13:8–13," *BibSac* 153 [July–September 1996]: 348–49). He concludes, in agreement with Fee, that "the change in verb and voice in 1 Corinthians 13:8—from prophecy that 'will be

done away' and knowledge that 'will be done away' to 'tongues will cease'—is nothing more than rhetorical style. The change emphasizes the temporary nature of these gifts in contrast to the permanence of love." See also Gordon D. Fee, *God's Empowering Presence* (Peabody, MA: Hendrickson, 1994), 206.

10. Gary Steven Shogren demonstrates quite convincingly in his review of patristic and recent reflection on this text that "the majority viewpoint is and always has been that it is eschatological, thus: 'We know in part, we prophesy in part but when the perfect comes . . .' (13:10) is parallel to 'now I know in part, and then I shall know' (13:12) and both have reference to seeing Christ at the Parousia, 'face to face' in 13:12 being drawn from the Old Testament language of divine epiphany." See Gary Steven Shogren, "How Did They Suppose 'the Perfect' Would Come?" *Journal of Pentecostal Theology* 15, (October 1999): 99–121.

11. Augustine, *The Enchiridion on Faith, Hope, and Love*, ed. Henry Paolucci (Washington, D.C.: Regnery Gateway Editions, 1991), 135.

Chapter 17—Gifts Are for Ministering to the Body

1. I agree with Fee that Paul does not "damn tongues with faint praise." The correct approach is not "disuse," but "proper use." I disagree, however, in what that might look like (see Gordon D. Fee, *The First Epistle to the Corinthians*, TNICNT [Grand Rapids: Eerdmans, 1987], 575–76, 653).

2. Jean Hering, *The First Epistle of Saint Paul to the Corinthians*, trans. from the 2d French ed. by A. W. Heathcote and P. J. Allcock [London: Epworth, 1962], 149.

3. The use of *phrene* here balances the instruction in chapter 1 in which the writer's reference to the destruction of fleshly wisdom should not be construed as leaving their brains at the door (see ibid., 152).

4. Leon Morris, *The First Epistle of Paul to the Corinthians* (Grand Rapids: Eerdmans, 1976), 198–99.

5. Fee, *First Epistle to the Corinthians*, 699ff., succinctly notes, "Although these two verses are found in all known manuscripts, either here or at the end of the chapter, the two text-critical criteria of transcriptional and intrinsic probability combine to cast considerable doubt on their authenticity." See also notes 1–4. I agree that Bengel's first principle must be overruled in this instance. However, the manuscript tradition is so ancient and pervasive that I think we

must give the burden of proof to those who, with Fee, would consider it an interpolation. While it may not be possible to establish certainty as to Paul's precise intent by this instruction, several interpretive possibilities may be offered requiring neither the rejection of the Pauline authorship nor a contradiction with other clear Pauline teaching (e.g., chap. 11) on this matter. Kummel, *Introduction* 203, defends the traditional reading with: "The command 'Let a woman be silent in church' . . . does stand in tension with I 11:3 ff. But the contradiction is explained by the almost universally shared view that in I 14:33b–35 only 'disputation' is forbidden. Hence the supposition of an interpolation here is also unnecessary." See also Hering, 154. As Susan T. Foh, *Women and the Word of God* (Nutley, NJ: Presbyterian and Reformed, 1980), has noted, it is not necessary to understand 1 Corinthians 14 as a blanket prohibition and at the same time see it as a contradiction to chapter 11. John Calvin, (*The First Epistle of Paul to the Corinthians,* English translation by John Fraser [Grand Rapids: Eerdmans, 1960], 231), understands chapter 14 as the completion of Paul's argument regarding women. That is to say, they are to wear a covering *and* they are to remain silent.

6. See Dillow, *Speaking in Tongues* (Grand Rapids: Zondervan, 1975), 170; Paige Patterson, *The Troubled Triumphant Church* (Nashville: Thomas Nelson, 1983), 266.

7. See Fee, *First Epistle to the Corinthians,* 704–5, n. 26, for salient discussion.

8. Ibid. Fee despairs so of any resolution to the apparent textual and theological problems that he dismisses it as a very early insertion into the text. See note above.

9. See, e.g., Kummel, *Introduction,* 203, C. K. Barrett, *The First Epistle to the Corinthians* (New York: Harper and Row, 1968), 331–33; and Hering, *First Epistle of Saint Paul to the Corinthians,* 154. The likely scenario is that some of the women were challenging their husbands openly—perhaps in the context of verse 29 in the "judging" of the prophetic message (viz. D. A. Carson, "Silent in the Churches," in *Recovering Biblical Manhood and Womanhood,* ed. John Piper and Wayne Grudem (Wheaton: Crossway, 1991), 140–53; or perhaps it was nothing more than idle chatter unrelated to the service (*lalein* in classical Greek had this sense as an onomatopoeia). See Fee, *First Epistle to the Corinthians,* 703, n. 20); Patricia Gundry,

Woman, Be Free! (Grand Rapids: Zondervan, 1977), 70; Krister Stendahl, *The Bible and the Role of Women,* trans. Emilie T. Sander (Philadelphia: Fortress Press, 1966), 30; Foh, *Women and the Word of God,* 119–21.

10. Defending the appropriateness of this in the context of the writer's discussion, Hering notes, "The Apostle has just restated the principle of decorum, which must be observed in Church gatherings (14:33). So it is quite natural that he should go a step farther and reduce to silence the women who, contrary to Jewish and Greek custom, wished to take part in discussions" (*First Epistle of Saint Paul to the Corinthians,* 154).

11. Fee, *First Epistle to the Corinthians,* 711.

Chapter 18—The Resurrection

1. This theory was explored extensively a half-century ago by Norman de Witt, in his *St. Paul and Epicurus* (Minneapolis: University of Minneapolis Press, 1954). Due to his excessive analysis, the theory has since been generally neglected by serious scholars. More recently the suggestion once again has been supported by Graham Tomlin of Wycliffe Hall, Oxford. I am indebted to him for much of my analysis. See his "Christians and Epicureans in 1 Corinthians," *JSNT* 68 (December 1997): 51–72.

2. Ibid. See also Richard E. Demaris, "Corinthian Religion and Baptism for the Dead (1 Corinthians 15:29): Insights from Archaeology and Anthropology" *JBL* 114, no. 4 (winter 1995): 661–82. And see Joel R. White, "Baptized on Account of the Dead": The Meaning of 1 Corinthians 15:29 in Its Context," *JBL* 116, no. 3 (fall 1997): 487–99, for a balanced assessment of DeMaris.

3. Donald Engles, *Roman Corinth: An Alternative Model for the Classical City* (Chicago: University of Chicago Press, 1990), 73. Tomlin comments on Engles, noting that there was a "shift in ethnic and cultural identity from Roman (Latin) to Greek which took place in Corinth through the middle of the first century. . . the original social elite of the city, arriving in the new colony from Rome, tried to resist this process of Hellenization, wanting instead to preserve their Italian identity over against their new Greek cultural context. . . . Philosophies such as Epicureanism, which they would originally have brought with them from Rome, would quite probably have formed an important part of this Italian identity" ("Christians and Epicureans," 54).

4. James D. G. Dunn, "1 Corinthians 15:45—Last Adam, Life-giving Spirit," in *Christ and Spirit in the New Testament,* ed. B. Lindars and S. Smalley (Cambridge: Cambridge University Press, 1973), 127–41.

5. That is to say, the text contains the characteristic features of deliberative rhetorical discourse. See Saw, *Paul's Rhetoric* 193ff.

6. Since Martin Debilius's work, *From Tradition to Gospel,* trans. B. L. Woolf (New York: Scribner, n.d.), 18–21, there has been general agreement that the words *paredoka,* "delivered," and *parelabon,* "received," (here and in 11:23) are "technical terms used in connection with a carefully preserved tradition" (Ron Sider, "The Nature and Significance of 1 Corinthians XV 1–19," *NT* 19, no. 2 [April 1977]: 124–41). On *paralambano,* Delling notes correctly that Paul's use of this term is not to be associated with its use in the mysteries, "even where it would have been natural for him to do so (1 Cor. 15:51; Eph. 1:9; 3:3; 6:19; Col. 4:3). *Paralambanein* does not denote the direct supernatural revelation which is what Paul has in view, but personal or oral impartation." See "*paralambano,*" in *TDNT,* ed. G. Kittel, vol. 4 12. But he does not seem to recognize the contradiction when he then goes on to stress Paul's existential experience in arguing that it is not "human bearers" of this revelation that Paul has in mind in this text (see p. 14). The evidential value of the passage has been developed in John Kloppenborg's important study "An Analysis of the Pre-Pauline Formula in 1 Cor. 15:3b–5 in Light of Some Recent Literature," *CBQ* 40 (1978): 351–56. In a soon to be published study of the apologetic value of such an early "creed," see Gary Habermas, *The Risen Jesus and Future Hope* (Lanham, MD: Newman and Littlefield, 2003). Habermas shows that the consensus of scholarship agrees that 1 Corinthians 15:3–5 represents a tradition that dates from the third decade of the first century (see n. 12 below).

7. Gordon D. Fee, *The First Epistle to the Corinthians,* TNICNT (Grand Rapids: Eerdmans, 1987), 715.

8. Ibid.

9. Jean Hering, *The First Epistle of Saint Paul to the Corinthians,* trans. from the 2d French ed. by A. W. Heathcote and P. J. Allcock (London: Epworth, 1962), 158.

10. B. Siede, "Receive" in *NIDNTT,* ed. Colin Brown, vol. 3, (Grand Rapids: Zondervan, 1978), 748.

11. C. K. Barrett, *The First Epistle to the Corinthians* (New York: Harper and Row, 1968), 336.

12. Habermas has amassed an exhaustive list of recent English, French, and German scholars who agree that Paul draws from a common tradition from the earliest strata of Christian history. They include Lapide, Fuller, Kloppenborg, Murphy-O'Connor, Hengel, Ludemann, Conzelmann, Perrin, Wedderburn, Wilckens, Meier, Sanders, Fitzmyer, Hans-Ruede Weber, Robinson, Bultmann, Marxsen, Durrwell, Grass, Cullmann, Higgins, Goppelt, Hunter, Ramsey, Pannenberg, Ladd, G. B. Kelly, Samuel, Merklein, Cranfield, Lindars, Barclay, Stuhlmacher, Keck, and many others. He notes O'Collins, who knows of no scholars who date Paul's reception of this creed after the A.D. 40s. See Habermas, nn. 78–86.

13. Some have even argued for a Semitic original. See J. Jeremias, *The Eucharistic Words of Jesus* (London: SCM, 1966), 101–5. While Palestinian origins are generally conceded, a Semitic original is difficult to substantiate. See Kloppenborg, "Analysis of the Pre-Pauline Formula," 351–57; Hans Conzelmann, "On the Analysis of the Confessional Formula in 1 Corinthians 15:3–5" *Interpretation* 20, no. 1 (January 1966): 15–25.

14. Ibid. 351–67; and J. Murphy-O'Conner, "Tradition and Redaction in 1 Cor. 15:3–7," *CBQ* 43 (1981): 582–89.

15. Randall Webber is likely correct in following X. Leon-Dufour's suggestion on a probable source ("A Note on 1 Corinthians 15:3–5," *JETS* 26, no. 3 [September 1983]: 268).

16. Murphy-O'Connor, "Tradition and Redaction," 583, notes that the use of *kai hoti* indicates that Paul is assembling a series of independent statements, "a profession of faith." See also R. Fuller, *The Formation of the Resurrection Narratives* (London: SPCK, 1972), 13–14. And see the identical expression in 8:4, which reads, "and that *[kai hoti]*, there is no God but one."

17. Some exclude the last phrase (Hering, *First Epistle of Saint Paul to the Corinthians*, 158–59; Barrett, *First Epistle to the Corinthians*, 338–41). Most include the fourth phrase; some stop at the first *eita*, "then." Some (e.g., Jeremias and Klappert) see an Aramaic original, while others (e.g., Conzelmann and Vielhauer) argue for a Greek original (see Fee, *First Epistle to the Corinthians*, 723, nn. 49, 50). It is difficult to underestimate its value in demonstrating the antiquity of the "tradition" concerning the death, burial, and resurrection of Christ. It demonstrates (versus the critics) that there is no time after the resurrection of Christ to allow for the development of a "mythology" concerning these events. See note 12 on Habermas above.

18. Barrett, *First Epistle to the Corinthians,* 338.

19. See Woodrow M. Kroll, *The Book of Romans: Righteousness in Christ,* Twenty-first Century Biblical Commentary, ed. Mal Couch and Ed Hindson (Chattanooga: AMG Publishers, 2002), xiv.

20. Barrett, *First Epistle to the Corinthians,* 339.

21. Fee, *First Epistle to the Corinthians,* 724.

22. Gordon H. Clark, *First Corinthians: A Contemporary Commentary* (Nutley, NJ: Presbyterian and Reformed, 1975), 253.

23. Fee, *First Epistle to the Corinthians,* 727–28.

24. Kloppenborg, "Analysis of the Pre-Pauline Formula," 361–64.

25. It should be noted that most of the language throughout these verses has been judged to reflect the influence of a non-Pauline source. Again, the force of such an observation is not to question its authenticity but to reinforce it as coming from the apostles and the earliest followers of the Lord. Cf. Habermas and Murphy-O'Connor.

26. Murphy-O'Connor, "Tradition and Redaction in 1 Cor. 15:3–7," 586.

27. Clark, *First Corinthians,* 254.

28. Murphy-O'Connor, "Tradition and Redaction in 1 Cor. 15:3–7," 589. He also adds, "He could not claim equality with the Twelve (v. 5) because that would imply membership in a group whose constitution antedated Paul's conversion. Hence, in order to move from the last member of the creed to his own status he needed a middle term to serve as transition. This is precisely what the traditional formula 'James and the apostles' provided."

29. If one takes the view that Paul is still referring to the fact that the risen Lord's appearance to him was as to one "abnormally born," then this would have reference to Paul's experience of Christ, not of himself per se. However, his use of the definite article, the fact that this suggests a "premature" birth, not a "late" one, and that it came to have a metaphorical sense of "freakish" in the literature, cause us to seek an alternative. There is the suggestion that it is a play on Paul's name—*Paulus,* meaning "little one." Compared to the other apostles, such as Peter, and better preachers, such as Apollos, Paul was a lightweight. Taking the meaning in this way, we have a better explanation of his subsequent digression regarding the character of his apostleship against their distortions of what such an honor should bring. See Fee, *First Epistle to the Corinthians,* 733. W.

Schneider, *"ektroma,"* in *TDNT*, ed. G. Kittel, vol. 2 464–67, takes it in only "a very general sense" in agreement with most to suggest that Paul uses it as a pejorative to speak of himself as a person who was "not born at the right time."

30. Fee, *First Epistle to the Corinthians*, 734.

31. This seeks the interpretive key in the context that follows and in Galatians 1:1–4, 11–17. Here there are two possibilities: Paul is simply noting how "monstrous" a person he was (as a persecutor of the church) to be called as an apostle. Or, as Nickelsburg has suggested, the reference is associated with Paul's calling "from his mother's womb." That is, when God called him he was still in his unformed "Jewish" state. I prefer the former interpretation. For discussion see George W. E. Nickelsburg, "An *'ektroma,'* Though Appointed from the Womb," in *Christians among Jews and Gentiles: Essays in Honor of Krister Stendahl on His Sixty-fifth Birthday* ed. George W. E. Nickelsburg and G. W. MacRae (Philadelphia: Fortress Press, 1986), 198–205.

32. See also John Calvin, *The First Epistle of Paul to the Corinthians*, English translation by John Fraser (Grand Rapids: Eerdmans, 1960), 318. "This is the reasoning behind the argument that is to be drawn 'from Christ to us': 'Christ did not die or rise again for Himself, but for us, therefore His resurrection is the substance *(hypostasis)* of ours; and that which was effected in Him must be brought to completion in us also.'"

33. Hering, *First Epistle of Saint Paul to the Corinthians*, 163.

34. Fee, *First Epistle to the Corinthians*, 746.

35. Clark, *First Corinthians*, 261. Fee, *First Epistle to the Corinthians*, 746–47, agrees that there are two critical realities regarding Paul's outlook that must be kept in mind as one examines this passage. The first is that "whatever else, Paul's thinking is thoroughly eschatological." He understands that with the resurrection of Christ and the coming of the Holy Spirit, the "end times" are upon us. The second is that "Christ did not rise from the dead, but God raised him. Therefore the inevitable chain of events set in motion by Christ's resurrection has ultimately to do with God's own absolute authority over *all things*, especially death." Eduard Schweizer would add that Paul's teaching here is fully consistent with the teachings of Jesus that this kingdom is *future* and that it "in no way has been delivered into the hands of man. It remains at the disposition of God, who will permit it to come in his own time" (Eduard Schweizer, "1 Corinthians

15:20–28 as Evidence of Pauline Eschatology and Its Relation to the Preaching of Jesus," in *Saved by Hope*, ed. James I. Cook [Grand Rapids: Eerdmans, 1978], 120–21).

36. A point correctly underscored in Schweizer, "1 Corinthians 15:20–28," 123, as responding to those enthusiasts at Corinth who seemed to think they were already in the kingdom.

37. Fee, *First Epistle to the Corinthians*, 750–51.

38. This insight is owed to David Fredrickson. For the evidence supporting this approach, see "God, Christ, and All Things in 1 Corinthians 15:28," *Word and World* 18, no. 3 (summer 1998), 262.

39. Ibid., 263.

40. Demaris, "Corinthian Religion," 662, n. 4, says, "Chrysostom *(Hom. in 1 Cor. 40)* attests to the Marcionite adoption of this practice, but ancient Christian writers rarely or never mention baptism for the dead. Mathis Rissi has collected the few ancient and medieval references, 'Die Taufe fur die Toten: Ein Beitrag zur paulinischen Tauflehre,' *ATANT* (Zurich: Zwingli, 1962), 42: 6–22."

41. Leon Morris, *First Epistle of Paul to the Corinthians* (Grand Rapids: Eerdmans, 1976), 219

42. Charles Hodge, *An Exposition of the First Epistle to the Corinthians* (Grand Rapids: Eerdmans, 1974), 337

43. White, "Baptized on Account of the Dead," 490, nn. 14, 15.

44. Ibid.

45. Luther's rather creative solution seems to be an adaptation of this. He suggested that the Corinthian believers were actually being baptized over the graves of the dead. However, this "local sense" had long since gone out of currency in the Greek language of Paul's day. See Rissi, *"Die Taufe fur die Toten,"* 53; White, "Baptized on Account of the Dead," 491.

46. White, "Baptized on Account of the Dead," 493–94. *Hoi baptizomenoi* is taken literally, *huper* is understood in its causal sense, and a metaphorical interpretation is posited for *ton nekron* (meaning "the apostles"), while *nekroi* is construed as a reference to the literal dead.

47. Ibid., 494–99. White supports this with an analysis of four "thesis-like summaries of Paul's understanding of the significance of his suffering as an apostle. These four texts . . . either invoke as a controlling metaphor the image of the Roman triumphal procession, which

ended in the execution of the prisoners at the end of the procession" or are found in proximity to tribulation texts. These include in addition to this text 1 Corinthians 4:9; 2 Corinthians 2:14; 4:7–12; and 6:1–10. White summarizes Paul's argument:

> [B]oth Christ's sufferings as a part of his redemptive mission and Paul's own sufferings as a part of his apostolic mission are validated by the fact of the resurrection. By rejecting the resurrection, then, the Corinthians were rejecting not only the very redemptive work of Christ which they professed to believe but also the compelling testimony to the resurrection which Paul had lived out before them through his own willingness to suffer on their behalf just as Christ, before him, had done.

48. John D. Reaume, "Another Look at 1 Corinthians 15:29, 'Baptized for the Dead'" *BibSac* 152 (October–December 1995): 457–75.

49. Cited in Robert M. Grant, *Gods and the One God* (Philadelphia: Westminster, 1986), 24–25.

50. Ibid.

51. For discussion, see Fee, *First Epistle to the Corinthians*, 772.

52. Joachim Jeremias, "Flesh and Blood Cannot Inherit the Kingdom of God," *NTS* 2, no. 2 (fall 1956): 151–59.

53. See discussions in Fee, *First Epistle to the Corinthians*, 803–4, and Walter J. Harrelson's "Death and Victory in 1 Corinthians 15:51–57: The Transformation of a Prophetic Theme," in *Faith and History*, ed. John T. Carroll, Charles H. Cosgrove, and E. Elizabeth Johnson (Atlanta: Scholars Press, 1990), 149–59.

54. M. E. Dahl, *The Resurrection of the Body* (Naperville, IL: Allenson, 1962), 84. Despite his Bultmannian treatment of 1 Corinthians 15, it is evident that he has eloquently captured the closing benediction of the apostle.

Chapter 19—A Great Door Is Opened

1. See comments above regarding the significance of this expression.

2. Hutson shows that the common caricature of Timothy as timid and cowardly is a misreading of those texts, such as 2 Timothy 1:6–14 and our text here, which reflects a "rhetorical device that appeals to youthful sensitivity regarding honor and shame. Such a device is common in philosophical exhortation addressed to youth in the early empire." Citing Margaret Mitchell's work on New Testament envoys, he suggests,

"The issue is not that Timothy is a greenhorn whom the Corinthians might fail to take seriously. Indeed, an envoy who required such coddling could scarcely have been effective in dealing with the divisions in Corinth. Rather it is that the Corinthians are liable to incur judgment if they fail to regard the coming of an agent of the Lord. As Margaret Mitchell has shown, Greco-Roman mores of hospitality and diplomacy dictated that an envoy 'should be treated according to the status of the one by whom he was sent, not the status he individually holds'" (Christopher R. Hutson, "Was Timothy Timid? On the Rhetoric of Fearlessness [1 Corinthians 16:10-11] and Cowardice [2 Timothy 1:7]," *BR* 42 [1997]: 58–73; Margaret M. Mitchell, "New Testament Envoys in the Context of Greco-Roman Diplomatic and Epistolary Conventions: The Example of Timothy and Titus," *JBL* 111 [1992]: 649–51). See also Abraham J. Malherbe, *Moral Exhortation* 135–43.

3. C. K. Barrett, *The First Epistle to the Corinthians* (Harper and Row, 1968), 391–92.

4. Hutson, "Was Timothy Timid?" 65.

5. F. W. Grosheide, *Commentary on the First Epistle to the Corinthians*, NIC (Grand Rapids: Eerdmans, 1953), 403.

6. For a review of salient literature see the discussion in Hurd, *The Origin of 1 Corinthians* 48–50 and notes. He also comments on the import of this reference along with the other various occasions of this letter for the critical challenge to the unity of this epistle. It is nonetheless generally conceded that all of this information came to Paul in a relatively short period of time and that the letter was written in response to the report from Chloe's people, the church's list of questions to him, and the report of the men listed here.

7. Gordon D. Fee, *The First Epistle to the Corinthians*, TNICNT (Grand Rapids: Eerdmans, 1987), 837.

8. Baird, *The Corinthian Church* 201.

9. Patterson, 321.

10. Floyd V. Filson, *The New Testament Against Its Environment* (London: SCM, 1963), 38.

11. Matthew Black, "The Maranatha Invocation and Jude 14, 15 (I Enoch 1:9)," in *Christ and Spirit in the New Testament*, ed. B. Lindars and S. Smalley (Cambridge: Cambridge University Press, 1973) 192.

12. As Leon Morris (*The First Epistle of Paul to the Corinthians* [Grand Rapids: Eerdmans, 1976], 248) has noted, the subscript of the KJV—

"The first epistle to the Corinthians was written from Philippi by Stephanas, and Fortunatus, and Achaicus, and Timotheus"—does not belong to the original letter and has no support from the earliest manuscripts.

Abbreviations

ATANT	*Abhandlungen zur Theologie des Alten und Neuen Testaments*
BA	*Biblical Archaeologist*
BARev	*Biblical Archaeology Review*
Bib	*Biblica*
BibRes	*Biblical Research*
BibSac	*Bibliotheca Sacra*
BZ	*Biblische Zeitschrift*
CBQ	*Catholic Biblical Quarterly*
EvQ	*Evangelical Quarterly*
Exp	*The Expositor*
ExpT	*The Expository Times*
HTR	*Harvard Theological Review*
ICC	*International Critical Commentary*
JBL	*Journal of Biblical Literature*
JSNT	*Journal for the Study of the New Testament*
JTS	*Journal of Theological Studies*
LXX	*The Septuagint*
NIC	*New International Commentary*
NIDNTT	*New International Dictionary of New Testament Theology*
NovT	*Novum Testamentum*
NovTSup	*Novum Testamentum Supplements*
NTS	*New Testament Studies*
TDNT	*Theological Dictionary of the New Testament*
TS	*Theological Studies*
TynB	*Tyndale Bulletin*

About the Author

Dr. Daniel R. Mitchell is academic dean of Liberty Baptist Theological Seminary and professor of theological studies. Dan has been in full-time ministry since 1964, serving as a chaplain, pastor, and seminary professor. He has been with Liberty since 1976. He is a graduate of Washington Bible College (B.A.), Capital Bible Seminary (Th.M.), and Dallas Theological Seminary (S.T.M.; Th.D.). He was general editor of the *King James Study Bible* (Nelson) and consulting editor of the recently published *KJV Study Bible* (Zondervan). He has pastored two churches in Virginia, during which time he preached through 1 Corinthians in anticipation of writing the present volume. In addition to Liberty, he has taught at Western Seminary, Tyndale Theological Seminary (Amsterdam, Holland), and the Associacao Brasileira de Ensino Cultura, Assistecia E Religiao (ABECAR) in Sao Paulo, Brazil. Dan lives with his wife, Nancy, in Forest, Virginia. They have four grown children.

About the General Editors

Mal Couch is founder and president of Tyndale Theological Seminary and Biblical Institute in Fort Worth, Texas. He previously taught at Philadelphia College of the Bible, Moody Bible Institute, and Dallas Theological Seminary. His other publications include *The Hope of Christ's Return: A Premillennial Commentary on 1 and 2 Thessalonians, A Bible Handbook to Revelation,* and *Dictionary of Premillennial Theology.*

Edward Hindson is professor of religion, dean of the Institute of Biblical Studies, and assistant to the chancellor at Liberty University in Lynchburg, Virginia. He has authored more than twenty books, served as coeditor of several Bible projects, and was one of the translators for the New King James Version of the Bible. Dr. Hindson has served as a visiting lecturer at both Oxford University and Harvard Divinity School as well as numerous evangelical seminaries. He has taught more than fifty thousand students in the past twenty-five years.